Quod scriptura, non iubet vetat

The Latin translates, "What is not commanded in scripture, is forbidden."

On the Cover: Baptists rejoice to hold in common with other evangelicals the main principles of the orthodox Christian faith. However, there are points of difference and these differences are significant. In fact, because these differences arise out of God's revealed will, they are of vital importance. Hence, the barriers of separation between Baptists and others can hardly be considered a trifling matter. To suppose that Baptists are kept apart solely by their views on Baptism or the Lord's Supper is a regrettable misunderstanding. Baptists hold views which distinguish them from Catholics, Congregationalists, Episcopalians, Lutherans, Methodists, Pentecostals, and Presbyterians, and the differences are so great as not only to justify, but to demand, the separate denominational existence of Baptists. Some people think Baptists ought not teach and emphasize their differences but as E. J. Forrester stated in 1893, "Any denomination that has views which justify its separate existence, is bound to promulgate those views. If those views are of sufficient importance to justify a separate existence, they are important enough to create a duty for their promulgation . . . the very same reasons which justify the separate existence of any denomination make it the duty of that denomination to teach the distinctive doctrines upon which its separate existence rests." If Baptists have a right to a separate denominational life, it is their duty to propagate their distinctive principles, without which their separate life cannot be justified or maintained.

Many among today's professing Baptists have an agenda to revise the Baptist distinctives and redefine what it means to be a Baptist.

Others don't understand why it even matters. The books being reproduced in the *Baptist Distinctives Series* are republished in order that Baptists from the past may state, explain and defend the primary Baptist distinctives as they understood them. It is hoped that this Series will provide a more thorough historical perspective on what it means to be distinctively Baptist.

The Lord Jesus Christ asked, *"And why call ye me, Lord, Lord, and do not the things which I say?"* (Luke 6:46). The immediate context surrounding this question explains what it means to be a true disciple of Christ. Addressing the same issue, Christ's question is meant to show that a confession of discipleship to the Lord Jesus Christ is inconsistent and untrue if it is not accompanied with a corresponding submission to His authoritative commands. Christ's question teaches us that a true recognition of His authority as Lord inevitably includes a submission to the authority of His Word. Hence, with this question Christ has made it forever impossible to separate His authority as King from the authority of His Word. These two principles - the authority of Christ as King and the authority of His Word - are the two most fundamental Baptist distinctives. The first gives rise to the second and out of these two all the other Baptist distinctives emanate. As F. M. Iams wrote in 1894, "Loyalty to Christ as King, manifesting itself in a constant and unswerving obedience to His will as revealed in His written Word, is the real source of all the Baptist distinctives." In the search for the *primary* Baptist distinctive many have settled on the Lordship of Christ as the most basic distinctive. Strangely, in doing this, some have attempted to separate Christ's Lordship from the authority of Scripture, as if you could embrace Christ's authority without submitting to what He commanded. However, while Christ's Lordship and Kingly authority can be isolated and considered essentially for discussion's sake, we see from Christ's own words in Luke 6:46 that His Lordship is really inseparable from His Word and, with regard to real Christian discipleship, there can be no practical submission to the one without a practical submission to the other.

In the symbol above the Kingly Crown and the Open Bible represent the inseparable truths of Christ's Kingly and Biblical authority. The Crown and Bible graphics are supplemented by three Bible verses (Ecclesiastes 8:4, Matthew 28:18-20, and Luke 6:46) that reiterate and reinforce the inextricable connection between the authority of Christ as King and the authority of His Word. The truths symbolized by these components are further emphasized by the Latin quotation - *quod scriptura, non iubet vetat* - i.e., "What is not commanded in scripture, is forbidden." This Latin quote has been considered historically as a summary statement of the regulative principle of Scripture. Together these various symbolic components converge to exhibit the two most foundational Baptist Distinctives out of which all the other Baptist Distinctives arise. Consequently, we have chosen this composite symbol as a logo to represent the primary truths set forth in the *Baptist Distinctives Series*.

BAPTIST PRINCIPLES RESET

BAPTIST PRINCIPLES RESET

CONSISTING OF ARTICLES ON

Distinctive Baptist Principles,

A SERIES BY THE LATE

Jeremiah B. Jeter, D. D.,

AND ALSO ARTICLES BY

President HENRY G. WESTON, D.D., LL.D., of Crozer Theological Seminary
President Emeritus ALVAH HOVEY, D.D., LL.D., of Newton Theological Institution.
President E. Y. MULLINS, D.D., LL.D., of the Southern Baptist Theological Seminary.
HOWARD OSGOOD, D.D., LL.D., of Rochester Theological Seminary.
FRANKLIN JOHNSON, D.D., LL.D., of the Divinity School, University of Chicago.
B. O. TRUE, D.D., LL.D., of Rochester Theological Seminary.
J. B. GAMBRELL, D.D., of Texas.
A. E. DICKINSON, D.D., of Richmond, Va.
MADISON C. PETERS, D.D., of Baltimore, Md.
W. R. L. SMITH, D.D., of Richmond, Va.
R. H. PITT, D.D., of Richmond, Va.
B. H. CARROLL, D.D., of Texas.

NEW AND ENLARGED EDITION.

RICHMOND, VA:
THE RELIGIOUS HERALD CO.
1902

he Baptist Standard Bearer, Inc.
NUMBER ONE IRON OAKS DRIVE • PARIS, ARKANSAS 72855

Thou hast given a *standard* to them that fear thee;
that it may be displayed because of the truth.
-- *Psalm 60:4*

Reprinted in 2004
by

THE BAPTIST STANDARD BEARER, INC.
No. 1 Iron Oaks Drive
Paris, Arkansas 72855
(479) 963-3831

THE WALDENSIAN EMBLEM
lux lucet in tenebris
"The Light Shineth in the Darkness"

ISBN #1-57978-527-1

Table of Contents

Baptist Distinctives Series Logo Explanation.. Page ii
Half Title.. Page v
Complete Title... Page vii
BSB Logo Explanation.. Page viii
Table of Contents.. Page 1
2nd Half Title .... Page 3
Preface... Page 5
Preface to the Third Edition.. Page 11

PART I - Distinctive Baptist Principles
by Jeremiah B. Jeter

Introduction... Page 16
Chapter 1 - A Spiritual, or Regenerate Church Membership................................ Page 23
Chapter 2 - Baptism: A Condition of Church Membership.................................. Page 32
Chapter 3 - Believers the Only Subjects of Baptism.. Page 39
Chapter 4 - Believers the Only Subjects of Baptism (cont.)................................. Page 45
Chapter 5 - Believers the Only Subjects of Baptism (cont.)................................. Page 54
Chapter 6 - Only Immersion is Baptism... Page 62
Chapter 7 - Only Immersion is Baptism (cont.).. Page 69
Chapter 8 - Only Immersion is Baptism (cont.).. Page 77
Chapter 9 - Only Immersion is Baptism (cont.).. Page 85
Chapter 10 - Communion at the Lord's Table Confined to Churches.................. Page 93
Chapter 11 - Communion at the Lord's Table Confined to Church Members..... Page 101
Chapter 12 - Is Open Communion Demanded for the Edification of the Churches.. Page 109
Chapter 13 - Incidental Points Pertaining to Close Communion.......................... Page 118
Chapter 14 - Religious Freedom.. Page 125
Chapter 15 - Obligations of Baptists to Their Principles...................................... Page 133

Table of Contents

PART II - Distinctive Baptist Principles
by Various Authors

Chapter 1 - Regenerate Church Membership - *Henry G. Weston*............................ Page 147
Chapter 2 - The Subjects of Baptism - *Alvah Hovey*.. Page 159
Chapter 3 - The Case for Immersion at Present - *Edgar Y. Mullins* .... Page 169
Chapter 4 - Archaeology of Baptism - *Howard Osgood*... Page 187
Chapter 5 - Baptism the Door to the Lord's Supper - *Franklin Johnson*................. Page 201
Chapter 6 - Baptism the Door to the Lord's Supper (cont.) - *Franklin Johnson*..... Page 216
Chapter 7 - Baptism the Door to the Lord's Supper (cont.) - *Franklin Johnson*..... Page 229
Chapter 8 - Baptists and Religious Liberty - *Benjamin O. True*.............................. Page 245
Chapter 9 - Obligations of Baptists to Teach Their Principles - *J. B. Gambrell*..... Page 259

PART III - Baptist Principles, etc.
by Various Authors

Chapter 1 - What Baptist Principles Are Worth to the World - *A. E. Dickinson*..... Page 277
Chapter 2 - Why I Became A Baptist - *Madison C. Peters*...................................... Page 307
Chapter 3 - Candid Scholarship - *W. R. L. Smith*.. Page 317
Chapter 4 - Sunday Observance and Religious Liberty - *R. H. Pitt*........................ Page 323
Chapter 5 - One Hundred Years Ago - *B. H. Carroll*... Page 333

APPENDICES A-D

A - Immersion Essential to Christian Baptism - *John A. Broadus*.......................... Page 353
B - The Evils of Infant Baptism - *Alvah Hovey*... Page 421
C - Protestant Paedobaptism & the Doctrine of the Church - *Howard Osgood*......... Page 475
D - The Position of Baptism in the Christian System - *H. H. Tucker*..................... Page 511

INDEX... Page 563

BAPTIST PRINCIPLES RESET

PREFACE.

Dr. J. B. Jeter died February 18, 1880. In the autumn of 1876, in execution of a purpose formed long before, he began a series of articles on "Distinctive Baptist Principles." He was at this date, had been for many years, and continued till his death the first among his brethren. His mind was not only rich in accumulated stores of information, well digested, but it was characterized by a manly vigor and a most uncommon candor, which commanded the respect and admiration of all who knew him. Dr. Jeter was a model controversial writer. Scrupulously fair in his statement of an opponent's views, he never descended from the high plane of courteous debate to indulge in personalities. He was incapable of subterfuge or indirection. He took no short cuts in discussion. The articles from his pen which we print in this volume illustrate these characteristics. No word of bitterness will be found in them. They are not marred by any attempt at smartness. They are never extravagant, never hysterical. They are marked by a sober and conscious strength, which makes them very convincing. It is only just to Dr. Jeter to say that these papers were prepared for the *general* reader. While not a technical and professional scholar, he was well acquainted with the conclusions of the best scholarship, and these are embodied in his articles. But we venture the opinion that the reader will find no obscure sentence, nothing abstruse or recondite. They are plain, clear, coherent. Moreover, let no one neglect the papers under the impression that they will be dull and lifeless. The writer's remarkable command of his mother tongue, his kindly humor, his style, marked by vivacity as well as sobriety, most of all his clear and well-reasoned conviction of the unshakable truth of his contention, will give growing interest to the series.

✣ ✣ ✣

While these articles were reappearing in one of our journals, the editors determined to follow them with another series, written by the ablest and most representative of our living Baptist brethren. Accordingly the articles which are found in Part II. of this volume were, at their request, prepared and printed. Dr. Henry G. Weston, President of Crozer Theological Seminary—vigorous, clear, scholarly—contributes the first article, on that fundamental tenet of Baptists, "A Regenerate Church Membership." Dr. Alvah Hovey, President Emeritus of Newton Theological Seminary, who through his long, useful, and distinguished life has been growing "in the grace and knowledge" of his Lord—a most judicious interpreter of the Scriptures—compresses a most remarkable article on "The Subjects of Baptism" within very brief limits.

It is distinguished company into which our young and gifted President Mullins, of the Southern Baptist Theological Seminary, comes; but he is worthy to take his place with these venerated and experienced teachers. His article, on "The Case for Immersion at Present," is one of the best.

In Dr. Jeter's fine series one aspect of the baptismal question was not discussed—its archæology. It is not extravagant to say that there is no living man more competent to deal with that matter than Dr. Howard Osgood, who is among the very foremost conservative scholars of our day and time. His article on "Archæology of Baptism—The Bath Under the Old Testament" is intensely interesting and highly informing.

When President Harper was gathering around him his great corps of teachers for the University of Chicago, he brought to the Divinity School Dr. Franklin Johnson. Dr. Johnson had already given evidence of his intellectual power—notably in a volume meeting and combatting the destructive criticism which was attacking the Bible. When his strong and stalwart articles on "The Lord's Supper" appeared, competent judges declared that he had covered the ground with surpassing skill. We do not know of any argument on the whole question so simple, strong, and conclusive.

Dr. Benjamin O. True, of Rochester Theological Seminary (Church History), one of the most accurate and sympathetic students of history, has brought us all greatly in debt to him by the fine and comprehensive glimpse which he has given of "Baptists and Religious Liberty." He makes us all long for more.

Then, to complete this remarkable series and to round out this distinguished company, we laid violent hands on our Baptist commoner, our philosopher-preacher, Dr. J. B. Gambrell, at present of Texas, but in spirit, in the sweep of sympathy and intelligence, a real "citizen of the world."

※ ※ ※

Now, in printing the articles by the revered and lamented Jeter, and in adding these by seven of the most distinguished and representative Baptist scholars and leaders in the world, it is modestly maintained that this volume is unique. Among all the treatises on denominational teaching that have appeared, we know of none like this. Dr. Jeter's articles were first published nearly a quarter of a century ago. They set forth views which had been formed probably twenty-five years earlier. In the first part of this volume, then, we have the product of one mind, thinking his theme through from start to finish. The articles in Part II. have been printed within the past few months. Seven men—one in Massachusetts, one in Pennsylvania, two in New York, one in Illinois, one in Kentucky, and one in Texas—furnish them. They write wholly independent of one another. Each develops his theme without considering how his discussion will fit in with those of his brethren.

Now, then, we come out upon a most remarkable result. First, they do make a singularly consistent and harmonious whole. The Jeter articles do not fit one another more perfectly than these. Secondly, they harmonize entirely with the articles by Dr. Jeter. Probably fifty years lie between the Jeter articles and these by our living brethren. They have, too, been years of theological change—in some respects change that has been almost revolution. Great denominations have been rent and great institutions have been alienated from denominational control by theological controversies. The seminaries have been hot-beds of heresy. But every important Baptist theological seminary in the land, except one, is represented in this series, and Drs. Jeter and Gambrell fitly represent the many who have not taught or learned in these schools of the prophets. Still, with no authoritative formulary, with no doctrinal court to settle differences, the Baptists continue to think and believe alike. Thus this book illustrates, in a way all the more impressive because unintentional, that solidarity of doctrine is best preserved where human formularies have no voice of authority, and the true secret of denominational and of Christian unity is a free and reverent approach to Christ, the centre of our hopes and the object of our faith.

May God bless the book to the honor of his name and the spread of the truth!

R. H. Pitt.

Richmond, Va., February 25, 1901.

Preface to Third Edition.

The first edition of this book was so quickly exhausted that it became necessary to issue a second edition. In this the original volume was enlarged by the addition of Dr. A. E. Dickinson's monograph on "What Baptist Principles Are Worth to the World," Dr. Madison C. Peters' paper on "Why I Became a Baptist," Dr. W. R. L. Smith's article on "Candid Scholarship," and a brief paper by the undersigned on "Sunday Observance and Religious Liberty." We make this third edition still more valuable by printing an admirable article by Dr. B. H. Carroll, Principal of the English Bible Course in Baylor University, and by printing good likenesses of the contributors.

R. H. PITT.

Richmond, Va., February 20, 1902.

"In the estimation of all true Baptists *the Kingship of Christ* is a vital fact. To them he is in very deed the King of the Saints. They behold him on the throne, and hasten to 'crown him Lord of all.' They accept fully the declaration of the great apostle to the Gentiles, that 'Christ is the Head of the Church,' and thence they conclude that he is her one supreme Lawgiver. Hence, his will is to them the end of all controversy. In the most practical way they call him 'Master' and 'Lord,' by making his Word their highest rule of doctrine and duty. With them his voice silences doubt, debate and dissent, for it is the voice of their King, and its utterance is the final word, from which there is no appeal.

Remembering his words, 'One is your Master, even Christ, and all ye are brethren,' they insist upon an absolute equality of rights among brethren, and an absolute subjection of all to that one Master. Their churches, consequently, are in themselves so many simple democracies, in which all the members have equal rights; but, considered in its relation to our Lord, each of those churches is a pure Christocracy, knowing no law and, in matters of faith and practice, confessing allegiance to no authority but that of Christ alone . . . *this loyalty to Christ as King, manifesting itself in a constant and unswerving obedience to his will as revealed in his Written Word, is the real source of all the peculiarities observable among Baptists.*

The average Baptist has no natural partiality for immersion . . . But Jesus has commanded immersion, and Jesus is King, and true Baptists have no choice in the matter, an authority which they dare not disobey has fully determined it. And the same thing is true of all their other peculiarities. They adhere to them simply because loyalty to the King requires it . . . the command of the King is all the warrant they require for any practice that may challenge acceptance. With them Christ's prerogative is indisputable. In everything it is his to command, and ours unhesitatingly to hear and obey.

Thus *the Kingship of Christ is the formative, the fundamental idea among Baptists*. It controls them everywhere and always, determining their beliefs and their practices from first to last. Their rejection of sprinkling, and their faithful adherence to the practice of immersion, are due to this idea alone. So, too, their practice of believer's baptism only, and their persistent rejection of the baptism of infants, are due to the same fundamental principle. And in like manner . . . the practice of restricted communion, is due to the same controlling idea, the practical recognition of the Kingship of our Lord in everything relating to his people and to his house. For his authority is as complete in the order of the ordinances as in any principle or precept of his gospel, and we may not set it aside . . . *this practical recognition of the Kingship of Christ is really the most vital of all the matters at issue between Baptists and Pedobaptists.* Theoretically all who call themselves Christians confess that Christ is King. But theory is one thing, and far too often practice is another and widely different thing. Theoretically our Pedobaptist friends say Christ is King, and almost constantly they sing, 'Crown him Lord of all;' but practically they reject his Kingly authority in the matter of baptism, and instead of rendering a joyful and implicit obedience to his command, they change that command to suit their own tastes, and then calmly tell us that their new way will do as well. Does this seem a grave charge against a vast body of the professed disciples of our Lord, and one that ought not slightly to be made? Well, I admit it. It is a grave charge, but it is as true as it is grave, and the evidences of its truth abound on every side. The current defense of sprinkling, viz., that it will do as well as immersion, deliberately sets aside the Kingship of Christ . . . In other words, it weighs the command of our Lord in the scales of its own petty human reason, and dares to set it aside, and to substitute for it a something different, which it pronounces just as good. If this is not a practical rejection of the Kingship of our Lord, what is it?"

F. M. IAMS
"The Kingship of Christ"
<u>Before The Foot-Lights</u>
(Louisville: Baptist Book Concern, 1884).

JEREMIAH BELL JETER, D. D.
1802-1880.

Pastor of 1st Baptist Church, Richmond, VA
and Editor of The Religious Herald, Richmond, VA.

PART I.

Distinctive Baptist Principles

By the Late J. B. JETER, D. D.,

Editor The Religious Herald.

DISTINCTIVE BAPTIST PRINCIPLES.

Introduction.

We promised a series of articles on this subject, so soon as we could dispose of other matters claiming our attention. The time has come for us to begin to redeem that pledge. An elaborate discussion of the various points comprehended in our scheme must not be expected. We can attempt nothing beyond a brief and simple statement of Baptist principles, and the main arguments by which they are defended. Our statements or arguments may not be satisfactory to all our readers; but, in presenting them, we will endeavor to be candid, courteous, and fair. We shall earnestly aim so to write that, if any person should be offended, the fault shall be his, and not ours. We are so firmly convinced of the soundness of our principles that we can well afford to discuss them with calmness and good-will to all men.

Before we enter on an examination of the distinctive principles of Baptists, it is proper that the points regarding which they are in full and hearty accord with most Protestant Christians should be stated. The Baptists are united in the support of what is generally known as *Evangelical Christianity*. This system embraces the plenary inspiration of the Scriptures—their sufficiency as a rule of faith and practice; the existence of God in three persons—Father, Son, and Holy Ghost; the perfection of the divine law in its precepts and in its penalty; the apostasy and guilt of man; his utter inability to attain to righteousness or justification by deeds of law or good works; the incarnation, obedience, sufferings, and death of the Son of God; his resurrection, ascension, and assumption of universal empire; salvation by grace through his atoning blood; the necessity of the Holy Spirit's influence in the regeneration of the soul; free justification by faith in Christ; the necessity of good works as the fruit and evidence of faith; the resurrection of the dead, both of the just and of the unjust; the general judgment; the eternal blessedness of the redeemed and the eternal punishment of the wicked.

We have presented these points, not as exhaustive of the evangelical system, but as comprehending its main articles. These constitute the fundamental, vital, soul-saving facts and teachings of the gospel. In their support and diffusion, Baptists are happy to unite with Christians of every name and party. We rejoice that they are received by most Protestant sects, and that, wherever they are heartily embraced, they bring forth the fruits of righteousness. We are ready to concede, too, that these points are far more numerous and important than those concerning which we differ from them.

It may be proper to add that Baptists generally hold to what may be termed, for the sake of distinction, "moderate Calvinism." They are far from acknowledging Calvin as authority in matters of religion; but the system of doctrine which bears his name, as it has been modified by the study of the Scriptures, is now commonly accepted by Baptists. Fifty years ago, they mostly adhered to high Calvinism, as maintained by Dr. John Gill, of London. Since that time their views have been considerably changed, through the writings of Andrew Fuller and others. These differences of views, however, have not disturbed their harmony or hindered their co-operation, except with a small dissenting party, whose Antinomian views led them to proclaim their hostility to missions and to all liberal efforts for the diffusion of Christianity.

Before we enter on a discussion of Baptist principles, it may be proper to state them briefly, that the reader may see the ground which we propose to traverse. A spiritual church membership lies at the foundation of all Baptist peculiarities. In harmony with this principle, Baptists maintain that only believers, or regenerated persons, are proper subjects of baptism; that only immersion on a profession of faith is true baptism; that only baptized believers are entitled to the privileges of church membership, and consequently that only church members should be admitted to the Lord's table. The last-named principle is held, not by all Baptists, but a large majority of them.

There are some principles held by Baptists in common with other Christian denominations, and to which Baptists give peculiar prominence. Among these may be mentioned the sufficiency of the Scriptures for guidance in religious matters, and the independence of the churches, under Christ, in the exercise of discipline. All Protestant sects, so far as we know, except those of rationalistic tendency, adopt the first of these principles, though many of them seem to us to be sadly swayed, in the interpretation of the Scriptures, by tradition, creeds, and ecclesiastical relations. The second principle is held as firmly by the Independents of England, the Congregationalists of this country, and other minor sects, as by Baptists; though, perhaps, the latter give it greater prominency, and follow it more fully to its logical consequences than others do. These principles, however warmly they may be cherished by Baptists, cannot be classed among their distinctive views.

The peculiar principles of Baptists, while they do not constitute the main doctrines of Christianity, deeply affect the purity, progress, and triumph of the kingdom of Christ. If these views are erroneous, Baptists are more profoundly interested than any other people to discover the error. If they are deceived, they are exerting—unintentionally, but most unfortunately—a disturbing influence among the disciples of Christ. As we do not claim to be infallible, we should cultivate a candid spirit, diligently search the Scriptures, earnestly pray for divine guidance, and be ready to sacrifice reputation for truth. If these views, however, are true, it is the solemn duty of those who receive them to expound, defend, and proclaim them in such manner as shall best secure their prevalence and final triumph. The differences between Baptists and Pedobaptists are not a mere question as to whether much or little water shall be used in baptism. They fundamentally affect church organization. They are all concentrated in this inquiry: Shall churches be composed only of believers, who profess their faith in the divinely appointed way, and prove their sincerity by lives in harmony with the gospel of Christ? To us, it seems that conformity to this method would free Christianity from more than half the evils by which it is brought into reproach and its progress and final triumph are hindered. It is clear that its adoption would deliver the world from all hierarchies, all connections between Church and State, except that created by mutual good-will, all pontiffs and lordly ecclesiastics, all persecution for conscience' sake, and all the immense expenditures lavished in support of the palaces and splendors of princely prelates; and the true friends of Christ would be left to support and extend his cause by the sanctity of their lives, the purity of their doctrine, the faithfulness of their labors, their liberal sacrifices, and the divine blessing on their efforts. Would not this be a gain?

It is to be lamented that Christians cannot discuss their differences with equanimity, fairness, and affection. They serve a common Lord, and he is the God of truth. He takes no pleasure in error, however plausibly it may be defended. They have a common interest to promote, and that is the extension of the kingdom and the manifestation of the glory of their Redeemer. It is only by the knowledge and the diffusion of divine truth that they can promote the end for which they were translated into the kingdom of God's dear Son. It is vain, however, to hope that the discussion of controverted religious questions, except in rare instances, will be conducted with a simple desire to discover and to maintain truth. The pride of opinion, the desire of victory, sectarian zeal, the prejudices of education, and personal interests, are likely to give more or less inspiration and heat to religious controversy, by which its proper end is, in a great measure, defeated.

As our arguments will be based chiefly on the common version of the Scriptures, it is proper to notice a few things concerning it. It was made, not by Baptists, but by Pedobaptists. The translators were instructed by King James to retain the "old ecclesiastical words" found in the existing versions. Whether baptism belonged to this category, we need not decide. Certain it is that the translators did not render *baptize* and its derivatives into English, but merely gave them an English termination and spelt them with Latin letters. The English reader is left to infer their meaning from their connection and the circumstances of the act which they denote. The reader must perceive that a version made by Pedobaptist scholars, under such a restriction, can have no unfair leaning to Baptist principles; and yet we expect to show, by a proper use of it, their soundness.

CHAPTER I.

A Spiritual, or Regenerate, Church Membership.

A spiritual, or regenerate, church membership, as already stated, lies at the foundation of all Baptist peculiarities. On this point, Baptists and the few small sects that agree with them differ from the whole Christian world. If numbers were an infallible sign of truth, we should be constrained to abandon our principles. But they are not. On this supposition, Protestantism would be compelled to yield to Romanism, and Christianity itself to paganism. The oracles of God are the only infallible test of truth. To these we appeal.

The Israelitish theocracy, or commonwealth, differed widely from the Christian church, or, more properly, churches. That institution—a politico-religious organization—consisted only of the descendants of Abraham, in the line of Jacob, or Israel, with such foreigners as chose, by submission to a painful and bloody rite, to become incorporated with the nation. Citizenship in the commonwealth was hereditary, and was maintained, not by regeneration and a life of piety, but by the observance of various costly rites. The government was designed and admirably adapted to preserve the nation from commingling with the neighboring heathen. To the Israelites were committed the oracles of God and the honor of maintaining his worship amid the gloom of surrounding idolatry. From that favored race the Messiah was to descend, in whom all nations were to be blessed.

In the fulness of time, Jesus of Nazareth made his appearance. He claimed to be the promised Messiah, and confirmed his title to the office by the wisdom of his words and the number and greatness of his miracles. He came, not to establish or to modify the "commonwealth of Israel," but to introduce a new dispensation, or order of things. After a brief, but most instructive, ministry, terminating in his sacrificial death, he endowed his apostles with plenary inspiration and the power of working miracles, and entrusted to them the duty of carrying into effect his gracious and sublime mission.

In the execution of the plan, the apostles organized churches, first in Judea, then in Samaria and Galilee, and afterwards among the heathen nations throughout the Roman empire. These churches were not a continuation of the Jewish hierarchy. They differed from it widely in members, doctrine, rites, worship, and discipline. No man was entitled to a place in a Christian church because of his connection with a synagogue. Nicodemus, a ruler of the Jews, could not share in the blessings of the new kingdom without regeneration. Under the changed order of things, circumcision, which was a passport to the privileges of the synagogue, availed nothing. All the rites and ceremonies of the Levitical economy were abolished under the new dispensation. The truth, which had been symbolically and dimly revealed to the Jews, was clearly taught in the churches. Repentance, faith, regeneration, were conditions of admission to their fellowship, and holy lives were essential to its continuance. Instead of the blood sacrifices of the Jews, the churches offered up "spiritual sacrifices, acceptable to God by Jesus Christ." In fine, the commonwealth of Israel was a hierarchy; but the churches are voluntary associations. That was typical, preparatory, and temporary; these are spiritual and permanent.

Having made these general remarks, we will now proceed to prove their correctness. John the Baptist, the morning star of the new dispensation, was an eminent reformer. He preached repentance and the necessity of godly lives, laid the axe at the root of the trees which did not bear good fruit, and proclaimed that descent from Abraham, which secured all the benefits of Judaism, would avail nothing under the reign of the Messiah. He baptized the penitent for the remission of sins; but he organized no church among his disciples. His mission was to prepare the way of the Messiah, by awaking an expectation of his coming, making ready a people to receive him, and introducing him into his public ministry; and, having done these things, his work was ended. Matt. iii. 1-12; Mk. i. 1-11; Lu. iii. 2-22; Jno. iii. 28-31.

The personal ministry of Jesus was preparatory to the constitution of churches. His preaching was eminently searching, and fitted to reform men and make them spiritual and devout; but during his life no church was organized, and his disciples were subject to no discipline, and their labors, except so far as they were directed by his personal attention, were without concert.

On the day of Pentecost, after the ascension of Jesus, the apostles, by the descent of the Holy Spirit, were fully qualified to carry forward and complete the work that John and Jesus had begun. The first church was formed in Jerusalem, and this soon became the mother of other churches in various countries. We have at present no concern with them, but to show that they were composed exclusively of believers—converts to Christianity—or persons who made a credible profession of piety. The mother church was clearly a spiritual one. The 120 disciples who held a continuous prayer meeting in Jerusalem were its nucleus. Acts i. 14, 15. To these were added 3,000 believers on the day of Pentecost. Acts ii. 41. Additions were daily made to the church, but only of such as were saved. Verse 47. To this company was added Joses, surnamed Barnabas, who signalized his conversion by his liberality to the cause of Christ. Acts iv. 36, 37. After the death of Ananias and Sapphira, the ungodly were deterred from joining the church; "but believers were the more added to the Lord, multitudes both of men and women." Acts v. 13, 14. After the appointment of deacons, "The word of God increased, and the number of disciples multiplied in Jerusalem greatly; and a great company of the priests were obedient to the faith." Acts vi.

7. This was *the true church*. Are we not justified in affirming that it was composed of believers, and of believers only? There is not the slightest trace in the copious inspired record that, in this large, primitive, model church, there were unconverted seekers, or infants or hereditary members. The church was organized under the immediate guidance of the Holy Spirit and according to the will of Christ, and we have a full and infallible account of its membership, for the instruction of church builders in all ages. Is it possible that, on the Pedobaptist theory of church construction, there should have been no reference to its infant members? Among the thousands of believers added to the church, did none claim the covenant blessing for their children? Or did the faithful historian fail to mention so important a fact? Can anybody believe that, if Pedobaptists were favored with such a wonderful increase of members, their account of it would contain no allusion to the reception of the infant offspring of the converts into the church?

Had we no other proof that the primitive churches were composed exclusively of believers, the history of the church at Jerusalem should fully satisfy us on that point. It is perfectly fair to conclude that all the churches were conformed, in their membership, as in other things, to the mother church. On this point, however, evidence is ample. The second church was probably organized in Samaria. We have not so full an account of its constitution as we have of that at Jerusalem, but quite enough to guide us to a right conclusion. After the persecution of the disciples consequent on the death of Stephen, "Philip went down to Samaria and preached Christ unto them." Many of the Samaritans gave heed to his words and were joyfully converted. "When they believed Philip preaching the things concerning the kingdom of God and the name of Jesus Christ, they were baptized, both men and women." Acts viii. 12. We have no definite account of the organization of the church, but there can be no reasonable doubt that these believing men and women were its constituent members. Children were not among the baptized, nor can we reasonably suppose that they were admitted into the church.

In the Acts of the Apostles, covering a period of more than thirty years, and recording the labors of the apostles and their assistants in founding and edifying churches in a large part of the Roman empire, there is not the slightest evidence, or shadow of evidence, except that supposed to be furnished by household baptisms, (which will be hereafter examined,) that any persons were admitted to membership in the churches except on a credible profession of faith, or retained in them, by apostolic sanction, without lives in harmony with their profession.

The proof furnished by the apostolic epistles in favor of the spiritual membership of the primitive churches is quite as conclusive as that drawn from their inspired history. Let us briefly examine it.

Paul addressed his first epistle in the canon, "To all that be in Rome, beloved of God, called to be saints," and thanked God that their faith was "spoken of throughout the world." Rom. i. 7, 8. If the church contained other members, either adults or infants, the fact does not appear in the long letter. Human ingenuity has not been able to find in all its chapters a single allusion, or shadow of allusion, to any other than a regenerate membership.

The next epistle in course was directed by the apostle "Unto the church of God in Corinth"; but, that there might be no mistake as to its membership, he adds, "to them that are sanctified in Christ Jesus, called to be saints," &c. 1 Cor. i. 2. The second epistle was addressed by Paul and Timothy, "Unto the church of God which is at Corinth, with all the saints which are in all Achaia." 2 Cor. i. 1. We think that it is impossible to find in these letters, copious as they are in instruction, the slightest sanction of an unregenerate church membership.

The next epistle was addressed by Paul, not to a single church, but to the churches of the large province of Galatia. "Grace be to you and peace," he said, "from God the Father, and from our Lord Jesus Christ." The apostle did not use such language as this to the unconverted. Only believers are the recipients of grace and peace. Of the unbelieving his language was: "If any man love not the Lord Jesus Christ, let him be anathema maranatha." We can find in this epistle no trace of infant church membership.

We must abridge our labors on this point. The epistle to the Ephesians was addressed "to the saints which are at Ephesus, and to the faithful in Christ Jesus." Eph. i. 1. The letter to the Philippians was directed "to all the saints in Christ Jesus," &c. Phil. i. 1. The epistle to the Colossians was addressed "to the saints and faithful brethren in Christ which are at Colosse." Col. i. 2.

If there were unconverted seekers or infants in the apostolic churches, is it not strange and inexplicable that the apostle in his epistles should have taken no notice of them? They must have constituted a large and important part of the churches. Many questions must have arisen concerning the relations which they bore to the churches and the responsibilities arising from them. Were they members in full fellowship or only nominal members? Were they entitled to partake of the Lord's supper? Were they subject to discipline as other members? Should they be formally expelled from the churches, if they furnished no evidence of piety? If they ceased to be members by lack of piety, at what age and under what circumstances did their membership terminate? These and similar questions have greatly perplexed modern Pedobaptists. Is it possible that these difficulties should not have arisen in the primitive churches, if they contained infant members? How is it to be explained that the Spirit of inspiration, so full of light and love, left the churches in utter ignorance on questions so vitally affecting their interests?

All these difficulties are obviated and all these questions are explained by a spiritual church membership. The primitive churches were composed of believers, and of believers only, and all the facts recorded in the inspired history and all the instructions in the inspired epistles are in perfect harmony with this fundamental principle of church organization.

CHAPTER II.

Baptism a Condition of Church Membership.

Baptism is a Christian ordinance. It originated in the wisdom, goodness, and authority of God. John was divinely commissioned to baptize. Jno. i. 3. Jesus honored the ordinance of baptism by receiving it at the hands of John. Matt. iii. 16, 17. When Jesus entered on his public ministry, he continued the administration of baptism, through the agency of his disciples. Jno. iv. 2, 3. The ordinance occupies an important place in the great commission which Jesus, after his resurrection, gave to the apostles for evangelizing the world. Matt. xxviii. 19, 20. No man can intelligently and candidly read the New Testament without perceiving that baptism is of solemn import, and designed to exert a momentous influence in the kingdom of Christ.

It has been already shown that the first church was organized in the city of Jerusalem, after the ascension of Jesus, and was composed entirely of believers. This church was formed exclusively of Jews. No Gentile was admitted, or could have been admitted for some years after its constitution, to a participation of its privileges. The Jews were not received into it in virtue of their descent from Abraham, or their interest in the covenant that God made with him, or their circumcision, or their good standing in the hierarchy. Still more, they were not admitted into it simply because of their repentance, faith, and regeneration. Peter, standing in the midst of the great pentecostal assembly, with a cloven tongue of fire upon him, to symbolize his plenary inspiration, said: "Repent and be baptized, every one of you, in the name of Jesus Christ for the remission of sins." Acts ii. 38. Repentance was an indispensable duty—it implied faith and the new birth—a great moral change; but it was not enough to secure a participation in the privileges of the church then in the process of formation. It was a visible body, and a divinely prescribed outward act, in confession of repentance, faith, and the remission of sins, through the name of Jesus Christ, was an essential condition of a formal union with it. To this inspired order the converts all conformed. "Then they that gladly received" Peter's "word were baptized; and the same day there were added unto them about three thousand souls." Verse 41. There is no misconceiving the meaning of this language. The converts were baptized before they entered the church. Of the multitudes, on that day of excitement and of wonders, not one was added to the church without baptism.

We must notice briefly the significance of this transaction. Jesus, after he was risen from the dead, remained forty days with his apostles, "speaking of the things pertaining to the kingdom of God." Acts i. 3. We cannot doubt that his instructions were comprehensive and minute. The apostles were liable, however, to misunderstand or forget his teaching; but, to preserve them from the possibility of error, they were commanded to remain until they "should be endued with power from on high"; that is, receive the baptism of the Holy Spirit. Lu. xxiv. 49; Acts i. 5. Are we not bound to believe that the apostles, on the day of Pentecost, having been "endued with power from on high," said and did just what was according to the will of Christ, and designed to be for the guidance of his disciples in all ages? What they required of the Jews on the day of Pentecost, in order to admission into the church, was required of them at all places, at all times, and under all circumstances, for the same purpose.

If baptism was demanded of the Jews as a prerequisite of church membership, we may reasonably conclude that the Gentiles were not admitted to the privilege except on the same condition. The Jews, as some Pedobaptists maintain, were already members of the church, and had received the rite of circumcision, for which baptism is merely a substitute; and yet the Jews—even rulers of the Jews, and priests, though they had been circumcised and were devout—could not be admitted into the church at Jerusalem, or into any other church, without baptism. Certainly, then, the heathen, ignorant of God and his worship, were not received into the churches without this divinely appointed, public, solemn, and impressive acknowledgment of the authority of Christ and the enjoyment of the remission of sins through his blood.

We are not, however, left to any uncertain inference on this momentous subject. We have definite scriptural information concerning it. Peter, instructed by a vision from heaven, went from Joppa to Cæsarea, where he found Cornelius, a Roman officer and a Gentile, who had been directed by a holy angel to assemble "his kinsmen and near friends," all Gentiles, to hear the words of the apostle. Peter preached the gospel to them; and while he was speaking, "the Holy Spirit fell on all them that heard the word." It was a renewal of the wonders of the day of Pentecost. The Christian Jews accompanying Peter were astonished at this effusion of the Holy Ghost on the Gentiles. They had not anticipated such a display of divine grace on behalf of the heathen. The miracle, however, was undeniable, and Peter, guided by the Spirit of inspiration, promptly saw and admitted all its consequences. He did not say: God has received these Gentiles, and they may dispense with baptism; they have received the baptism of the Holy Ghost, and water baptism can do them no good; as God has accepted them, the church also is bound to accept them. No; the events of the pentecostal reformation had not faded from his memory. He recollected the divine order concerning the Jews, and, seeing that it was applicable to the Gentiles, said: "Can any man forbid water, that these should not be baptized, which have received the

Holy Ghost as well as we?" Their baptism was not a matter of choice, or taste, or convenience, but a solemn duty. "He commanded them to be baptized in the name of the Lord." Acts x. 24-48.

There can be no good reason to suppose that, as these first Gentile converts were baptized under the immediate direction of the Holy Spirit, preparatory to church membership, other Gentiles were admitted into the churches without baptism. There surely can be no solid reason furnished why the ordinance, which was obligatory on the first and most favored converts from heathenism, is not the duty of all Gentile believers.

The apostolic churches, so far as we have definite information of their constituency, were all composed of baptized believers. Paul, writing to the saints at Rome, and classing himself among them, said: "We are buried with him (Christ) by baptism into death." Rom. vi. 4. Paul preached the gospel in Corinth, and "many of the Corinthians, hearing, believed and were baptized." Acts xviii. 8. These baptized believers doubtless constituted the church in that city. Writing to them afterwards, and reproving them for their divisions, he inquired, "Were ye baptized in the name of Paul?" He takes it for granted as well that they had been baptized as that they had not been baptized in the name of Paul. He had baptized Crispus and Gaius and the household of Stephanas; but there is no cause to conclude that, as these members were baptized by the apostle, other members were left without the ordinance. 1 Cor. i. 13-16. Moreover, Paul, in writing to the church in Corinth, after enumerating the gross vices prevalent among the Gentiles, says: "And such were some of you; but ye are washed, but ye are sanctified, but ye are justified in the name of the Lord Jesus, and by the Spirit of our God." 1 Cor. vi. 11. In this passage, "washed" is generally supposed by commentators to mean "baptized"; and, indeed, as distinguished from "sanctified" and "justified," we do not see what else it can mean. We may fairly conclude, then, that the church in the city of Corinth was composed exclusively of baptized persons. Lydia and her household, and the jailer and his family, who constituted the nucleus of the church at Philippi, were all baptized; and there is no ground to conclude that the other members of the church did not submit to the ordinance. Acts xvi. 15, 33. To the church in Colosse the apostle wrote: "Ye are * * * buried with him (Christ) in baptism." Col. ii. 12.

As both Jews and Gentiles were admitted into the church by baptism, as several of the churches we know were composed wholly of baptized members, and as all the churches were under the same Lord and the same law, it is clear that baptism was a condition of membership in the primitive churches.

Baptism is not essential to salvation, but is in many cases essential to obedience, and obedience is essential to salvation. "The Pharisees and lawyers rejected the counsel of God against themselves, not being baptized with the baptism of John." Lu. vi. 30. Those who reject the counsel of God cannot be wise or in safety, and the apostolic baptism is not less the counsel of God than was that of John. Jno. xv. 14. Christ has made it obligatory on all who would enter his church, and that is enough to control the conduct of those who love him.

We have, perhaps, unnecessarily extended this argument. No evidence, or semblance of evidence, can be furnished from the Scriptures that any person was ever received into an apostolic church without baptism. Indeed, there is no point concerning which Christians of all denominations and parties are more united than in maintaining the necessity of baptism to church membership. There is no large and settled church or sect that does not make baptism a condition of admission to its privileges.

CHAPTER III.

Believers the Only Subjects of Baptism.

If, as we have shown, the churches of Christ were composed exclusively of believers who had been voluntarily baptized, we may reasonably expect to find the ordinance restricted to believers. Our knowledge on the subject must be derived wholly from the New Testament. As the rite is peculiar to the new dispensation, the Scriptures of the Old Testament contain no allusion to it. Let us come, then, to the common version of the New Testament, and examine it honestly and carefully, that we may learn what it teaches concerning the subjects of baptism.

That the baptism of John was restricted to the penitent is, so far as we know, unquestioned. "John did baptize in the wilderness, and preach the baptism of repentance for the remission of sins." In our opinion, the differences between the baptism of John and that of the apostles, after the ascension of Jesus, were circumstantial, and not fundamental. The discussion of this question, however, would lead us too far from our purpose, and it is not necessary for its accomplishment. We have introduced the subject to make a single remark. If John's baptism and the baptism of Christ's disciples, before his crucifixion, were limited to penitent believers, and the apostolic baptism, after his resurrection from the dead, was extended to the unconverted children of baptized believers, is it not strange and inexplicable that so radical a change should have taken place in the administration of the ordinance without any distinct mention of it, or even a slight reference to it? If there was no such change, the omission is easily understood.

Baptism is a positive or legal institution. It is of no obligation except from the divine will, and as that will is revealed to us. The question concerning it should be—not, What thinkest thou? but, How readest thou? It is what God wills it to be—nothing more and nothing less. Let us turn, then, to the law of Christian baptism? Matt. xxviii. 19, 20: "Go ye, therefore, and teach all nations, baptizing them in the name of the Father, and of the Son, and of the Holy Ghost; teaching them to observe all things whatsoever I have commanded you." All positive laws must be strictly construed. The command to make disciples and baptize them differs widely from the command to baptize persons and then make disciples of them. How did the apostles understand their grand commission? "Teach all nations, baptizing them"—not nations in the gross, good, bad, and indifferent, but the taught, disciples; "teaching them"—the baptized disciples—"to observe all things," &c. This was the plain construction of the language. How would the training of the apostles lead them to understand it? They were not ignorant on the subject of baptism. They had attended on the ministrations of John and seen that his baptisms were limited to penitents, who brought forth the fruits of repentance. Some of them certainly, probably all of them, had received baptism at his hands. Jno. 1. 37, 40. They and their fellow-laborers had baptized more disciples than John. They knew nothing of any baptism except the baptism of disciples. How is it possible, then, that they should have understood their commission except in its plain sense? It changed the formula, but not the subjects of the rite?

The interpretation which the apostles put on the language of their commission we may learn clearly and certainly from their practice. They proceeded, in a few days, under the infallible guidance of the Holy Spirit, to the execution of their sacred trust. On the day of Pentecost—the most memorable day in the history of Christian churches—only those were baptized who "gladly received his (Peter's) word"; that is, who heartily embraced the gospel. Acts ii. 41.

In every subsequent account of the administration of baptism (except in the cases of household baptisms, which will receive timely consideration), it is clear that the rite was limited to believers. Philip was the first evangelist who carried the gospel beyond the limits of Judea. He went down to Samaria and preached Christ with great success. "The people with one accord gave heed unto those things which Philip spake." "There was great joy in that city." Now surely we shall learn how the apostles and their fellow-disciples understood the law of baptism. The evangelist followed the example of the pentecostian laborers. "When they (the Samaritans) believed Philip preaching the things concerning the kingdom of God and the name of Jesus Christ, they were baptized, both men and women." Acts viii. 12.

It is not necessary to mention at length the baptism of the Ethiopian treasurer (Acts viii. 36-38), of Saul of Tarsus (ix. 18), of Cornelius and his friends, the first Gentile converts (x. 47), and the Corinthians (xviii. 8), who, according to the terms of the commission and the practice of the apostles, before and after the resurrection of Jesus, were all baptized after they were made disciples.

We will close this argument with the statement of an interesting event illustrative of it. Rev. Luther Rice was one of the most clear-headed men that we have ever known. He was sent by the Congregationalists as a missionary to India. It was his lot to make the voyage in company with two English Baptist missionaries. With one of them, a man of some learning and acuteness, he frequently discussed the subject of baptism. Rice found no difficulty in replying to his arguments, and took great pleasure in perplexing him by questions. One evening, at the close of a protracted discussion, the other Baptist missionary, a plain, sensible man, who had listened silently to the debate, said: "If a man had never heard of infant baptism, he might read through the New Testament without ever thinking of it." Rice hastily thought of the Scriptures relating to baptism, but felt a little disconcerted at his inability to remember a text that certainly had reference to the practice. The remark haunted him. He resolved to examine the Scriptures more carefully on the subject. The more he searched them, the more painfully he was convinced of their silence concerning infant baptism. He had no doubt but that they taught it; but just where or how he could not perceive. He had great confidence in the learning and astuteness of Judson, who had preceded him in the voyage to India. He resolved to postpone the investigation of the subject until he could have the aid of his able fellow-missionary.

On reaching his destination and meeting Judson, he proceeded at length and very carefully to state his difficulties regarding infant baptism. Judson, having heard him patiently, quietly replied that his objections were unanswerable. Rice was confounded at the concession, and greatly grieved to find that Judson was on the point of being immersed on a profession of his faith.

Rice resolved at once to dismiss the subject from his mind. He had been sent out by the Congregationalists, and was dependent on them for support. His defection would hinder the success of the mission, or might even destroy it. Whatever might be true in regard to baptism, it would be unwise to pursue a course fraught with so many evil consequences. Thus he reasoned; but his conscience was truer than his head. Meditation and prayer brought him to the conclusion that it is better to please God than men, and that the way to be useful is to do right. So soon as he was willing to follow the convictions of his conscience, his doubts and difficulties were all dissipated. The path of duty was straight and plain before him. He was baptized, returned to the United States, awakened the Baptist denomination on the subject of missions and of education, and contributed more than any man, dead or living, to their prosperity, growth, influence, and usefulness.

Let us not lose sight of the argument in our interest in the story. If infant baptism is a divine ordinance, it is obligatory on all Christian parents. The Scriptures were written for their instruction in righteousness. Is it not strange that they should contain no clear information concerning the rite? The duty of the Israelitish parents to circumcise their children, and of all believers to be baptized, is plain enough—a child may see it written as with a sunbeam; but the duty of parents to have their children baptized can be found only by diligent search and ingenious interpretations of Scripture, and multitudes cannot find it at all.

CHAPTER IV.

Believers the Only Subjects of Baptism.

Pedobaptists are not agreed as to the reasons for baptizing infants. Some baptize them because they are holy and worthy to receive it, and others because they are sinful and need its influence. Some derive their right to the ordinance from household baptisms, and others from the Abrahamic covenant and circumcision. Many, admitting that it is not of divine authority, practise it because it is a beautiful, appropriate, and useful ceremony. We must notice some of these pleas for the rite.

Before entering on an examination of the baptized households, we must offer a few general remarks. First, then, all families do not contain children, and particularly young children. In every neighborhood, houses may be found in which there are no infants. To base a positive Christian institution on the possibility or probability—for *certainty* there cannot be—that there were little children in the three or four families of whose baptism we read in the Scriptures, and that these children were baptized, is quite adventurous. Statute law is specific and positive, not inferential, and surely leaves no place for conjecture. Moreover, families are frequently spoken of in distinction from infants or without regard to them. If it is affirmed that a man has an intelligent or a pious family, nobody concludes that he has no infants in his household, or that they are intelligent or pious. The remark is naturally and universally supposed to refer to that part of the family of whom intelligence or piety may be reasonably predicated. The person who should infer from the statement that the family contained infants, and that they were distinguished for their knowledge or godliness, would prove himself to be a sophist, or something more unfortunate.

How would the baptism of households be understood by the primitive Christians? The command was to baptize disciples, and all the early baptisms, if household baptisms be excepted, were in harmony with the command. How natural, then, was it for them to understand by household baptisms the baptism of such members of the families as were capable of complying with the prescribed conditions of the ordinance—such as had been instructed, and, under the influence of instruction, had repented and believed the gospel. They could hardly have imagined that these baptisms set aside the divine law of baptism and disregarded the example of the apostles, given under circumstances of so great solemnity in Jerusalem and Cæsarea. Surely nothing short of inspired testimony could have convinced them that household baptisms differed so widely from baptisms administered by the apostles under the immediate guidance of the Holy Spirit, and on occasions of the most profound interest.

Let us now examine the household baptisms in

detail, that we may see what light they shed on infant baptism. We have an account of the baptism of four households in the New Testament—those of Cornelius, Stephanas, the jailer, and Lydia. We will notice them in the order in which we have named them.

The baptism of the family of Cornelius, the Roman centurion, is not definitely mentioned; but the fact is unquestionable. By divine direction, he sent to Joppa for Peter, to learn what he ought to do. Cornelius waited for the apostle in Cæsarea, and "called together his kinsmen and near friends" to hear him. Peter preached to them the gospel. It was the first sermon delivered to the Gentiles, and God accompanied it with an extraordinary demonstration of his favor. "The Holy Ghost fell on all them which heard the word," and they spake "with tongues and did magnify God"; and the apostle "commanded them to be baptized in the name of the Lord Jesus." That the family of Cornelius were all included among the converts, there is no ground to question. They would surely have been called with his other kindred to hear so important a message, under circumstances of such thrilling interest; especially as we are informed that the centurion "feared God, with *all* his house." This household baptism offers no support to infant baptism, but is in perfect harmony with the law of baptism and the apostolic practice on the day of Pentecost. Cornelius was the head of a family that reverenced the true God, heard the gospel, received the gift of the Holy Ghost, glorified God, and were baptized in the name of Jesus. We are decidedly in favor of the baptism of all such households. Acts x. 2, 24, 44, 46-48.

"I baptized," said Paul, "the household of Stephanas." 1 Cor. i. 16. The apostle visited Corinth about A. D. 54 or 55, where he remained "a year and six months, teaching the word of God among them." Acts xviii. 11. During this time, he baptized Stephanas and his family. In the year A. D. 59, or thereabouts, he wrote his first letter to "the church of God" in that city. In the epistle he makes special reference to the house of Stephanas. "I beseech you, brethren," said he, "(ye know the house of Stephanas, that it is the first fruits of Achaia, and that they have addicted themselves to the ministry of the saints,) that ye submit yourselves unto such," &c. 1 Cor. xvi. 15, 16. Several points are worthy of notice in this text. The family of Stephanas were "the first fruits of Achaia." This term is applied to the regenerate. "Of his own will begat he us with the word of truth, that we should be a kind of first fruits of his creatures." Jas. i. 18. See, also, Rev. xiv. 4. The word is never used, so far as we know, to denote unconscious or unregenerate infants. This family, in four or five years after their baptism, devoted "themselves to the ministry of the saints," whether in preaching the word or supplying the wants of the poor, we do not know. It was a benevolent, noble service, commended by the Spirit of inspiration. If they were infants baptized by Paul, four or five years previously, they were the most precocious children that we have read of. Nor is this all. The apostle besought the Corinthian saints, renowned throughout the world for their spiritual gifts (1 Cor. i. 7), to "submit" themselves "unto such" as "the house of Stephanas." They were not only the benefactors of the church, but fitted to bear rule in it. They were not infants, not children; nor were they at the time of their baptism. It ought in fairness to be conceded that the baptism of the house of Stephanas yields no support to infant baptism, but lends its full weight to the exclusive baptism of believers.

We must now notice the baptism of the household of the Philippian jailer, recorded in Acts xvi. 24-34. Paul, divinely guided, passed for the first time into Europe, and commenced his ministrations at a Roman post called Philippi. Here several persons were converted and baptized, and a great persecution was commenced against Paul and Silas. They were arrested, scourged, and committed to the hands of the jailer, under strict charge to keep them safely. He cast them into the dungeon and made their feet fast in the stocks. They were delivered from their bondage by divine interposition, and the jailer was saved from suicide by the friendly counsel of Paul. We shall notice the narrative only so far as it relates to the point under discussion. The jailer brought Paul and Silas into his house, and "they spake unto him the word of the Lord, and *to all that were in his house.*" Verse 32. We might infer, from the excitement and importance of the occasion, that all the jailer's family were present; but there is no room left for conjecture. The historian tells us positively that the word was preached "to *all* that were in the house." What was the result of this instruction? The jailer, in the "same hour of the night, * * * was baptized, he and all his, straightway." Verse 33. That there might be no possible plea for infant baptism found in this narrative, the inspired writer adds: "He (the jailer) brought them (Paul and Silas) into his house, * * * and rejoiced, *believing in God, with all his house.*" Verse 34. It is incomprehensible to us that any man of intelligence and candor should doubt that the jailer's family were converts to Christianity. There is precisely the same evidence of their conversion that there is of his. Did he hear the word of the Lord? So did they. Did he believe in Christ? So did they. Was he baptized? So were they. The whole narrative corresponds with the apostolic commission and practice in Jerusalem and Cæsarea. The order observed was instruction, faith, baptism. The ingenious reasoner who can derive authority for infant baptism from this narrative can find it anywhere.

Only the baptism of Lydia's household remains to be considered. Acts xvi. 14, 15: "A certain woman named Lydia, a seller of purple, of the city of Thyatira, which worshipped God, heard us; whose heart the Lord opened, that she attended unto the things which were spoken of Paul. And when she was baptized, and her household," &c. Were there infants in Lydia's family? The burden of proof lies on the advocates of pedobaptism, who would derive authority for their practice from this passage. We have shown incontrovertibly, as it seems to us, that in three baptized households there were no children, or that they were not included among the baptized. Does not this fact create a strong presumption that there were none in Lydia's house? We will perform, however, a work of supererogation. While we cannot positively prove that Lydia had no infant children, we can show the extreme improbability that she had any. She was a dealer in purple goods, of the city of Thyatira, in the province of Asia, several hundred miles distant from Philippi. She was probably an adventurer, with no permanent home. She, it is likely, had no husband. She said to Paul and Silas, "Come into *my* house and abide." If she had a husband, he seems to have been of no importance in the family. If she were married, there is no proof that she had children; and if she had children, there is no evidence that they were infants or minors. Her family probably consisted of the servants and helpers in her mercantile shop. When Paul and Silas were released from prison, and forced hastily to leave the city, they "entered into the house of Lydia; and when they had seen the brethren, they comforted them and departed." Verse 40. Who were these brethren in Lydia's house? They were not infants or young children, but persons capable of receiving religious consolation and encouragement. If there were nothing to bias the mind, it would be almost impossible to avoid the conclusion that the brethren referred to were Lydia's baptized household. If infant baptism has no better foundation than the probability that there were infants in the family of Lydia, and that they were baptized, it ought to be abandoned.

Let us test the strength of the argument drawn from the baptism of households in support of infant baptism by a parallel case. There were believing as well as baptized households. Of the nobleman of Cana it is said: "Himself believed, and his whole house." Jno. iv. 53. We read: "Crispus, the chief ruler of the synagogue, believed on the Lord, with all his house." Acts xviii. 8. What would we think of the acumen of a logician who should reason after this manner: We read in the Scriptures of believing families; infants are found in most families; therefore, in the apostolic times, infants believed the gospel. The conclusion is a manifest absurdity, and consequently nobody reasons in that way; but the argument is quite as logical and the inference quite as conclusive as that which attempts to deduce infant baptism from the baptism of households.

The argument in favor of infant baptism derived from household baptisms proves quite too much for those who employ it. If families are to be baptized on the faith of their parents, why should the baptisms be limited to infants? Are not adult children, as well as servants, as often found in families as infants? If families are to be baptized, why not baptize the whole of them? By what authority is the ordinance limited to infants and little children? The jailer "was baptized—he and *all his*." If family connection is a plea for baptism, why should it not avail for adults as well as infants?

Perhaps it will be said that faith is required of adults, in order to their baptism. Certainly it is, of those who act on their own responsibility; but households, according to the Pedobaptist theory, are baptized on the faith and by the authority of the parents. If households are to be baptized in virtue of their relation to their pious heads, why should any portion of the family be excluded from the privilege? The Israelites were required to circumcise all the males in their families, free and bond, at the age of eight days; but if, from any cause, the rite was neglected, it was proper to perform it at any period of life. Gen. xvii. 13 and Josh. v. 8. Circumcision was a family institution, and all its male members were entitled to its benefits. Baptism is supposed by the advocates of the infant rite to be a substitute for circumcision. By what plea, then, do they limit the baptism of households to the baptism of infants? That is not household baptism. It is the baptism of a part, usually a small part, and that, too, the least important part, of the family; and the discrimination, so far as we can discern, is arbitrarily made.

CHAPTER V.

Believers the Only Subjects of Baptism.

A popular argument in support of infant baptism is drawn from the Abrahamic covenant and the rite of circumcision. It is said: God entered into covenant with Abraham, and required him to have his male children circumcised as a sign or token of the covenant; that it is still in force; that baptism, under the new dispensation, is the sign of the covenant, as circumcision formerly was; that the sign should be applied to the children of believers, as circumcision was applied to Abraham and his descendants; and that baptism should be administered to female as well as male children, because the ordinance is suited to both sexes.

Let us examine this subject. When Abram was ninety years old, God entered into a covenant with him. Among its provisions, on God's part, Abraham was to have a numerous progeny—to be "a father of many nations"; kings were to come of him; the covenant was to be established with his seed, to be "an everlasting covenant"; the land of Canaan, in which he was a stranger, was to be given to him and to his seed "for an everlasting possession," and that God would be their God. Abram—whose name was then changed to Abraham—was, on his part, bound to walk before God and be perfect, and, in token of the covenant, to circumcise every male child, eight days old, born in his house or bought with his money. Gen. xvii. 1-14. This sign or seal was to be perpetuated in the family of Abraham. It was a visible, enduring mark in the flesh, testifying what God had promised to the patriarch, and what he required of him and his posterity. Is baptism a token of this covenant? Does it certify that Abraham should have a numerous progeny? that kings should descend from him? that his posterity should possess the land of Canaan? If we did not know that pious and intelligent men have insisted that baptism is a token of this covenant, we should suppose that the opinion did not come within the range of human credulity.

Let us consider this matter further. Moses incorporated circumcision among the statutes that he gave to Israel. Lev. xii. 3. The rite has been observed by the descendants of Israel, in the line of Judah—that is, the Jews—down to the present time. It is maintained by them as a family distinction, and a token that they worship the God of Abraham. Is baptism a substitute for this family or national rite? The Scriptures give us no intimation of the substitution. No Jew was admitted to Christian privileges in virtue of his circumcision. There are great and irreconcilable differences between circumcision and baptism. Their *subjects* are different. Circumcision was administered only to the male descendants of Abraham and to the male slaves born in their families or bought with their money; baptism was administered to penitent believers, of all nations and of both sexes. The *time* of their administration differed. Circumcision was administered to infants, by express command, when eight days old; baptism was administered to its subjects at any age and when convenience permitted. Acts viii. 36, 38. Circumcision was administered, not *officially* by priests, but by *parents* or *masters;* baptism was administered, not by parents, but by *apostles* or *ministers* of the gospel. No *moral quality* was required in order to circumcision (Josh. v. 1, 2); repentance and faith were the invariable prerequisites of baptism (Matt. iii. 7, 9. The *design* of the two rites was entirely different. Circumcision was a token in the flesh of the covenant in which God promised to Abraham and his posterity both temporal and spiritual blessings, on condition of their devotion to his service; baptism is a symbol of the resurrection of Christ and of the remission of sins. Rom. vi. 4; Acts xxii. 16. In short, circumcision belonged to the ceremonial dispensation, and passed away with its various sacrifices and bloody rites; and baptism is a gospel ordinance, to be perpetuated to the end of time. Matt. xxviii. 19, 20.

That there may be resemblances traced between circumcision and baptism, need not be denied. There are not two things in nature which do not bear a likeness to each other. There are no two rites in all the systems of religion, true or false, which do not have a resemblance to each other. But what of that? Water and fire resemble each other; but one cannot be substituted for the other.

Various resemblances may be pointed out between circumcision and baptism; but the latter differs so widely from the former in all its essential characteristics that, to infer the subjects of baptism from those of circumcision, is illogical and fallacious.

The *onus probandi* lies on those who affirm that baptism is a substitute for circumcision. We are not required to prove a negative. We will, however, in this case, come as near to doing it as possible to miss it. No subject caused the early churches so much perplexity and trouble as the introduction of Gentile converts into them without circumcision. The Jewish Christians were very zealous in support of the rite. They had received it from the fathers, it was incorporated among their national ceremonies, and was held in the highest estimation by all the Israelites. The introduction of Gentiles into the churches without this sacred and venerated rite seemed to these Jewish Christians to be a desecration and an outrage. They taught that, except men were circumcised after the manner of Moses, they could not be saved. Repentance, faith, baptism, holy lives, could avail them nothing, without circumcision. There was dissension and disputation among the brethren on this subject. A council was called in the city of Jerusalem to consider the matter and give their opinion concerning it, for the guidance of the churches. The convention consisted of the apostles, and elders, and the whole church. The believing Pharisees maintained "that it was needful to circumcise" the Gentile converts, "and to command them to keep the law of Moses." The subject underwent a full discussion, in which Peter (the apostle, not Pope), Barnabas, Paul, and James participated. The council reached the conclusion that circumcision was not obligatory on Gentile believers. It was a burden which God had not laid upon them.

The discussion and the decision of the council contained not the slightest reference to the substitution of baptism for circumcision. We will not affirm that, admitting the substitution was divinely required, it was *impossible* that the discussion should have occurred without an allusion to it. We know not the limit of possibilities. We will, however, say that, under the circumstances, it seems to us *extremely improbable*, conceding the divine authority of the substitution, that it was not mentioned as an important element in the settlement of the matter. Consider the facts of the case. The question was whether it was necessary to circumcise the Gentile converts. They had been baptized, and, if baptism was a substitute for circumcision, they had been virtually circumcised. This explanation would have satisfied the Gentiles, and, at least, have silenced the Pharisees. Indeed, it was absolutely necessary to an understanding of the matter in debate. Is it reasonable to suppose, does it come within the scope of credibility, that Peter and Barnabas, Paul and James, should have publicly discussed this perplexing subject without the slightest reference to the principle that would have freed it from all difficulty? We do not believe that they did. The matter is all plain when we suppose that the council, under the inspiration of the Holy Ghost, knew nothing of the substitution of baptism for circumcision. They could not have learned it from the Scriptures, and, if they learned it from direct inspiration, they failed to record it for the benefit of future generations.

Several passages of Scripture have been quoted in support of infant baptism, which we need not examine. A careful attention to their contexts will show their irrelevancy to the subject; or an examination of the comments of candid and learned Pedobaptists will usually disclose the same truth. These texts do not mention infant baptism, or refer to it, or reveal any principle which can logically lead to it.

Infant baptism seems to be a harmless rite. It appeals strongly to parental affection, is invested with poetic charms, and refers for its support to a venerable antiquity, and to the number, learning, and respectability of its advocates. What harm, it is asked, can a rite so simple, appropriate, and beautiful do to the child or its parents? The influence of pedobaptism, in this country, has been greatly modified by the prevalence of Baptist views. In many places and some religious sects it has fallen greatly into desuetude. If the rite is not neglected, it is observed as an empty ceremony. It has no regenerating and no sin-cleansing efficacy. In four-fifths of the Christian world, however, infant baptism is viewed in a very different light. It is held and practised as a regenerating, sin-purifying ordinance. This doctrine is taught without equivocation and without reservation. Infants, born in sin, are supposed to be renewed in nature and delivered from guilt by the application of a few drops of water, in the name of the Father, Son, and Holy Spirit, by a duly qualified priest, or, in cases of necessity, by parents, physicians, or nurses. The regenerated child is made a member of the mystical body of Christ and an inheritor of the kingdom of heaven. He grows up in the church. His membership is perpetuated by the rite of confirmation.

To this system we have grave and weighty objections. It finds no countenance in the oracles of God. We read, indeed, in a book containing many excellent truths and precepts, that by baptism infants are regenerated, made members of the mystical body of Christ, and inheritors of the kingdom of heaven; but we find no such teaching in the Scriptures. The tendency of this doctrine has been, in all ages and in all countries, to obliterate the distinction between the church and the world. In almost every land where pedobaptism has enjoyed uncontrolled sway, the limits of the church and the world have been coextensive. All the infidelity, corruption, and blasphemy of the people have been within the church. Its discipline has been overthrown, or exercised only in regard to those who have questioned its authority. The Romish and

Grecian hierarchies, wherever they have been established, have confirmed these statements; and Protestant hierarchies, though restrained by the influence of dissent in their tendency, have quite clearly exemplified the same remarks.

The influence of the doctrine of baptismal regeneration is even worse on individuals than on communities. Persons who grow up under the persuasion that they are regenerated, children of God, and inheritors of his kingdom, are laboring under a perilous delusion. They misconceive the plan of human redemption. They cherish a hope that neither Scripture nor reason can sanction. They vainly imagine that they have some claim to divine mercy, some advantages for securing salvation, that others have not. Will not this persuasion inevitably beget a false peace, inspire a deceptive hope, and tend to prevent repentance unto life? Parents, too, must have less solicitude for the salvation of their children, as they have been placed within the limit of the covenant and made heirs of the heavenly kingdom.

CHAPTER VI.

Only Immersion is Baptism.

The inspired writers use only one term, with its derivatives, to denote the act required by the ordinance under consideration. That word, it has been elsewhere stated, as expressed in Roman letters and changed in form to suit the English idiom, is *baptize*. What does it mean?

Some writers maintain, and multitudes of people believe, that baptize signifies equally to sprinkle, to pour, or to immerse. We will not affirm that a word might not be employed with a meaning so comprehensive and yet so indefinite. We have no knowledge of any such term. There is certainly no such word in the English tongue. If there is any such term in any language, modern or ancient, it has not come to our knowledge. We do not perceive what use could be made of so vague a word. Sprinkling, pouring, and immersing are entirely distinct acts, and are never confounded in human conception. Terms to express these different acts are needed in the intercourse of society, and are found, we doubt not, in all languages; but a word denoting them all would not only be a *nondescript*, but tend merely to confuse or mislead. If baptize means sprinkle or pour, it does not mean immerse.

Other persons insist that baptize signifies neither sprinkle, pour, nor immerse, but wash or cleanse; that it denotes an effect, not an act. This definition will be found to be utterly irreconcilable with the inspired use of the term.

We maintain that baptize means immerse or dip, and that, like these terms, though it may be used in a figurative sense, it invariably has reference to its primary import. To learn the meaning of the word, let us go, not to lexicons, but to the common version of the Scriptures. We decline an appeal to lexicons, not because we have any dread of the result, but because we wish to present an argument in support of our views that may be fully understood and appreciated by every intelligent reader of the Scriptures.

It must be borne in mind that the translators of the English version were Pedobaptists, and, either from the order of King James or their own views of propriety, failed to translate the Greek term *baptizo*, with its cognates, used in the Scriptures to denote the act required by the ordinance. We must, therefore, learn its meaning from its various connections in the New Testament.

We may infer the import of baptism from the *places* of its administration. John, having received his commission to baptize from heaven, commenced preaching "the baptism of repentance for the remission of sins"; and "then went out unto him all the land of Judea, and they of Jerusalem, and were all *baptized of him in the river Jordan*." Mk. 1. 5. No intelligent person, reading this passage with an unbiassed mind, would have any doubt that these multitudes were immersed in the river.

To suppose that they went into the stream merely to have water sprinkled or poured upon them, is, in our view, a puerility undeserving a reply.

Read again: "John was baptizing in Ænon, near to Salim, because there was much water there; and they came and were baptized." Jno. iii. 23. The necessity of "much water" for the purpose of immersing is quite plain; but it was not needed for sprinkling or pouring. It is said, however, by the advocates of sprinkling, that great multitudes attended the ministry of John, and that "much water" was needed to quench their thirst and that of their beasts. This is not what the evangelist says. His words are, not that John was preaching or encamped at Ænon, because there was "much water" there, but that "John was *baptizing in Ænon, because there was much water there.*" If language can make anything clear, it is plain that John baptized in Ænon on account of its furnishing an ample supply of water for the purpose.

It is sometimes said that these passages refer to John's baptism, and not to Christian baptism. This is true; but we are simply inquiring for the meaning of the word baptize. The thing which John did, Christ commanded his apostles to do. If he immersed, they immersed. It can hardly be supposed that the meaning of the word "baptize" was changed in the short period from the commencement of John's ministry to the beginning of the apostolic ministry.

The baptism of the jailer and his family, at

Philippi, is supposed by some to furnish proof that the rite was administered by sprinkling or pouring. He was baptized, it is said, in the prison, at night, without previous preparation for the administration of the ordinance, and it is not probable that there was any convenience in the jail for immersion. This argument cannot rise above probability. There might have been ample means for immersion. If the word "baptize" means immerse, there is nothing in this case to create the slightest doubt that the jailer and his family were immersed. On the contrary, the recorded facts furnish strong probability in favor of their immersion. The jailer, alarmed by an earthquake, brought Paul and Silas "out"—doubtless out of the "inner prison"—and inquired for the way of salvation. "And they spake unto him the word of the Lord, and to all that were *in his house.*" This teaching clearly occurred in the jailer's house—probably a portion of the prison set apart for his occupancy. In the same hour of the night, he "was baptized, he and all his, straightway." Now, notice, after the baptism, he "brought them into his house." Why had they left it? If the baptism had been sprinkling or pouring, there would have been no need for going out of it. Immersion, in all probability, rendered it necessary to leave the jailer's house, and, the ordinance having been administered, the company very naturally returned to the house for refreshments. Acts xvi. 25-34.

The meaning of the word "baptize" is clearly indicated by the *import of the prepositions* used in connection with it. Notice the following passages: "Baptized *in* Jordan"—Matt. iii. 6; "Jesus, when he was baptized, went *up* straightway *out of* the water"—verse 16; "They went down both *into* the water, *both* Philip and the eunuch, and he baptized him; and when they were come up *out of* the water," &c. The prepositions used in these texts are in perfect harmony with the practice of immersion, but are utterly discordant with that of sprinkling or pouring. The unbiassed mind, in reading these passages, would never imagine that baptism was anything but immersion.

The attempt has been made to weaken the force of this argument by appealing to the ambiguity of the Greek prepositions contained in these Scriptures. That they were used with considerable latitude and indefiniteness need not be denied. It must be conceded, however, that the best Pedobaptist scholars have translated the prepositions as we have them in the above passages. So far as we know, there is not a respectable version of the Scriptures in the English tongue in which these prepositions are not rendered substantially as in the common version.

There is, however, in this version a notable exception to the rendering of the preposition under consideration. We read in Matt. iii. 11: "I indeed baptize you *with* water unto repentance." This preposition cannot be well construed with immerse. It would be awkward and bad English to say, "I *immerse with* water." The language, "I *sprinkle* you *with* water," sounds well; but it would be intolerable to say, "I *pour* you *with* water."

It seems strange that the Greek preposition *en*, which in the 6th verse is rendered *in*—"*in* Jordan"—should in the 11th verse be translated *with*—"*with* water." Uniformity of translation is desirable, if not forbidden by the sense of Scripture. In these passages, there is nothing to prevent a uniform rendering. It would be incongruous to say "with Jordan"; but it is in perfect harmony and good taste to translate the passages "*in* Jordan" and "*in* water." Dr. George Campbell, of Edinburgh, a learned Presbyterian divine, and president of Marischal College, not only translates the passage "*in* water and *in* the Holy Ghost," but makes the following comments on the subject:

"All the modern translations from the Greek which I have seen render the words as our common version does, except Le Clerc, who says, *dans l' eau—dans le Saint Esprit*. I am sorry to observe that the Popish translators from the Vulgate have shown greater veneration for the style of that version than the generality of Protestant translators have shown for that of the original; for in this the Latin is not more explicit than the Greek. Yet so inconsistent are the interpreters last mentioned that none of them have scrupled to render *en to Jordane*, in the 6th verse, *in Jordan*, though nothing can be plainer than that, if there be any incongruity in the expression *in water*, this *in Jordan* must be equally incongruous. But they have seen that the preposition *in* could not be avoided there, without adopting a circumlocution, and saying *with the water of Jordan*, which would have made their deviation from the text too glaring. The word *baptizein* (baptize), both in sacred authors and in classical, signifies *to dip, to plunge, to immerse,* and was rendered by Tertullian, the oldest of the Latin fathers, *tingere,* the term used for dyeing cloth, which was by immersion. It is always construed suitably to this meaning. Thus it is *en udati* (in water), *en to Jordane* (in Jordan). But I should not lay much stress on the preposition *en,* * * * which may denote *with* as well as *in,* did not the whole phraseology in regard to this ceremony concur in evincing the same thing. * * * When the Greek word *baptizo* is adopted, I may say, rather than translated, into modern languages, the mode of construction ought to be preserved, so far as may conduce to suggest its original import. It is to be regretted that we have so much evidence that even good and learned men allow their judgments to be warped by the sentiments and customs of the sect which they prefer. The true partisan, of whatever denomination, always inclines to correct the diction of the Spirit by that of the party."— "The Four Gospels," Boston Edition, Vol. IV., pages 23, 24.

CHAPTER VII.

Only Immersion is Baptism.

Another proof of our proposition may be derived from the incidental and figurative references to baptism in the Scriptures. Several of these claim our notice.

Baptism is a burial. "We are," says Paul, "buried with him (Jesus Christ) by baptism into death." Rom. vi. 4. This language is figurative; but it must have reference to the import of the word "baptism." There is a resemblance between immersion and a burial, clear to every intelligent mind. In either case the body is covered, concealed. A burial by sprinkling is a thing unknown. It would, indeed, be possible to bury a body by the sprinkling of earth; but how could it be buried by the sprinkling of water? A conception so unnatural and grotesque surely never found a lodgment in the brain of the pupil of Gamaliel. A burial by pouring water is little less wild and improbable; while a burial by washing or cleansing is a simple absurdity. But, supposing—what Dr. Doddridge says it is the part of candor to admit—that there is in the language "an allusion to the manner of baptizing by *immersion*, as most usual (universal, as we maintain) in these early times," the figure is plain, striking, and impressive.

It is asserted by some, in their efforts to weaken the argument drawn from this text in favor of immersion, that the baptism referred to was not literal, but spiritual. Our only present use for the text is to prove that baptism is immersion. It serves our purpose quite as well whether it be interpreted literally or spiritually. Paul, who was a master of language, and guided by the Spirit of inspiration, called baptism a burial; which figure is clear, pertinent, and instructive, if baptism means immersion, but forced, meaningless, and misleading, if it signifies sprinkling, pouring, or cleansing.

Washing is an effect of baptism. "Arise," said Ananias to Saul of Tarsus, "and be baptized, and wash away thy sins." Acts xxii. 16. Washing is not an effect of sprinkling. The conception of washing by sprinkling is unnatural. It may be used to moisten or soften, but not to wash. Washing may be an effect of pouring; but the text cannot be construed in harmony with this term. It is an obvious absurdity to say: "Arise, and be poured, and wash away thy sins." A man can be poured upon, but only liquids or solids in dust or grains can be poured. The language, "Arise, and be *immersed*, and *wash away* thy sins," is in perfect harmony with our conceptions of the effect of immersion. We immerse for the purpose of washing. The removal of filth is the usual consequence of immersion.

Baptism denotes overwhelming distress and suffering. "I have," said Jesus, "a baptism to be baptized with; and how am I straitened (or pained) till it be accomplished!" Lu. xii. 50. It is evident from the context that the Saviour had reference in this language to his approaching sufferings and death. He calls them, figuratively, a baptism—an immersion. The figure is natural, common, and impressive. We speak of overwhelming sufferings, of being drowned in sorrow, and of being immersed in cares. Everybody perfectly understands the language. Jesus called his sufferings a baptism because of their severity. The same conception of sufferings is expressed by the Psalmist in different language: "Then the waters had overwhelmed us, the stream had gone over our soul; then the proud waters had gone over our soul." Psa. cxxiv. 4, 5. Dr. Campbell, the learned Pedobaptist already referred to, thus translates the text: "I have an immersion to undergo; and how am I pained till it be accomplished!" The thought is solemn and affecting. The Saviour said, in anticipation of his sufferings on the cross: "I have an immersion to undergo"—I am to be overwhelmed in sorrow and in sufferings; and I am "pained"—filled with anxiety and grief—till the fearful trial is over. How tame and unmeaning, not to say incongruous, does the text become, if it be rendered: "I have a pouring, or sprinkling, or cleansing to undergo." Who would think of representing the sufferings of the Saviour by sprinkling a few drops of water on the face or pouring a cupful of water on the head? To call the sufferings of Christ a washing or cleansing, would be a grievous offence against taste.

Some writers, to evade the force of this passage in favor of immersion, have maintained that the Saviour was baptized by his own sweat and blood. His sufferings are, in several passages of Scripture, described as the shedding of his blood. Matt. xxvi. 28; Heb. ix. 22. By a common figure of speech, a part is put for the whole, or the effect for the cause. The shedding of Christ's blood was a notable part of his sufferings, and the cause, or one of the causes, of his death. It would not have been strange, if, in anticipation of his sufferings, he had described them as a blood-shedding; but to call them a sprinkling or a pouring has no sanction, so far as we are informed, from analogy, and greatly weakens and obscures the sense of the passage. How much more in accordance with its intent and force is the comment of Lange: *"To be baptized—An image of the intensity of his suffering, like a baptism performed by immersion."*

Baptism is a covering. "Our fathers * * * were all baptized unto Moses in the cloud and in the sea." 1 Cor. x. 2. This was not a literal, but a figurative baptism. There was a resemblance between the passage of the children of Israel through the Red Sea and immersion. It is plain to every discerning mind. In both cases there was a covering up, a shutting in. Dr. Whitby, an Episcopalian, who cannot be suspected of any partiality for Baptist views, describes it: *"They were baptized unto Moses in the cloud;* i. e., into the doctrine taught by Moses; for the cloud was not only for direction, but for a covering over them, according to the words of the Psalmist, 'He spread out the cloud for a covering.' Psa. cv. 29. *And in the sea*—for they were covered with the sea on both sides. Ex. xiv. 22. So that both the cloud and the sea had some resemblance to our being covered with water in baptism. Their going into the sea resembled the ancient rite of going into the water."

Dr. McKnight, the learned Scotch commentator, though less explicit in his language than Dr. Whitby, evidently put the same interpretation on the passage. He says: "*In the cloud and in the sea.* Because the Israelites, by being hid from the Egyptians under the cloud, and by passing through the Red Sea, were made to declare their belief in the Lord and in his servant Moses (Ex. xiv. 31), the apostle very properly represents them as 'baptized unto Moses in the cloud and in the sea.'"

This sense of the passage commends itself to the enlightened and impartial mind. Another interpretation, however, is given to it, in the interest of sprinkling or pouring. The Israelites, it is maintained, were baptized by the sprinkling or pouring of water from the cloud, and by spray from the sea. This exposition demands the change of the common rendering of the Greek preposition *en* from *in* to *by*—a change which it admits, but which is sanctioned by no translator within our reach. This change, however, will avail the advocates of sprinkling but little. The interpretation is inconsistent with the history of the case. God wrought a miracle to deliver his people from the power of the Egyptians. "The Lord went before them by day in a pillar of a cloud, to lead them the way; and by night in a pillar of fire, to give them light; to go by day and night." Ex. xiii. 21. The cloud and fire were a symbol of the divine presence, designed to cover and guide, and not to sprinkle, the escaping Israelites. Nor were they moistened by the spray of the sea. "The Lord caused the sea to go back by a strong east wind all that night, and made the sea dry land, and the waters were divided." Ex. xiv. 22. It would certainly have derogated from the completeness of the miracle and the glory of God, had they reached the eastern shore of the sea drenched with showers and bedraggled with mud. The miracle was dishonored by no such imperfection. "The children of Israel walked upon *dry land* in the midst of the sea, and the waters were a wall unto them on their right hand and on their left." Verse 29. This was undoubtedly a dry baptism, but a figurative one. The person who can find sprinkling, pouring, or cleansing in this baptism will have no difficulty in finding it anywhere. The servant of James Hervey, the author of "Meditations Among the Tombs," said his master could make a sermon out of a pair of tongs, and no doubt he could. It does not, however, require half the ingenuity to make a sermon on a pair of tongs that is demanded to extract water baptism from the pillar of a cloud and the sea walls that protected the Israelites in their escape from Egypt.

We will notice a passage, of the class of Scriptures under consideration, relied on by many in the defence of sprinkling or pouring. "He (Jesus) shall baptize you with the Holy Ghost and fire." Matt. iii. 11. Nothing, beyond a fair translation, is needed for the understanding of this text. The attentive reader has already seen that Dr. Campbell not only renders the language "*in* the Holy Ghost and fire," but expresses his surprise that the translators of King James should have abandoned the ordinary sense of the preposition *(en)*, which they were compelled to accept in the 6th verse. The best, we think, that can be said in favor of the common version is that the particle *may be* rendered *with*. In the first ten chapters of Matthew, *en* occurs about ninety-five times. In seventy-four places it is rendered *in*, or by terms of equivalent import; in sixteen passages it is translated by other words, and only in five places by *with*. The almost uniform import of the preposition seems to have made it obligatory on the translators not to depart from it without necessity. In the 11th verse the necessity did not exist. Lange, in his commentary, agrees with Dr. Campbell as to its proper rendering. He says: "Verse 11. *He shall baptize*, or immerse, *you in* the Holy Ghost and *in* fire."

The language is figurative; but its import is clear. When it is affirmed that a man is immersed in cares, or politics, or debt, or trouble, nobody has any doubt as to the meaning of the words. A man is immersed in cares when they absorb his thoughts and occupy his time. A man is immersed in the Spirit when he is fully under the influence of the Spirit—is enlightened, strengthened, guided, and endowed with extraordinary gifts by him. Baptism in the Spirit denotes that wonderful communication of the Spirit by which the apostles and their colaborers were fitted for their important mission.

It is maintained by the advocates of pouring and sprinkling that the baptism of the Holy Ghost was by pouring. In support of this view, several passages are quoted: "Having received of the Father the promise of the Holy Ghost, he (Jesus) hath shed forth this which ye now see and hear." Acts ii. 33. "On the Gentiles was poured out the gift of the Holy Ghost." Acts x. 45. "The Holy Ghost fell on them, as on us at the beginning." Acts xi. 15. These expressions, "shed forth," "poured out," and "fell on," denote the manner of the copious communication of the Spirit and his gifts; but they do not describe the baptism of the Spirit. That was the result of this abundant communication of the Spirit. He was "shed forth," "poured out," "fell," in such great measure that those who received the gift were not only filled with the Spirit, but immersed in him—brought entirely under his influence, as a body covered with water is saturated with it. The baptism of the Holy Ghost has no reference to the manner of his communication, whether it be by shedding, pouring, or falling; but to his abundant influence. The apostles were immersed in the Holy Spirit just as a guinea would be immersed in a vessel filled by water poured into it.

CHAPTER VIII.

Only Immersion is Baptism.

The word "immerse" and its derivatives may be substituted for "baptize" and its derivatives in every place where they occur in the New Testament, making good sense, without the slightest incongruity or violence to the language; and this is not true of the term "sprinkling, pouring, washing, or cleansing."

When we insert a key in a lock, and it fits every ward and easily turns the bolt, we know that we have the right key. Just so it is in the definition of a word. If it is properly defined, the definition may be put in every place in which the word is rightly used, without force or bad taste; but, if the definition is incorrect, while it may be substituted in many sentences for the original term without obvious inaccuracy, it cannot be so substituted in an extensive use of the term without bad taste, ambiguity, or nonsense. To this principle of language, so far as we know, there is no exception. Let us subject the definitions of the word "baptize" to this test. The process may lead to the repetition of statements made in preceding articles; but its importance will justify the operation.

"And were all baptized of him *in the river Jordan*." Mark i. 5. It is obvious that pouring candidates in the river is not good English. That word must stand aside.

"*Buried* with him *in baptism.*" Col. ii. 12. Buried in sprinkling, or in pouring, or in washing, or in cleansing, are all barbarisms. These substitutes for baptism must be ruled out.

"Be baptized and wash away thy sins." Acts xxii. 16. To be sprinkled for the purpose of washing is incongruous; but to be washed or cleansed for that object is simply preposterous.

"By one Spirit are we all baptized into one body." 1 Cor. xii. 13. "As many of you as have been baptized into Christ." Gal. iii. 27. To be sprinkled, or poured, or washed, or cleansed into a body, or into Christ, is language that no scholar, or writer of clear conceptions, would employ.

By the laws of language, sprinkling, pouring, washing, and cleansing are equally excluded as substitutes for baptism. Immersion is the key that fits all the wards of the philological lock, by which so many commentators and critics have been needlessly perplexed. Immersion and its cognates will substitute baptism and its cognates, through all their moods, tenses, and declensions, without obscurity, confusion, or the slightest violence to the prepositions and other terms used in connection with them. On this point the reader may find conclusive evidence in the Revised Version of the New Testament, published by the American Bible Union.

Immersion was so evidently practised by the early Christian churches, except in cases of sickness or of supposed necessity, it seems strange that an intelligent person should deny it. Any number of credible witnesses on this point might easily be furnished; but it will be sufficient to present two or three quotations—which, for the sake of convenience, we copy from the "Star Book," a valuable little treatise on baptism:

MOSHEIM: "In this century [the first], baptism was administered in convenient places, without the public assemblies, and by *immersing* the candidates wholly in water."

NEANDER: "In respect to the form of baptism, it was, in conformity with the original institution and the original import of the symbol, performed by *immersion*, as a sign of entire baptism into the Holy Spirit, and of being entirely penetrated by the same."

WADDINGTON: "The sacraments of the primitive church were two—that of baptism and the Lord's supper. The ceremony of *immersion*, the oldest form of baptism, was performed in the name of the three persons of the Trinity."

SCHAFF: "Finally, so far as it respects the mode and manner of baptizing, there can be no doubt that *immersion*, and not sprinkling, was the original normal form." *Star Book*, pages 37, 38.

Not only was immersion practised by the early Christian churches, but it has been continued by the Greek church, next to the Roman Catholic, the largest of all the Christian sects, and containing the people who have inherited the language in which the New Testament was written, down to the present time. Every well-informed person is acquainted with this fact; but we will quote a single testimony in proof of it:

COLEMAN: "The Eastern church has uniformly retained the form of *immersion* as indispensable to the validity of the ordinance; and repeat the rite, whenever they have received to their communion persons who have been baptized in another manner." *Star Book*, page 45.

The Greek church practises *trine immersion*, which we consider a corruption of the apostolic baptism; but this fact does not weaken its testimony in favor of immersion. The repetition of the act might easily grow out of an erroneous interpretation of the command, "baptizing them in the name of the *Father*, and of the *Son*, and of the *Holy Ghost*"; but we see no reason for changing sprinkling into immersion. All the motives of convenience, comfort, and taste draw in the opposite direction.

The Roman Catholic church continued immersion, except in extreme cases, to the close of the thirteenth century. On this point the most abundant testimony can be furnished. We need quote but two authorities:

DR. BRENNEN: "*Thirteen hundred years* was baptism generally and originally performed by the *immersion* of the person under water, and only in extraordinary cases was sprinkling or affusion permitted. These latter methods were called in question, and even prohibited."

AUGUSTI: "*Immersion* in water was general until the *thirteenth century* among the Latins. It was then displaced by sprinkling, but retained by the Greeks." *Star Book*, pages 40, 41.

The English Episcopal church, in its rubric on baptism, strictly enjoins that the child shall be *dipped*, unless it be duly certified that it is sickly or weak and unable to endure dipping; and in that case, pouring or sprinkling may suffice.

The *baptisteries* still preserved in Italy and in the East furnish conclusive evidence that *immersion was the practice of the early Christian centuries*. These buildings, some of them dating as far back as the third or fourth century, were erected at great expense, and were furnished with ample conveniences for immersing adults, as well as infants. The fonts are in the centre of the buildings, circular in form, three or four feet deep, and sufficiently spacious for the immersion of half a dozen adults at one time. These structures furnish proof, not only that immersion was practised, but of the great importance attached to it. No modern church or sect has furnished proof of their zeal for immersion comparable in strength with that given by the early Christians in the erection of their baptisteries.

If sprinkling was not the primitive baptism, it may very properly be asked when and how was it introduced. On this subject we quote from the Edinburgh Encyclopædia, which cannot be suspected of any partiality for Baptists:

"It is impossible to mark the precise period

when sprinkling was introduced. It is probable, however, that it was invented in Africa, in the second century, in favor of clinics. But it was so far from being approved by the church in general that the Africans themselves did not account it valid. The first law for sprinkling was obtained in the following manner: Pope Stephen III., being driven from Rome by Astulphus, king of the Lombards, in 753, fled to Papin, who, a short time before, had usurped the crown of France. Whilst he remained there, the monks of Cressy, in Brittany, consulted him whether, in a case of necessity, baptism performed by pouring water on the head of the infant would be lawful. Stephen replied that it would. But, though the truth of this fact should be allowed, which some Catholics deny, yet pouring or sprinkling was only admitted in cases of necessity. It was not till 1311 that the legislature, in a council held at Ravenna, declared immersion or sprinkling to be indifferent. In this country (Scotland), however, sprinkling was never practised, in ordinary cases, until after the Reformation; and in England, even in the reign of Edward VI., trine immersion—dipping first the right side, secondly the left side, and last the face of the infant—was commonly observed. But, during the persecution of Mary, many persons, most of whom were Scotsmen, fled from England to Geneva, and there greedily imbibed the opinions of that church. In 1556, a book was published at that place, containing 'The form of prayers and ministration of the sacraments, approved by the famous and godly learned man, John Calvin,' in which the administrator is enjoined to take water in his hand and lay it upon the child's forehead. These Scottish exiles, who had renounced the authority of the Pope, implicitly acknowledged the authority of Calvin; and, returning to their own country, with Knox at their head, in 1559, established sprinkling in Scotland. From Scotland this practice made its way into England. in the reign of Elizabeth, but was not authorized by the Established church. In the Assembly of Divines, held at Westminster in 1643, it was keenly debated whether immersion or sprinkling should be adopted. Twenty-five voted for sprinkling and twenty-four for immersion; and even this small majority was obtained at the earnest request of Dr. Lightfoot, who had acquired great influence in that assembly. Sprinkling is, therefore, the general practice of this country. Many Christians, however, especially the Baptists, reject it. The Greek church universally adhere to immersion."—*Art. Baptism.*

The origin of sprinkling and pouring for baptism is of historical interest, and tends to confirm the position that "only immersion is baptism." They are clearly of post-apostolic origin. Our chief reliance, however, for the support of immersion is on the import of the word "baptize," as its meaning is disclosed in the Scriptures and confirmed by the highest lexicographical authority. If, as Moses Stuart says—and this country has produced no scholar more eminent than he was—"all lexicographers and critics of any note are agreed" that "*baptizo* (baptize) means to dip, plunge, or immerse into any liquid," then to baptize by sprinkling or pouring is a gross solecism. The incongruity of the language appears, if we substitute immerse for baptize. To immerse by sprinkling is an absurdity. To immerse by pouring is equally impossible, if the pouring is not sufficiently copious to overwhelm. How can a man be immersed by pouring a cup of water on his head?

CHAPTER IX.

Only Immersion is Baptism.

Admitting that baptism means immersion, and never sprinkling or pouring—that the apostolic baptism was immersion; that immersion was practised, except in cases of supposed necessity, for several centuries, and that it was generally practised till the beginning of the fourteenth century—it is maintained by some that it is not essential to the validity of the ordinance. The dispensation, it is said, is spiritual; ceremonies are of little importance; baptism is symbolic of a moral cleansing, and is equally expressive, whether the candidate be immersed or water be applied to him in some other way. Immersion is good, but not better than sprinkling or pouring, as a sign of purification. We have not the work of Professor Moses Stuart on baptism before us; but, if our memory is not at fault, the above is substantially the ground which he occupied in regard to baptism.

In our view, this is the most plausible argument in favor of sprinkling or pouring. It is plausible, but not sound. The Greek language had a copious variety of words, denoting sprinkling, pouring, washing, purifying, wetting, and the like; and yet Jesus chose *baptize*, meaning, as conceded in the argument, *immerse*. Why did he select this word to signify the act required in the ordinance? There must have been a reason for it, and a good one.

He was infinitely wise, and righteous, and kind, and comprehended perfectly the design of the institution, and all the abuses that would be made of it. It is noticeable, too, that neither evangelists nor apostles ever employ any other term but this or its cognates, with reference to the rite. Immersion, also, is suited to all climates, all countries, and all times. The notion that there are habitable countries so dry as to furnish no water for immersion, or that there are regions so cold that water can neither be found nor prepared for that use, is unworthy of refutation. Immersion may be inconvenient, and involve some expense and trouble; but what of that? Jesus travelled from Galilee to Judea, sixty or seventy miles, probably on foot, to be baptized of John in the river Jordan; and shall we set aside his command because it is not according to our convenience, or because we imagine that something else would suit us better?

Christ has made no provision for changing the ordinance. Neither churches, nor synods, nor general assemblies, nor ecumenical councils, nor pontiffs, nor any earthly power, have the shadow of authority for altering it. It is their province to obey, not to legislate. "Ye are my friends," said Jesus, "if ye do *whatsoever* I command you." Roman Catholics changed the rite from immersion to sprinkling—and, with their views of church power, acted consistently; but Protestants, or Christians who take the Bible as their standard of practice, can have no apology for making such an alteration.

Even supposing that churches had authority for changing the ordinance, why should they do it? Are they wiser than their Lord? Sprinkling and pouring, it is said, symbolize moral purification. Do they do it better than immersion? Cleansing is not all that is symbolized by baptism. It represents the death and the resurrection of Christ, and conversion under the idea of a resurrection. "Know ye not," says Paul, "that so many of us as were baptized into Jesus Christ were baptized into his death? Therefore, we are buried with him by baptism into death; that, like as Christ was raised up from the dead by the glory of the Father, we shall be also in the likeness of his resurrection." Rom. vi. 3, 4. All commentators not writing in the defence of sprinkling and pouring agree with Archbishop Tillotson in their interpretation of this passage: "Anciently, those who were baptized were *immersed*, and *buried* in the water, to represent their death to sin; and then did rise up out of the water, to signify their entrance upon a new life. And to these customs the apostle alludes." *Star Book*, page 29. Now, we ask whether sprinkling or pouring, by any stretch of the imagination, can be made to symbolize a death and resurrection. The only reason for changing the ordinance would be simply this: Christ deemed immersion proper, and commanded its observance; but we consider it inconvenient, if not indelicate—unsuited to the taste and refinement of the age—and, therefore, we "abridge somewhat its form.'

We have a few plain and candid general remarks to make to sincere believers in Christ:

Immersion is certainly baptism. This has been conceded by all the Christian world, so far as we are informed, excepting a few Presbyterians of the present century. On this point they confront the learning and authority of Christendom. Roman Catholics and members of the Greek church, Protestants, Lutherans, Episcopalians, Calvinists, Methodists, Congregationalists—all sects, orthodox and heterodox, with the exception mentioned, not only concede that immersion is "permissible" baptism, but, at least, of equal validity with sprinkling or pouring. The Greek church, of more than 60,000,000, deny that sprinkling or pouring is baptism. The English church, with all its learning, enjoins dipping, and considers pouring, in exceptional cases, merely "permissible." All sects of Baptists maintain the exclusive validity of immersion. Roman Catholics, with perfect unanimity, accept sprinkling or pouring for baptism on a ground on which every consistent Protestant must reject it. Now, we ask any candid believer why he should receive sprinkling or pouring for baptism, of whose validity there is so much reason to doubt, and reject immersion, whose scripturalness is conceded by all Christendom, except a few modern polemics? In regard to his worldly interests, he would not so act. He would surely be governed by the commanding probability. Should he be less anxious to pursue the right course when the honor of his Master and the interests of his kingdom are at stake? We think not.

Baptism is not essential to salvation, and, therefore, it is maintained by some, the manner of its observance is of no great importance. We do not believe in the essentiality of baptism to salvation. On this point Baptists have been much misunderstood and misrepresented. In former times, they were censured for conceding the possibility of salvation without baptism; and in the present day, they are blamed for giving it undue prominence and importance. The rite may be over-estimated or under-estimated with facility. We should aim to give it the precise position that it holds in the Sacred Scriptures. While we admit that baptism is not essential to salvation, we maintain that *obedience* is. Christ is "the author of eternal salvation unto all them that *obey* him"; and only unto such. Heb. v. 9. Baptism is a divine commandment, obligatory on all believers. It is enforced, not only by the supreme authority, but by the winning example of the Son of God. Of persons ignorant, or misinstructed, or in doubt, or dilatory in regard to the ordinance, we say nothing. We leave them in the hands of a righteous Judge. Suppose, however, a person professing to trust in Christ believes immersion to be divinely commanded, and deliberately and persistently refuses to submit to it; can he be saved? We judge not. He will be lost, not for the lack of baptism, but because his disobedience will demonstrate his want of faith, and consequently his unregeneracy. His rejection of baptism proves his disloyalty to the King of kings.

On this point we do not speak from conjecture, but follow the teaching of the divine oracles. "The Pharisees and lawyers," we are told, "rejected the counsel of God against themselves, being not baptized of him" (John). Lu. vii. 30. John's baptism was "the counsel of God," and those who, in their pride and self-sufficiency, rejected it, set themselves in opposition to God. The guilt and danger of the rejection were doubtless proportionate to their light and obstinacy. Are they less guilty, and exposed to less peril, who wilfully reject the baptism commanded by Christ, enforced by his example, and administered amid the wonders of the day of Pentecost? It is wisest and safest and best to obey Christ in all things.

We have never known a Baptist dissatisfied with the manner of his baptism. We have been acquainted with some who were troubled with doubts as to their fitness for the reception of the rite, and many more who had cause to lament that their lives had been so little in accord with the vows made in its reception; but not one, among the multitudes who, during a ministry of more than fifty years, have consulted us concerning their spiritual perplexities and troubles, has ever expressed any question as to the validity of immersion. Every pious Baptist knows that he has been baptized. He remembers the time, place, and circumstances of his baptism, and found in it "the answer of a good conscience toward God." With Pedobaptists the case is very different. Many of them are harassed with doubts and fears all their lifetime as to the validity of their infant sprinkling. Some are sensitive on the subject, and carefully avoid all discussion of it. Others seek relief from their troubles in reading treatises in favor of infant baptism and in listening to the reasonings of their pastors. Not a few, after enduring for years the accusations of an unquiet conscience, break away from their early and loved religious associates and follow Christ into the Jordan.

We have a question to put to sprinkled believers. We do not use this term in disrespect. For many of them we entertain the highest regard, and shall continue that regard, whatever may be their course concerning baptism. Our question is this: If you knew that your salvation depended on your being baptized precisely according to the command and example of Christ, would you trust your sprinkling in infancy, or even in your mature age? Many, doubtless, would; but multitudes, we are persuaded, would not. We once conversed with a young lady, converted under our ministry, on the subject of baptism. She had been sprinkled in childhood; but her conscience was ill at ease. Before making up her mind as to her duty, she desired, very naturally, to see her pastor. After a few months, we saw her again, and inquired: "Miss, have you settled the question as to your baptism?" "I am perfectly satisfied with it," was her reply. "If your salvation," we added, "depended on your being baptized according to the will of Christ, would you be satisfied with it?" "I do not believe that my salvation depends on that," she promptly answered. "Very well," we said; "but suppose it did; would you be satisfied?" With increased emphasis, she repeated: "*I do not believe* that it does." It was quite clear, had she believed that her salvation depended on the exact conformity of her baptism to the will of Christ, she would not have been satisfied.

Baptists have great confidence that their views of baptism are plainly presented in the Scriptures. It is quite common for them to refer young converts to the Bible to learn their duty in regard to baptism. The common version of the New Testament, prepared by Pedobaptists, is the best book for guiding plain, honest inquirers in reference to the ordinance. Do the advocates of sprinkling ever direct inquirers for information on the subject of baptism to read the Scriptures? We have never heard of such a case. We doubt whether one can be cited. We judge that it would be decidedly impolitic and unsafe for the advocates of sprinkling and pouring to refer young converts to the Scriptures for the solution of their doubts and the guidance of their conduct in regard to the rite of baptism.

CHAPTER X.

Communion at the Lord's Table Confined to Churches.

Baptism and the Lord's supper are alike in being instituted or positive rites, deriving their authority solely from the will of the Lawgiver. Their observance is required, not because they are essentially right, but they are right because they are divinely required. They differ widely, however, in several respects. Baptism is an individual duty. The command is: "Repent and be baptized *every one* of you." The Lord's supper is a social or ecclesiastical duty. This is indicated by the term "communion," or joint participation, by which it is expressed. "The cup of blessing which we bless, is it not the communion of the blood of Christ? The bread which we break, is it not the communion of the body of Christ?" Baptism is a duty not to be repeated. Churches may celebrate the Lord's supper as often as time and opportunity may permit, and inclination may prompt. There is no law prescribing how frequently it shall be observed. "*As often* as ye eat this bread, and drink this cup, ye do show the Lord's death till he come." Baptism is preparatory to church membership, as we showed in another article. The Lord's supper follows baptism. To this rule there is no exception. No unbaptized person, so far as the Scriptures testify, ever partook of the Lord's supper. It was never spread but in the Lord's house, and never approached except by those formally admitted into his family.

Information concerning the observance of the Lord's supper in the primitive churches is not very full, but quite sufficient to guide the humble and docile. The feast was instituted by the Lord Jesus on the night previous to his crucifixion. Only the apostles, who constituted the church in its incipiency, partook of it. That they were baptized by John, or by the disciples acting under Christ's authority (John iv. 1, 2), there can be no reasonable doubt. It is not essential to the validity of our argument, however, to show that they were baptized. The first baptizer was necessarily unbaptized. In the introduction of Christianity, there might have been more than one unbaptized administrator of the ordinance, though we do not suppose there were. In the organization of the churches there might have been, and doubtless there were, measures adopted, from the necessity of the case, which were not intended to be perpetuated in the regularly constituted churches.

The place of the Lord's supper in the divine economy is clearly indicated in the apostolic commission. Teaching, faith, baptism, instruction in all Christian duties, is the divinely prescribed order of service. Faith should precede baptism. The first public duty enjoined on a believer is baptism; but faith does not more certainly precede baptism than does baptism precede church membership and communion at the Lord's table. This order is clearly prescribed, and assuredly should be followed, unless some obvious and solid reason can be furnished for departing from it.

On two points we may be certain: The apostles understood their commission, and they executed it. Their example is, therefore, an authoritative exposition of it. The first church was organized in the city of Jerusalem, and we have a pretty full account of its formation and worship furnished by the Spirit of inspiration, for the guidance of the churches in all ages. Preaching, repentance, baptism, church membership, the Lord's supper, worship, was the order followed. "Then they that gladly received his (Peter's) word were baptized—were added unto them (the disciples in Jerusalem)—continued steadfastly in the apostles' doctrine and fellowship (in the teaching of the apostles and in co-operation with the church)—and in breaking of bread (communing at the Lord's table, called breaking of bread, as that was a noticeable part of the service, Acts xx. 7)—and in prayers," or the public worship of God. Can there be any reasonable doubt that in this primitive, true, model church baptism preceded church membership, and church membership the breaking of bread? In other words, the Lord's table was placed within the church, and the unbaptized had no access to it.

The only other place in which the Lord's supper is mentioned in the inspired history is Acts xx. 7: "Upon the first day of the week, when the disciples came together to break bread, Paul preached unto them, ready to depart on the morrow." We have here merely an incidental allusion to the Lord's supper. It is, however, perfectly accordant with what we learn of the ordinance from the Scriptures. "The disciples"—doubtless the church—"at Troas"—the ancient Troy—"came together to break bread," or partake of the Lord's supper. It is fair to conclude that this church was composed, as were all the churches of whose membership we are informed, of baptized believers.

There is no distinct reference to the observance of the Lord's supper in the apostolic epistles, except in the first letter to "the church of God" at Corinth. There had been in that church an abuse of the ordinance. It had not only been converted into a common feast, but into an occasion of excess. "When ye come together into one place," said Paul, "this is not to eat the Lord's supper. For in eating every one taketh before other his own supper; and one is hungry and another is drunken." Their feast was no longer "the Lord's supper," but a bacchanalia. The church was reproved in sharp terms for permitting this shameful desecration of the ordinance. "What?" said the indignant apostle; "have ye not houses to eat and to drink in? or despise ye the church of God, and shame them that have not (that is, the poor)? Shall I praise you in this? I praise you not." This language implies more than it expresses. The apostle not only did not praise, but sternly rebuked this profanation of a sacred institution. The apostolic judgment was divinely approved; for on account of this perversion many among the Corinthian Christians were "weak and sickly," and many slept or died. The church could not have been justly held responsible for this desecration of the supper, if it had not been authorized to exercise full control over the communicants.

It may be noticed that the apostle says to individual church members: "Let a man *examine himself*, and so let him eat of that bread and drink of that cup." It is not only the duty of the church collectively to maintain the purity of its communion, but of its members individually to partake of it with due self-examination and reverence. It should be borne in mind, however, that this exhortation was addressed to members of the church in Corinth; and we have elsewhere shown that it was composed exclusively of baptized believers. It was not, then, to men of the world, not to unbelievers, not to pious persons without the pale of a church, but to church members—baptized believers—that the injunction was given to partake of the Lord's supper with self-examination. 1 Cor. xi. 17-34.

The authority for the communion of church members at the Lord's table is clear and indisputable; but, as already stated, in all the Scriptures no instance can be found of its administration, except within a church, and to regularly admitted church members. These unquestionable truths convinced the Christian world for eighteen centuries that baptism is a prerequisite to communion at the Lord's supper. On no one point, until quite recently, have Christians been so united in opinion as on this. Catholics, Greeks, Protestants, sects, orthodox and heterodox, disagreeing on almost all other articles of faith, were united on this. Baptists, in defending their close communion, had only to avail themselves of the *argumentum ad hominem*. They could say to their Pedobaptist friends: You require baptism as a condition of communion at the Lord's table; we do the same. The only difference is that you admit infant sprinkling to be valid baptism; we do not. Our difference respects the nature of baptism, not the terms of admission to the Lord's table.

In the early part of the present century, the eloquent Robert Hall, of England, in the advocacy of open communion, took the ground that there is no connection between baptism and the Lord's supper; that the supper may as well precede baptism as baptism the supper. This is certainly the point on which the question of free communion hinges. This Hall admits: "If we supposed there were a necessary, unalterable connection between the two positive Christian institutes, so that none were qualified for communion who had not been previously baptized, we could not hesitate for a moment respecting the refusal of Pedobaptists, without renouncing the principles of our denomination." Vol. I., page 403. We have shown that baptism preceded the supper in the order prescribed by the apostolic commission; that the supper was administered in the primitive churches, and that they were composed exclusively of baptized believers; that all instructions concerning the administration of the ordinance were directed to a church and its members; and that these facts convinced the Christian world for eighteen centuries that baptism is a prerequisite to the Lord's supper; and we now submit that the *onus probandi* lies on those who claim the right of the unbaptized to partake of it. It is a divinely instituted feast. Only those can properly share in it whom Christ has invited to it. If the unbaptized—persons having no church connection—claim the privilege of partaking of it, let them show divine authority in its support. In what chapter and verse is it recorded? Let us have the law, or the precedent, or the principle, or the logical inference to confirm their right. We repeat that in all the oracles of God there is neither proof nor semblance of proof that the Lord's supper was ever administered but within a church and to its baptized members.

It may be replied that partaking of the Lord's supper is not more dependent on the previous performance of baptism than are prayer, praise, and other religious duties. This is a mistake. These are moral duties, obligatory on all men, at all times, and in all places. They were practised before the institution of baptism and after its institution, by those who had not as well as those who had received it. The Lord's supper was instituted within and for the church, and none were admitted to its privileges without baptism.

We submit, then, that those who partake of the Lord's supper without baptism do so without divine warrant, on their own authority, and on terms that would lead to the abrogation of all church order and discipline.

CHAPTER XI.

Communion at the Lord's Table Confined to Church Members.

We have briefly stated our reasons for holding what is popularly called "close communion"; and we desire to make an appeal to the candid judgment of all who maintain the opposite view. It is not strange that there should be differences of opinion among sincere Christians on this subject. Human judgments are so imperfect, and are warped by so many influences of education, interest, association, and taste, that we need not be surprised that they reach diverse conclusions. The primitive churches, under the instruction and supervision of the apostles, fell into many serious errors. Indeed, liability to mistakes on religious, as well as on other subjects, is inseparable from human ignorance, and enters into man's earthly probation. We say these things, not to extenuate the evils of error, but to inspire the erring with the spirit of candor.

Suppose, then, that the Scriptures do teach—as we have endeavored to show that they do—that the apostolic churches were composed exclusively of baptized believers; that baptism was uniformly immersion; that none but the baptized were admitted into the fellowship of the churches, and that the Lord's supper was administered within the churches, and only to their members—what is the duty of Christians, having a clear and settled conviction that that was the divinely established order? Shall they adhere to it, or shall they, in deference to the views and feelings of brethren whom they love, and whom they would not willingly offend, depart from it? Shall they be governed by their own views or by the opinions of others in a matter so grave and important? Let us examine the subject with care.

It is evident that no church or churches, no association or convention, no prelate or pontiff, has a right to annul an ordinance of Christ or to revoke an order which he has ordained. If Christ has made immersion a prerequisite to church membership and placed communion within the church, then it is plainly the duty of his disciples, if they understand his arrangement, to give the weight of their example and their influence to its support. On this point there surely should be no difference of opinion among those who acknowledge the supreme headship of Jesus.

Among the disciples of Christ there are wide differences of opinion as to the order mentioned. Some persons believe that sprinkling or pouring, as well as immersion, is baptism; others that the sprinkling of an infant is Christian baptism. Some that baptism is not a Christian ordinance, and others that baptism is not a prerequisite of church membership or of a participation in the Lord's supper. This conflict of views brings up new questions for the consideration of Christians—questions unknown in apostolic times, and consequently not specifically decided in the Scriptures. What is to be done in this exigency? Certainly no party can reasonably claim that its opinions are infallible, and that persons who dissent from them are either ignorant or bigoted. The obvious duty of all Christians, arising from this diversity of views, is not to reproach or persecute each other, but to confess their liability to err, study the Scriptures with greater diligence and candor, give to others full credit for their intelligence and piety, and follow the convictions of their own understandings. Believing, as we do, that immersion is a prerequisite to partaking of the Lord's supper, we feel bound, not only to follow that rule, but to do what we can to extend its authority; but we do not condemn or dislike Christians who dissent from our views. We think they are erring brethren, and would gladly reclaim them from their error; but we love them for the truth which they hold and the many Christian virtues which they display.

We have somewhat against our open-communion brethren, whether they be Baptists or Pedobaptists. They go too far for the truth, but not far enough for consistency. There is no conscientious bar to the fellowship of intercommuning churches. Whatever may be their differences of opinion concerning doctrine or church organization and discipline, they are not such as to interfere with their fellowship and communion at the Lord's table. They have one Lord, one faith, one baptism, and one communion table. Why should they have different churches?

It may be said, and it is said, that they prefer different forms of church government and modes of discipline, and there is no good reason why they should not indulge their preference. Episcopalians like prelacy and liturgical services; Presbyterians hold to an eldership and presbyterial form of church government, and Methodists must have an itinerant ministry and love feasts; but these differences involve no breach of fellowship or communion. They are all substantially of one church. They are, as it is often said, different regiments in the same great army, and under the same invincible Commander.

Now, this friendly diversity appears very well; but let us look a little more carefully into it. Where it leads to no unholy rivalry, and secures a brotherly and efficient co-operation, it is quite consistent with the principle of free communion. But take the case of a town with a population of fifteen hundred. It would make an admirable parish for a single pastor. He might be generously supported, and all his powers would find sweet and constant employment in feeding his flock. Such towns and villages are scattered all over the land. Yet you will scarcely find one in which there is not a Methodist, a Presbyterian, and an Episcopal church, and sometimes several other intercommuning churches. All the congregations are small, feeble, struggling for existence, and perhaps supported in part by the contributions of their wealthier sister churches of the cities. They maintain three or four or five pastors, to do what one could do as well, or even better. They go to the expense of erecting and keeping in repair as many houses of worship as they have churches and pastors, when one could conveniently accommodate all the worshippers. Nor is this all, nor the worst. Constituted as human nature is, there must be rivalry, and, in many cases, antagonism and irritation between the different sects. The Episcopalian eagerly seeks proselytes, because his church is the true church and has the genuine apostolic succession; the Presbyterian pleads for the extension of his church, on the ground that its government is according to the scriptural pattern; and the Methodist is quite sure that all believers, and seekers, too, will find through his church the plainest, straightest, and safest way to heaven. We do not censure them for holding these views, provided they have been received after due examination and are maintained with becoming modesty. We have great respect for conscientious convictions. The point we make is this: These different opinions present no bar to communion. Those who hold them have no conscientious scruples about entering into a common fellowship and communion. It surely will not be maintained that persons who commune together occasionally cannot do so stately and continuously; or that those who can consistently commune together cannot belong to a common church and submit to a common discipline. They may prefer certain forms of ecclesiastical government and certain modes of worship; but their preferences lie not in the way of their fellowship and communion. Love, candor, and a desire for the glory of Christ could easily adjust these differences. All might join the oldest, or the strongest, or the most convenient church, and manifest their zeal for the unity of the church and the honor of their common Lord by holding their peculiar views in abeyance; or they might organize a church, retaining some of the distinctive tenets and practices of the several sects uniting in its formation. Where there is a will, there is a way.

Now, when our intercommuning Pedobaptist brethren shall follow out their own principles—blending the feeble churches of the towns and villages into a common body, to promote their efficiency and to save expense—shall, in short, show more solicitude to unite the discordant churches than to build up their several sects—we shall be strongly impressed with their consistent zeal for Christian union. While, however, they keep up, at vast labor and expense, their sectarian folds in our towns and villages, we must conclude that either their logic or their love is defective.

It may be asked: Are not the Baptists equally eager to maintain churches in towns where the people are already amply supplied with Pedobaptist preaching? Perhaps they are. They certainly ought to be. The cases, however, are widely different. The Pedobaptist churches are of a common communion—they are branches of a common church—their members are kept apart by no conscientious convictions. Baptists occupy entirely different ground. They differ from their Pedobaptist brethren on church organization and Christian ordinances, and these differences are deemed, whether wisely or unwisely, of sufficient moment to justify and to demand a breach of ecclesiastical fellowship and communion. Baptists having, as they conceive, scriptural views of the formation and discipline of churches, which are of great importance to the progress and final triumph of the kingdom of Christ, deem it their duty, without any abatement of their love to their Christian brethren who dissent from these opinions, to maintain and propagate them, not only by tongue and pen, but by pursuing a course in perfect consistency with them. They do not hesitate, therefore, to found and support churches in towns or neighborhoods well supplied with Pedobaptist churches and pastors, because it is considered their duty—at least, the duty of such of their members as truly believe in Christ—to be baptized and unite with Baptist churches. This conviction is neither bigotry nor intolerance. Do not Pedobaptists believe that Baptists should have their children baptized and become members of Pedobaptist churches? If they do not, they are not loyal to their own creeds; and we are pleased to say that Baptists, certainly with very few exceptions, have a firmer conviction of the truth of their distinctive principles. It all comes to this: If our principles are true, we are right in maintaining them, and all Pedobaptists—that is, all believers—should accept and be governed by them; and if, on the other hand, pedobaptism and open communion are scriptural, then Baptists and all other persons should accept these principles and govern themselves accordingly. If our readers should be led to a candid, thorough, and God-fearing examination of these subjects, in the light of divine revelation, our end will have been gained.

CHAPTER XII.

Is Open Communion Demanded for the Edification of the Churches?

The Scriptures furnish no certain example of the intercommunion of churches. The nearest approach to it was the case of Paul breaking bread with the disciples at Troas. He was a divinely authorized founder of churches; but whether he was a member of any local church, in the sense in which the phrase is now understood, is very doubtful. If he was a member of any church, we do not know which it was. If intercommunion was practised by the members of the primitive churches, it was, we suppose, granted as a courtesy, and not claimed as a right. There was no law requiring it, and no example, if the doubtful one of Paul above referred to be omitted, encouraging it. It might have prevailed—its prevalence, so far as we can discern, would have been consistent with the constitution and discipline of the churches—it was simply a matter of choice and of courtesy. We may reasonably take it for granted that, had it been necessary or even desirable for the edification of the churches and the increase of brotherly love, the Scriptures would contain some precept, or example, or intimation for its enforcement. For the joint participation of the Lord's supper by members of the same church, they furnish ample authority;

but on the intercommunion of churches they maintain a profound silence.

What, in the light of observation, is the value of open communion? It is, we think, but little prized by those Christians who accept it as an article of their creed. In discussing the subject with Baptists, they lay great stress on it; but practically they attach little importance to it. In the cities, the members of the different Pedobaptist sects rarely commune with one another. Why should they do it? They have regular communions in their respective churches, and do not need to go beyond them to secure the benefits of the Lord's supper. In country churches, where religious worship is held infrequently, and the Christian sects are more thrown together, instances of the intercommunion of the members of different denominations are more likely to occur; but, even in these cases, we have yet to learn that the privilege is much prized or productive of much benefit.

Why, then, do Pedobaptists plead so earnestly for open communion? We wish not to be uncharitable; but we cannot close our eyes to the principles which govern human nature. Doubtless there are many who plead for open communion with a catholic spirit, believing that it is promotive of brotherly love; but this cannot be said of all its advocates. It answers several purposes besides those which charity would accomplish. It has a great semblance of liberality, which, we have shown, is in many cases a mere semblance. It contrasts very favorably with what is represented to be the narrowness and bigotry of close communionists. We, it is said, place no bar to the Lord's supper—we invite all his friends to it—all who desire to do so may partake of it; but it is left to be inferred that close communionists are governed by a very different spirit—they surround the Lord's table with unwarrantable barriers, claim for themselves peculiar privileges, and unchristianize people as good as themselves. Nor is this the only use made of the doctrine of open communion. Baptists maintain that all believers, even those baptized in infancy, should be immersed on a profession of their faith. Young converts, with the New Testament in their hands, if they have not received a thorough Pedobaptist drilling, are almost sure to conclude that they should go to the water, and not that the water should be brought to them, for baptism. The baptizing by John "in the river Jordan," and the going down of both Philip and the eunuch into the water for baptism, quite satisfy the minds of warmhearted, obedient new converts that baptism is immersion; and it is not easy, in some cases, to efface this conviction. Close communion, however, is an admirable weapon to combat the supposed error. Are you willing to be shut out from communion with your kindred and friends, and to confine your Christian fellowship to a sect whose views on the subject of communion fall, in liberality and freedom, so far below those of other Christian denominations? This is an appeal to young converts which strongly impresses their feelings. Their sympathies are warm and lively, and they would be pleased to commune with the whole world. They have yet to learn that, not their own feelings, but the Word of God, should be their guide in religious matters—that "charity rejoiceth in the truth." While the duty of baptism is in no wise dependent on the terms of communion, it is fair to conclude that thousands have been turned away from immersion on a profession of faith by the impression that immersionists are narrow and illiberal in regard to communion at the Lord's table.

Open communion, on the part of Baptists, is not only unauthorized, but *impolitic*. If it were divinely required, there should be an end to all controversy on the subject. If it were merely permitted, churches should be left to the exercise of their own taste and judgment in deciding on the expediency of its adoption. We believe that it is substantially forbidden; but that, if it were not, it would be *impolitic* for Baptists, with their responsibilities and aims, to practise it. They believe that on them devolves the duty of restoring the ordinances of Christ to their primitive simplicity, design, and order, and of promoting the organization of churches according to the apostolic model. This is their mission, and they should avoid whatever tends to defeat it. Open communion clearly leads in this direction.

The experience of the English Baptists has shed much light on the influence of open communion on the prosperity of churches. The practice is advocated mainly on the ground that it promotes brotherly affection and co-operation among evangelical Christians, and a candid examination of Baptist principles. These are certainly very important ends to gain; but let us inquire in what degree they are secured by the measure. We will ignore the fact that these objects might quite as easily, and, as we think, far more scripturally, be secured by the abandonment of infant sprinkling and a return to the primitive practice of immersion. Conceding that for their attainment Baptists shall adopt the practice of open communion, what will be the result?

Mixed church membership follows open communion by a logical necessity. Communion at the Lord's table is a test of church fellowship. If Christians commune together, they may surely co-operate in whatever is needed to support and extend the communion. The adoption of open communion brings, not peace, but discord, to Baptist churches. It opens the question of mixed church membership, by which many of the English Baptist churches have been agitated and rent asunder. Of these churches, some are close communion, some are open communion, some are of mixed membership, and not a few are battling over the subject of mixed membership.

Yielding on the question of open membership— as yield they must, if they accept open communion, and are capable of feeling the force of an argument—the churches are met by the inquiry whether their officers shall be limited to Baptists. Why should they be, if the churches are composed of Baptists and Pedobaptists, immersionists and sprinklers? It is unreasonable, unjust, and offensive, if a church is composed of a mixed membership, to insist that its officers shall all be of one party. Such unfairness cannot be maintained. As a matter of fact, Baptist churches, adopting mixed membership, soon accept Pedobaptist deacons and pastors.

Even this concession does not put an end to controversy. The question necessarily arises: Why should a church, composed partly of Baptists and partly of Antibaptists, and having officers of either party, be called a *Baptist* church? The name is false, misleading, and cannot be reasonably defended for a moment. With the distinctive principles of Baptists, their name must take its departure. We know not how many, but certainly quite a number, of English Baptist churches, under the influence of open-communion principles, have ceased to be Baptist churches. The church in Bedford, to which John Bunyan ministered, is a notable instance of the transforming power of open communion.

The influence of open communion and mixed membership is decidedly unfavorable to the progress of Baptist principles. They are not adapted to a carnal and worldly taste. They are accepted only on divine authority, and that authority, to exert its proper influence, must be frequently held up to the attention and pressed on the consciences of men. They are pleasing to the humble, self-denying, and devout; but they are distasteful to the proud, the gay, and the fashionable. These would peril their salvation sooner than they would be publicly and solemnly immersed in attestation of their loyalty to Jesus. It is not so with pedobaptism. It strongly appeals to parental affection, does not offend the most delicate taste, is recommended by the graces of poetry and the charms of painting, and is practised by thousands as a beautiful and seemly ceremony, who do not admit its divine authority. It is entrenched in the creeds and honored in the practice of the most numerous, respectable, and influential Christian sects. It needs no advocates. Its history and associations give it influence and secure its perpetuity.

The obvious effect of mixed communion and mixed church membership is to stop the mouths of Baptist ministers concerning their distinctive principles. Suppose a minister is pastor of a mixed church. He derives his support partly from those who believe and partly from those who reject his peculiar principles. His influence, his happiness, and his usefulness depend on his securing the confidence, affection, and co-operation of the members of his church, of all parties. Can he be expected to preach plain, pointed sermons on the duty of all believers to be immersed, and on the evils of infant baptism? Why, the very act of receiving

Antibaptists into the communion of the church is a public and solemn admission that Baptist principles are of little worth and need not be contended for. A few ministers of deep conviction and of great boldness may rise above these embarrassments, and give faithful utterance to their principles; but it is contrary to all the motives that govern human action to imagine that the number of such preachers could be great, or that the bravest would not be hampered by their associations. That such is the perplexing and restraining influence of mixed church membership, we were fully convinced by our observations on English Baptist meetings. Their leaders, men of learning, eloquence, and power, were constrained, by the courtesy due to a mixed membership, to avoid any vigorous utterance of distinctive Baptist principles.

If these be the influence and results of open communion, it is not surprising that persons who believe that the peculiar views of Baptists are erroneous should favor the practice. They are governed by sound policy. They pursue the wisest course to counteract the influence of Baptist principles. With their views, they act consistently. We only question the validity of their claim to any special liberality in their course. That Baptists are unwilling to adopt a practice whose logical results are open church membership and a renunciation of their distinctive principles and name, especially when in doing so they forsake the order of the primitive churches, is surely not wonderful.

If their principles are scriptural, it is their plain and solemn duty to avoid all measures that tend to hinder their influence, and employ the most suitable means to secure their spread and triumph.

CHAPTER XIII.

Incidental Points Pertaining to Close Communion.

We are often asked by persons, heartily accepting Baptist principles in the main, why the immersed members of Pedobaptist churches and the members of churches practising immersion are not invited to commune in Baptist churches. We admit, say they, that baptism is a prerequisite to communion; but these believers have been immersed, and some of them by duly qualified Baptist ministers—why, then, should they not be admitted to the Lord's table? The question is important, and deserving of candid consideration.

Faith and baptism are conditions precedent of a participation of the Lord's supper; but they are not the only terms of admission to it. We have endeavored to show that the supper is a feast within, and not without, a church, designed for all its members, and only for its members, or for members of other churches maintaining the same terms of communion. The exercise of discipline and the privilege of communion are co-extensive. In the apostolic churches, none were permitted to commune who were not subject to ecclesiastical discipline. Paul, in the exercise of his apostolic authority, required the church at Corinth to put away from among them the incestuous member; and afterwards, when he furnished proofs of his repentance, to restore him to their fellowship. 1 Cor. v. 1-5; 2 Cor. ii. 5-8. This transgressor was, for a time, excluded from a participation of the Lord's supper. 1 Cor. iv. 11. By common consent, this act of exclusion from a church is called *excommunication;* that is, expulsion from communion. So thoroughly is this truth embedded in the popular mind, that communion and church membership are expressions used interchangeably. A member of a Presbyterian or an Episcopal church is called a communicant of the church.

Piety and baptism do not constitute one a member of a Baptist church. He must, in order to become a member of it, seek admission into it, adopt its essential principles, and submit to its discipline. To continue a member of it, he must walk in the commandments and ordinances of the Lord, if not without blame, at least without gross and persistent departures from them. "Now we command you, brethren," said Paul, to "the church of the Thessalonians," "in the name of our Lord Jesus Christ, that ye withdraw yourselves from every brother that walketh disorderly and not after the tradition which he received of us." 2 Thess. iii. 6. To walk "disorderly" is to live in vice, or in wilful transgression. By "tradition" the apostle meant the doctrine or teaching which he and his associates had received from Christ and imparted to the Thessalonians. To walk "disorderly" is, we judge, to walk "not after the tradition" received from the apostles. The latter phrase is explanatory of the former. No command can be more imperative than that laid on churches to withdraw from disorderly walkers, who respect not the teaching of the apostles. "We command you," said Paul and his companions, not in their own names, but "in the name of our Lord Jesus Christ, that ye withdraw yourselves from every brother that walketh disorderly," &c. This withdrawal was to extend to *"every brother"*—rich or poor, high or low, kinsman or stranger—who walked "disorderly"; that is, persistently pursued a course contrary to the apostolic teaching. No plea of friendship, ignorance, or expediency can set aside this law.

We must now inquire whether the connection of immersed believers with Pedobaptist churches, or with other religious bodies, deemed unsound in doctrine or irregular in practice, is disorderly walking and contrary to apostolic teaching. In this argument, we must take for granted the truth of Baptist principles. Conceding that churches should be composed exclusively of immersed believers, and that communion at the Lord's table should be restricted to church members, is the course of Baptists in uniting with Pedobaptist churches, or with other bodies, not sound in faith and practice, orderly and according to apostolic "tradition"? We think not. Their course is not in harmony with the admitted principles. They voluntarily withdraw themselves from a church scripturally organized, and give their influence and labors to the support of principles which they admit to be false. In principles, they are Baptists; in profession and influence, they are Pedobaptists. Clearly it is their duty to support and disseminate the principles which they admit to be true. We believe, say they, that only believers are proper subjects of baptism, and nothing is baptism but immersion; but their example is at war with their convictions. In short, they concede that Christ has established one order for the constitution of his church, and they, for convenience or respectability, or from indifference to his authority, follow another. Such a course could not have been pursued in the apostolic times without incurring the charge of walking "disorderly," and "not after the tradition" received by the Spirit of inspiration.

It may be pleaded, in behalf of these inconsistent Baptists, that they are pursuing the course dictated by their consciences. We are not considering specially what is their duty, but what is the duty of the churches in regard to them. We do not judge these irregular Baptists. We consider them in error; but what allowance is to be made for their lack of information, their temperaments, their associations, and their peculiar circumstances, we know not. Their Master will judge them. Let them have due respect for their conscientious convictions. These may govern their own conduct; but they are no guide for the churches. They should be controlled by the Scriptures, honestly and intelligently interpreted and faithfully applied. If these teach that communion should be limited to churches, that churches should withdraw from all disorderly walkers, and that those walk disorderly who abandon churches scripturally constituted, to support those that are defective and irregular in their formation, then the duty of Baptist churches regarding these erring brethren is clear and imperative.

It is a pity that all Christians cannot commune together. We have no sympathy with those who believe that divisions among churches are good. They are evil, and are fraught with incalculable mischiefs. It is certainly to be deplored that all Baptists cannot commune together, according to the inspired order. Their identity of principles, interests, and aims should draw them together; and we wish to address some remarks to Baptists unconnected with regular Baptist churches.

There can be no union and communion between these parties without a yielding on one side or the other. The mountain must go to Mohammed, or Mohammed must come to the mountain. The denomination cannot yield its principles. They are grounded in its convictions, incorporated in its literature, and are the bond of its union. No man nor set of men, no arguments nor influence, can swerve it from its long-cherished doctrines. The mountain cannot go to Mohammed. There can scarcely, however, be any insuperable obstacle to the union of individual Baptists with Baptist churches. These irregular Baptists may deem it their privilege—they can hardly consider it their duty—to commune with Pedobaptists. There is no divine law requiring them to commune in churches whose baptisms they consider invalid. It is their duty to partake of the Lord's supper in the prescribed order; but surely there is neither precept nor example binding them to commune in Pedobaptist churches. Admitting, for the sake of the argument, that it is their right to do so, still they would violate no law, sacrifice no principle, and do no injury in declining to exercise it. Mohammed can come to the mountain.

As matters stand in this country, a Baptist cannot commune, however much he may desire it, in both Baptist and Pedobaptist churches. He must make his election between them. Either he must unite with Pedobaptists, and give his example, influence, and labors, indirectly, at least, to the support of pedobaptism, or he must join the Baptists and enlist his energies in support of their principles. It is strange that he should hesitate for a moment in making his choice. With Baptists he differs on a single point—the terms of admission to the Lord's table; from Pedobaptists he dissents on the conditions of church membership and on the subjects and act of Christian baptism—principles deeply affecting the form and prosperity of the churches.

A Pedobaptist church is no home for a Baptist. Many years ago, we were conversing with a minister of another denomination, a most fiery advocate of open communion. We said to him: "If I were a member of your church, holding the principles that

I do, and deeming it my duty to maintain and make proselytes to them, what would you do with me?" He promptly replied: "We should expel you." "That would be according to your discipline," said I; "but should I unite with a Baptist church, and propose to commune with you, would you admit me to your communion?" He frankly answered: "It would seem to be inconsistent."

The truth is, no earnest Baptist can long remain in a Pedobaptist church. It is only by ignoring his principles or keeping them in abeyance that he can be received into such a church. If he is intelligently convinced of their truth and importance, and deems it his duty—as undoubtedly he should—to disseminate them, he will soon find that he is an unwelcome member. The church will have no use for him, if he speaks in disparagement of infant baptism and pleads for the immersion of believers. They would *excommunicate* him, as a teacher of false doctrine and a disturber of the peace of the church. There is but one consistent course for a Baptist, and that is to be a member of a Baptist church, and labor, lovingly and faithfully, by all the means within his power, to defend and diffuse his principles.

CHAPTER XIV.

Religious Freedom.

We cannot close this discussion on Baptist principles without a reference to religious freedom. The liberty to worship God according to the dictates of conscience, is the dearest of all human rights. That it should ever have been denied is one of the strongest proofs of human fallibility. Certain it is, however, that, a little more than two centuries ago, almost all religionists, Catholic, Greek and Protestant, maintained that either the civil or the ecclesiastical power had the right to regulate the public worship of God, and that all persons subject to its jurisdiction were bound, under pain of fines, imprisonment, and death itself, in its most appalling forms, to comply with the prescribed regulations. In the early ages, Christians suffered severely from their heathen rulers, because they persistently worshipped Christ and labored to bring the world into subjection to his authority. After Christianity gained the ascendency, and the churches were consolidated into a hierarchy and invested with secular authority, or were able to control it through its subservient minions, the acceptance of its creed and conformity to its rites, worship, and decrees, were enforced with an intolerance and severity which exceeded even pagan ferocity. The history of Romanism is a heart-rending record of spiritual tyranny—of chains, dungeons, tortures, and fires. When the churches of Northern Europe threw off the papal yoke, along with many and important reforms which they introduced, they retained the intolerant views and spirit of their recent rulers. Romanists, claiming infallibility, had the plea of consistency for their persecutions; while Protestants, admitting their liability to err, had not that poor defence for their relentless cruelties to those who called in question their spiritual authority or dissented from their religious creeds. The Protestant sects of the sixteenth century— Lutherans, Presbyterians, and Episcopalians—invested with civil authority, or able to influence secular rulers, were intolerant, and carried their tyranny not only to fines and confiscation, but to imprisonment, torture, and blood. Even the Independents, who fled from the persecutions of the English Episcopalians to the wilds of America, deemed it their duty to cherish the spirit and imitate the example of their oppressors.

We can hardly claim belief in religious liberty as being *now* a *distinctive* Baptist principle. A great change has taken place in the views and spirit of the Christian world on this subject, especially the Protestant portion of it, within the last two centuries, and more particularly since the beginning of the present century. In all Protestant countries, there is, at present, religious toleration, if not full freedom. In most Roman Catholic countries, dissenters are tolerated, or, at least, treated with less severity than in former times. The fires of the Inquisition have been extinguished, and that ecclesiastical court, so fiendish in its spirit and so fearful in its works of darkness and of blood, has everywhere been overthrown or stripped of its power for mischief.

Baptists, under all the names which they have borne, in different countries and in different centuries, have been unswervingly loyal to the principles of religious liberty. Whatever may have been their faults—and they have neither been infallible in judgment nor irreproachable in conduct—they have been free from the guilt of persecution. They have not only been the earnest advocates of religious liberty, but they have supported it in its fullest extent. They have not only claimed it for themselves, but have accorded it to others—Jews and pagans, as well as Christians.

It must be conceded that Baptists, with scarcely an exception, have been a minority under civil governments. Minorities, especially when oppressed and persecuted, are always favorable to extending the limits of freedom. It would be impossible that they should not desire liberty in regard to the matters which subject them to reproach and punishment. It must also be admitted that small and persecuted sects have deep sympathy for each other in their trials, and are easily led to make common cause in the defence or for the extension of the freedom in which they have a common interest.

We claim for Baptists, however, not merely that they have been the steadfast friends of religious liberty, but that their distinctive principles necessarily compel them to maintain this position. They cannot be consistently Baptists and not advocates of soul liberty. Before they can persecute for conscience' sake, they must renounce, or, at least, ignore their distinctive principles. They may not be free from the spirit of bigotry and intolerance; but it is directly antagonistic to their doctrines.

Let us carefully examine this matter, even if, in doing so, we must retrace ground already trodden. According to Baptist views, no man can become a church member who does not voluntarily accept Christ as his Master, and who does not willingly receive baptism in attestation of this submission. Moreover, having freely become a member, he cannot retain his place in the church, unless his life is in harmony with his profession. In short, faith and baptism are essential prerequisites to church membership, and a godly life is necessary to the continuance of the connection. If these principles are maintained, neither birth, nor baptism, nor education, nor wealth, nor office, nor profession, can secure a place in a Baptist church; nor can one retain his place in it without imbibing the spirit and imitating the example of the Redeemer. It is obvious that a church organized on these principles cannot be a persecuting body. For what purpose could it persecute? Not to force members to join it; for none can be admitted to its membership without qualifications which no persecution can secure. Not to keep members within it; for it can retain only such as love its members, doctrine, ordinances, and discipline, and force cannot produce these fruits. The conquests of such a church must be made, not by the sword of the executioner, but by "the sword of the Spirit." Other churches may employ carnal weapons, and inflict pains and penalties, to promote their prosperity; but Baptist churches, if they flourish, must succeed by moral suasion and the grace of God.

Hierarchies—churches established by law, and supported by civil, and, if necessary, by military power—have been the greatest curse of Christendom. They are utterly at variance with the spirit and doctrine of Jesus. His kingdom is not of this world. He came, not to destroy men's lives, but to save their souls; and, to fulfil his mission, he employed, not swords and spears, but truth and reason and kind persuasion. He established no hierarchy, and gave no authority for its establishment. The connection between Church and State is adulterous, and equally corrupting to the church and pernicious to the State. A hierarchy cannot be supported without a hereditary membership, the obliteration of the line of demarcation between the godly and the ungodly, and the limitation of discipline to dissent from the established faith and resistance to spiritual authority. As a matter of history, all hierarchies have been composed of the population in their respective territories, regardless of their moral qualities. In England, until quite recently, no man could hold office who was not a communicant in the Established church; and it may be easily seen how strong was the temptation to hypocrisy and the profanation of the Lord's supper among the aspirants for political and official preferment.

Pedobaptism, though not necessarily associated with a hierarchy, is adapted to encourage it, readily lends its aid to support it, and is essential to its development. No State church has ever existed, or ever can exist, without its help. According to the Pedobaptist theory, children of church members are born in the church or are regenerated and inducted into it by baptism. They grow up in it, with whatever of selfishness, impurity, and unbelief may be developed in them. In most such churches, they are, at a certain age, without any profession of conversion, confirmed in their membership, by appropriate ceremonies—remain in their connection, regardless of their impiety, to the end of their lives—and are then buried in consecrated ground, in proof of their good ecclesiastical standing. It is easy to perceive that infant baptism is "the ground and pillar" of the system. Without it, hierarchies would soon tumble and disappear, "as the baseless fabric of a vision."

Baptists have an honorable record on the subject of religious liberty. If they were not the first, they were certainly among the first to proclaim it as the indefeasible right of man. Roger Williams, a Baptist, founded the State of Rhode Island, the first government in which full religious liberty was ever secured. Of him Bancroft says: "He was the first person in modern Christendom to assert in its plenitude the doctrine of the liberty of conscience, the equality of opinions before the law, and in its defence he was the harbinger of Milton, the precursor and the superior of Jeremy Taylor." Dr. S. S. Cutting, in his introduction to the Struggles and Triumphs of Religious Liberty, by E. B. Underhill LL. D., of London, speaking of this testimony of Bancroft, says: "The truth, however, is that the contest in the colony of Massachusetts Bay was an imported contest. It came, with all its distinctively recognized principles, across the Atlantic, in the breasts of men who had fought the same battles in Holland and England. John Cotton and Roger Williams had had their teachers in such men as John Robinson and Thos. Helwys"—both Baptists. Largely through the influence of Baptists, the religious establishment of Virginia was overthrown, and perfect soul freedom guaranteed in the State. This, so far as we know, was the first instance in the history of Christendom in which a hierarchy was dissolved, except to be succeeded by another of a different creed, with an unchanged spirit of intolerance and tyranny. Baptists took an active, and, no doubt, influential part in procuring an amendment to the Constitution of the United States securing religious freedom to all its citizens. How much their efforts have contributed to the progress and triumphs of religious liberty, it is impossible accurately to estimate. It is cause, however, for gratulation that they were, not only the first to assert it in its plenitude, but that they have been its consistent and earnest advocates for centuries; have heroically suffered persecution from most Protestant sects, but have persecuted none; and have been permitted to see the steady progress of the doctrine which they once held almost alone and under reproach, until almost the whole Christian world has been constrained to admit its truth, and govern its course accordingly.

CHAPTER XV.

Obligation of Baptists to Their Principles.

These principles having been stated and briefly defended, need not be here repeated. If they are false, their prevalence is to be deplored, and none are so profoundly interested in their refutation as Baptists. We do not deprecate, but invite, their discussion. If they are unsound, we shall be deeply indebted to any polemic who can expose their rottenness and deliver us from our delusion. We, however, firmly believe them to be revealed in the Scriptures, and reason and conscience require that we should be governed by our belief. Accepting them as true, what obligations do they impose on us?

These principles, if divinely revealed, may be comparatively overestimated. All truth is precious, but all is not equally precious. The Saviour distinguishes between the least and the greatest commandments. Matt. v. 19; xxii. 38. Some truths are vital. The knowledge of them is essential to salvation. John xvii. 3. Others are promotive of piety and usefulness, but they are not fundamental in the Christian system. The principles for which we are contending are important, but not supremely important. A spiritual church membership is a divine arrangement of great moment to the prosperity of the Redeemer's kingdom; but one may be spiritual without belonging to any visible church.

Immersion is important, but it is far less important than the resurrection of Christ and the regeneration of a soul, which it symbolizes. Whatever may be said in commendation of the Lord's supper, its value is not to be compared to the atonement of Christ, which it sets forth. In our view, those who make baptism a regenerating ordinance misconceive its design, and assign to it an agency and an honor due only to the Holy Spirit; and those who make it a sin-remitting institution mistake the symbol for the substance, and ascribe to the water what is due only to faith in the blood of Christ. It cannot be doubted by any intelligent and unbiassed reader of history that great injury has been done to Christianity by the unscriptural and extravagant importance attached to its ordinances and to ecclesiastical authority and discipline. By multitudes the church has been substituted for Christ, and churchianity for Christianity.

On the other hand, Baptistic principles, if true, should not be undervalued. They are a part of a divine system, of transcendent importance, and are essential to its harmony and perfection. A church composed exclusively of spiritual members, or of persons who make a credible profession of piety, is the fittest symbol of heaven and the most suitable school in which to train pupils for the enjoyment of its bliss and glory. The change of immersion to sprinkling deprives the ordinance of its fitness to represent the death unto sin and the resurrection unto life, experienced by every proper subject of it, and of the copious measure of the Spirit in which the apostles and the early Christians were baptized. In short, these principles were, we think, designed, and are pre-eminently adapted, to prevent the union of the church and the world—one of the sorest curses under which mankind have groaned.

There is no cause to be ashamed of these principles. They are not congenial to the taste of the world. In most nations and in most communities they are unpopular. Immersion especially is held in undisguised contempt by many, particularly among the upper classes of society. If, however, these principles are divine, they are wise, beneficent, and noble—worthy of our confidence and respect. Let men despise, if God approves them. It was through reproach and fierce opposition that the gospel gained its early and its most glorious triumphs. Our fathers maintained their principles amid scorn, persecution, and sufferings; and we should prove ourselves degenerate sons, if we were ashamed of truths in which they gloried and for which they extorted respect from a gainsaying and reluctant world.

Believing these principles, Baptists are solemnly bound to *defend* them. They have always had, and probably to the dawn of the millennium will continue to have opponents. Learning, eloquence, wealth, fashion, taste the interests and influence of large and powerful Christian denominations, and the authority and resources of hierarchies venerable for age and renowned for their works, are arrayed against them in serried ranks; while their advocates are comparatively few, poor, and feeble. If these principles had not been indestructible, they had long ago perished. It is ordained by the God of truth that they who know it shall defend it. "Contend earnestly for the faith which was once delivered unto the saints" (Jude 3) was an inspired direction to the primitive disciples—an injunction obligatory on Christians to the present day. They should contend, not harshly, inopportunely, or indiscreetly, but bravely, kindly, candidly, wisely, and persistently, for "the faith once delivered unto the saints"—for every article of it, with due regard to its comparative value.

Baptists are bound, not only to defend, but to *disseminate* their principles. Christianity is in its very nature aggressive. It is in essential antagonism with the maxims, customs, aims, and practices of the world. "If any man love the world, the love of the Father is not in him." The command of the risen Jesus to his apostles was: "Go, teach all nations." That law is of wide import. It requires that all mankind shall be instructed in the doctrine and precepts of Christianity; and in the faithful performance of this service, the inculcation of the important principles under consideration cannot be omitted. This is an abiding law of Christ. The gospel was given to the apostles, in trust for their successors—not their official successors, for they had none—but their successors in faith, spirit, aims, labors, and usefulness—their true successors—

"alway, even to the end of the world." Baptists should teach their distinctive principles in their families, in their Sunday schools, in their pulpits, and in the world—by pen, and by tongue, and by type, and by every means which Divine Providence may place within their reach.

Especially are Baptists bound to *exemplify* and commend their principles in their lives and in the discipline of their churches. The whole value of these principles lies in their power to make individual Christians more spiritual and churches more devout, liberal, and efficient. If, tried by tests, they are found wanting, it is sad for those who boast of them. Baptists and Baptist churches are not what they ought to be, and not what, under better culture, we trust they will become; but their principles present an insuperable barrier to that blending of the church and the world, which abolishes all wholesome ecclesiastical discipline, secularizes the church, and converts it into an agency for the promotion of worldly ambition and the indulgence of intolerant bigotry. No hierarchy can be organized on Baptist principles. Those who have been immersed on a solemn profession of their death to sin and their resurrection to a new life should so walk, in sobriety, righteousness, and piety, as to prove the genuineness of their profession. A selfish, worldly, undevout Baptist is a disgrace to his name. Baptist churches should be careful to maintain a scriptural discipline, making due allowance for ignorance and infirmity, but by no means tolerating a persistence in sin. They should remember and put in force the solemn admonition of the apostle: "But I have written unto you not to keep company, if any man that is called a brother be a fornicator, or covetous, or an idolater, or a railer, or a drunkard, or an extortioner; with such an one no not to eat." (1 Cor. v. 11.) This prohibition had reference to church fellowship, as appears by the limitation made to it in the context: "I wrote unto you in an epistle not to company with fornicators; yet not altogether with the fornicators of this world, or with the covetous, or extortioners, or with idolaters; for then must ye needs go out of the world." (1 Cor. v. 9, 10.) Christians should eschew ecclesiastical association with the ungodly, but cannot wholly avoid social intercourse with them.

What ground, it may be asked, is there to hope for the *ultimate triumph* of Baptist principles? None, if they be not true; but, if true, their final success is secured by the immutable purpose and the unfailing promise of the living God. Truth is mighty and will prevail. We are permitted, however, to see signs of their progress and of their increasing influence. Wherever there is an open Bible and religious toleration, there Baptist principles, to a greater or less extent, prevail. They are written, as with a sunbeam, by the Spirit of inspiration. By means of ingenious translations, learned commentaries, plausible arguments, and the force of early religious training, they may be concealed or perverted; but many who read the Scriptures with their own eyes, and with earnest prayer for divine guidance, will reach the conclusion that these principles are revealed in the Scriptures and are worthy of cordial acceptance.

Their prevalence among Pedobaptist denominations is a pleasing indication of their progressive power. Many intelligent and estimable members of Pedobaptist churches refuse to have their children baptized, and the supposed duty cannot be enforced by ecclesiastical authority. In spite of all the efforts made to cast odium on immersion, almost all Pedobaptist denominations are compelled to take their converts, to satisfy their consciences, to rivers, ponds, or Baptist fonts, for the administration of the ordinance. Nor is this tendency checked by an occasional instance of an irreverent and awkward administration of immersion, adapted, if not designed, to cast reproach on it. We think it a favorable indication of the progress of these principles that some Pedobaptists have run to the extreme of denying that immersion is baptism at all. It is an opinion contrary to the learning, history, and practice of the Christian world in all past ages, to which the advocates of *pedorantism* have been driven by their logical necessities. We decidedly prefer to combat the error on that line. It is a change of front, and indicative of conscious weakness on their part.

Our hope is, not that all the world will formally become Baptists but that the distinctive principles for which they plead will gradually permeate all Christian sects, and that there will be a universal return to apostolic principles in regard to Christian ordinances and church organization. Suppose all the evangelical sects were gradually to abandon infant baptism, return to the ancient practice of immersion, and adopt a discipline suited to spiritual churches—would it not be a great gain to the cause of truth? Many questions would doubtless arise in such a religious revolution that would perplex and trouble the most honest and earnest inquirers after truth and duty; but we need not discuss them now. All approximation to right principles and practices among the religious denominations should be hailed with delight, and receive due encouragement from the friends of an unadulterated Christianity.

Baptists should remain united, maintain their principles firmly and charitably, pray for the divine blessing on their efforts to advance his cause, and patiently wait for their dismission from the Master's service.

"I take up today the first and fundamental doctrine of Baptists, which is that concerning the Bible. . . They believe that the inspired Word of God is all that men need as a religious guide -- as guide to religious faith and practice . . . They hold, therefore, that the Bible is the sole, sufficient, sovereign rule of faith and practice, of doctrine and duty. With regard to Christian institutions, they hold, of course, that the New Testament is the sovereign authority. The Old Testament gives us valuable information, in its history of God's dealings with His ancient people; it gives us revelations of His character; the morality of its decalogue is universal and perennial in its binding force. But while the Old Testament is worth so much as a revelation of God's character and as a history of the preparation for the coming of the Saviour, we can never go back to it for instruction about Christian institutions. To do that would be to ignore the great fact of progress in God's revelation [Hebrews 1:1-3, etc.], and it would be to go back among the shadows for the substance.

The Baptist doctrine concerning the Bible, then, is this: The Bible -- and, as to Christian institutions, the New Testament -- is the sole, sufficient, sovereign religious authority . . . There are people that say that we must not preach our 'peculiarities.' I am persuaded that people who talk that way have not thought the matter through. I think they do not understand all that is implied in what they say. They have not considered that, if Baptists hold important views, they ought to set forth those views, at proper times and in proper ways; and that, if they have not important views which distinguish them from other denominations of Christians, they ought to cease to be Baptists and disband. The same rule, I am sure, applies to all denominations. Any denomination that has views which justify separate existence, is bound to promulgate those views. If those views are of sufficient importance to justify a separate existence, they are important enough to create a duty for their promulgation. If they are not of sufficient importance to make it the duty of those who hold them to promulgate them, then they are not of sufficient importance to justify maintaining a separate organization as a denomination; and it is the manifest duty of such a denomination to disband and allow itself to be absorbed in some other denomination which does stand for doctrines worth promulgating and that justify its separate existence.

The man who says that denominational peculiarities should not be preached, is virtually saying that his denomination has no right to a separate existence. That is what he is saying without knowing that so much is implied in what he says. That is what he is saying, no matter to what denomination he belongs. It is a thousand pities that men should talk that way. My advice to all such talkers, if I had an opportunity to advise them, would be: Either think more on the subject or talk less. I am sure that, if they would think the matter through, they would take the right view of it; and then they would talk right about it. They would see that the very same reasons which justify the separate existence of any denomination make it *the duty of that denomination to teach the distinctive doctrines upon which its separate existence rests.*"

E. J. FORRESTER
The Baptist Position as to The Bible, The Church, and The Ordinances.
(Baltimore: R. H. Woodward & Co., 1893).

PART II.

Regenerate Church Membership,
Henry G. Weston, D. D., LL.D., President of Crozer Theological Seminary.

The Subjects of Baptism,
Alvah Hovey, D. D., LL.D., President Emeritus of Newton Theological Institution.

The Case for Immersion at Present,
Edgar Y. Mullins, D. D., LL.D., President Southern Baptist Theological Seminary.

Archaeology of Baptism—The Bath, Under the Old Testament,
Howard Osgood, Rochester, N. Y.

Baptism the Door to the Lord's Supper,
Franklin Johnson, D. D., LL.D., The University of Chicago.

Baptists and Religious Liberty,
Benjamin O. True, D. D., Rochester Theological Seminary.

Obligations of Baptists to Teach Their Principles,
J. B Gambrell, D. D., Texas.

HENRY GRIGGS WESTON, LL. D.
1820-1909.
President of Crozer Theological Seminary.

CHAPTER I.

Regenerate Church Membership.

BY HENRY G. WESTON, LL. D., PRESIDENT OF CROZER THEOLOGICAL SEMINARY.

The conditions of membership in a New Testament church are determined by the nature of the church, its purpose, character, and functions.

Our Lord Jesus Christ became incarnate that he might redeem man and his dwelling-place from the dominion of Satan and establish a kingdom in which the will of God should be done on earth as it is in heaven.

The approach of the kingdom was formally and officially announced by John the Baptist, the divinely appointed herald, who bade the people prepare for the coming Messiah. The religious and civil authorities rejected the counsel of God against themselves, refused to be baptized by John, and finally put him to death. Lu. vii. 30. It was apparent that the same fate was reserved for Jesus. In view of this, he withdrew from the metropolis, gathered a band of followers in Galilee, to whom he so revealed himself by his words, his works, and his life that they saw that he was the Son of God, the manifestation of the Father, and they accepted and acknowledged him as such. When this was accomplished, he made known to them that he was about to establish a church composed of those to whom the Son had been divinely revealed by the Father; that to this church the keys of the kingdom would be entrusted;* that the way to the throne was by death on the cross; and that those who are to follow him must partake of his death and life. Matt. xvi. 13-28.

We have now to do with the first of these great truths—the church. Its name *(ecclesia)* indicates that its note is selection and separation; its members are chosen and sanctified. This is explicitly stated by our Lord: "If ye were of the world, the world would love its own; but because you are not of the world, but I have chosen you out of the world, therefore the world hateth you." Jno. xv. 19. Peter, to whom, as the representative and spokesman of the apostles, Christ declared his purpose to build a church, interprets his words as meaning what I have indicated. He describes the church as "an elect race, a holy nation, its members as living stones built on the living stone, a spiritual

---

* The identification of the church with the kingdom is one of the fatal errors of the Roman Catholic Church. It has given the keys of the church to Peter, an interpretation which destroys the relation of the church to the kingdom, but which is in strict accord with the theory of that church's relation to the world. If any one is disposed to acquiesce in this identification, let him substitute "church" for "kingdom" in the passages in the New Testament in which the latter word occurs, beginning with the first, "Thy kingdom come," and ending with the last (except the Apocalypse), "For so will be richly supplied to you the entrance into the eternal kingdom of our Lord and Saviour Jesus Christ," and see what sense he will make.

house to offer up spiritual sacrifices." 1 Pet. ii. 5-10. Holiness is everywhere ascribed to the church, as righteousness is to the kingdom, and these characteristics are never interchanged. The members of the church are both holy and righteous, but the distinguishing characteristic of the church is holiness; its members are "the saints."

In that wonderful chapter, the seventeenth of John's Gospel, which might be entitled the report which Christ makes to the Father of his earthly work, he describes the nature of that eternal life which he gives to all whom the Father has given him. It culminates in that divine unity which finds expression in the words, "I pray that they all may be one; as thou, Father, in me and I in thee, that they also may be in us"—words that are often interpreted to mean the union of Christians in an external organization. They have an infinitely deeper meaning. It is unity of which Christ speaks—that unity in the Father and the Son which has been produced by the manifestation of the divine nature to the men given to Christ out of the world (verse 6). It is frequently said that the prayer of Christ is as yet unanswered. Can we conceive of such a thing—that the prayer of God's Son, uttered at such a time, should be unanswered? It was answered; it is answered; and it is because of that answer that there has been any recognition in the world of the claims of Christ—"that the world may believe that thou didst send me." What are called the evidences of Christianity have done very little in inducing men to submit to Christ. It is when men see Christ in the Christian, the glory which the Father gave to Christ and which Christ gave to his disciples, as he says—"the glory which thou gavest me I have given them, that they may be one as we are one"—it is then that men are won to the Saviour.

To the same purport are those wonderful words of Peter, addressing those who have obtained an equally precious faith with us: "To whom he has given exceeding great and precious promises, that through these ye might become partakers of the divine nature, having escaped from the corruption that is in the world." 2 Pet. i. 4. This identification of the people of Christ with their Lord, this unity with the Father and the Son, finds continual expression in the Epistles. Believers are said to be in Christ, and Christ is said to be in them; they have died with him, so that, if any one be in Christ, he is a new creation; if any man, no matter what he is or has been, wise or ignorant, moral or immoral, if he be in Christ, he is a new creature; old things have passed away, all things are become new. The change when one becomes a Christian is no reformation, no evolution; it is a new creation.

This unity of life, of spirit, and of nature makes the church the body of Christ. A body is that by which the spirit acts on the world. All the proper acts and functions of Christ on the world are performed by means of his body—the church. He is the head, inspiring, directing, ruling, but doing all things through his body. "And gave him to be head over all things to the church, which is his body, the fulness of him who filleth all in all." Eph. i. 22. "All this grace and fulness must find means of expression and dispensation through the church." Through the church his redeeming and saving purposes are fulfilled; for it is through those who believe that he, the source of life, becomes the source of life to others. "He that believeth on me, as the Scriptures have said, out of him shall flow rivers of living water." Jno. vii. 30. They are partakers in his death and resurrection; they have died to sin and risen to newness of life, and, although this death and life are not yet consummated, and will not be until the complete and final triumph over death at the resurrection at the last day, they have been so united to Christ that they bring forth the fruit of the vine of whose life they partake.

It would seem unnecessary to discuss farther the place which regeneration holds in the divine economy. The scriptural definition of a Christian, the nature of a Christian life, the relation of the church to Christ, the office and functions of the church, the uniform and abundant teachings of the Epistles, the example of our Lord, who in his revelation of heavenly things begins with the absolute necessity of regeneration, all bear testimony to the great fundamental truth. And in this all evangelical churches agree. For that matter, the great majority of nominal Christians, whether evangelical or not, unite in asserting the absolute necessity of regeneration; the difference between them lies in the method of regeneration. The sacramentalists teach that "in baptism we were made members of Christ, the children of God, and inheritors of the kingdom of heaven." Evangelicals say that the church and its ordinances are for those who have been born again by the Holy Spirit, and that a church should be composed of the regenerate. This is abundantly declared in their official documents and by their acknowledged representatives. I quote only from those authorities which happen to be in my library.

Dr. Henry M. Dexter is the acknowledged exponent of American Congregationalism. His works are standard. In his treatise on Congregationalism, in his definition of a true church, he says: "A true church must be composed of those who believe themselves to be and publicly profess to be Christians." He argues this by a citation of those texts which (1) describe the church as being a holy body; (2) those which describe the vital union between Christ and the church; (3) those which announce the design which Christ has in regard to the church; (4) those which affirm a radical distinction between the church and the world; (5) those which require such preparation for the reception of church ordinances as only believers can have; (6) those which require the discipline of unworthy members. Dr. Ross, in his lectures on Congregationalism, delivered before the Andover Theological Seminary, says (page 104): "The local, particular church should be composed of believers, or holy persons"; and to the proof of this devotes six octavo pages. The venerable Dr. Charles Hodge has an elaborate article in the Princeton Review (1853) on "The Idea of the Church," in which he argues at great length that "the church must consist of true believers." About the year 1842, Dr. Hodge gave to the public a book, published by the American Sunday-School Union, entitled, "The Way of Life." It was prepared for "those who are anxious to know what they must believe and what they must experience in order to be saved." The first sentence in the preface is: "It is one of the clearest principles of divine revelation that holiness is the fruit of truth"; and the book is in accord with that sentence. It is full of evangelical truth, admirably expressed. His statements concerning the ordinances of the church are in exact harmony with our contention that a church should be composed of the regenerate. Witness the following, from page 267: "The Scriptures teach that the ordinances are not appointed to convey in the first instance pardon and sanctification, but to be signs and seals of these blessings to the penitent believer; and that to him, and to him only, are they efficacious means of grace." Again (page 279): "Thus a knowledge of the truth concerning God, concerning sin, atonement, and regeneration is essential to a proper participation of the ordinance of baptism." A dozen similar statements might be quoted from the chapter on "Profession of Religion."

In the British and Foreign Evangelical Review, October, 1860, is an article by Principal Cunningham, principal and professor of Church History, New College, Edinburgh, on "Zwingli and the Doctrine of the Sacraments." The article, with others from the same author, has been republished in a volume entitled, "The Reformers and Theology of the Reformation." Principal Cunningham argues that "the Reformers, in preparing their confessions of faith, proceeded on the assumption that those partaking in the ordinances were duly qualified and rightly prepared; and more particularly that the persons baptized, in whom the true and full operation of baptism was exhibited, were adults—adult believers." In support of this position he quotes Martin Vitringa's "complete and comprehensive summary of the doctrine of the Reformed churches upon this point; that the sacraments have been instituted only for those who have already received the grace of God—the called, the regenerate, the believing, the converted, those who are in covenant with God" (page 264). Vitringa has produced his evidence at length. His quotations fill about twenty pages, and are certainly amply sufficient to establish his position. They prove that the quotation we have cited contains a correct summary of the doctrine of the Reformed churches in regard to the proper subjects of the sacraments. Vitringa gives extracts from eight or ten of the confessions of the Reformation period, and from about fifty of the most eminent divines of that and the succeeding century (pages 265, 266). Two or three of his authorities we quote. Samuel Rutherford: "Baptism is not that whereby we are entered into Christ's mystical and invisible body as such, for it is presupposed we be members of Christ's body and our sins pardoned already, before baptism comes to be a seal of sin pardoned" (page 279). Thomas Boston: "The sacraments are not converting, but confirming, ordinances; they are appointed for the use and benefit of God's children, not of others; they are given to believers as believers, so that none others are capable of the same before the Lord" (page 282). Dr. John Erskine, "probably the greatest divine in the Church of Scotland in the latter part of the last century": "Baptism, then, is a seal of spiritual blessings; and spiritual blessings it cannot seal to the unconverted" (page 283).

How the positions thus avowed can be reconciled with the practice of infant baptism is not for me to say. Principal Cunningham says: "The views we have set forth on this subject may, at first sight, appear to be large concessions to those who deny the lawfulness of the baptism of infants," and he devotes two or three pages to the endeavor to show that these concessions are only in appearance. He says that infant baptism holds a peculiar place, and the ignorance or disregard of this fact has introduced much error and confusion into men's views upon this whole subject. "The peculiarity is that infant baptism really occupies a sort of subordinate and exceptional position."

We have probably said enough by way of establishing our proposition. History illustrates the importance of adhering to the scriptural position and practice in this matter. New England was settled by a people who held evangelical doctrine above all price. To attain it and retain it, they sacrificed everything. In an evil hour their descendants lost sight of the true nature of the church, adopted what was styled "The Half-way Covenant," and admitted to church membership those who gave no evidence of regeneration. The natural result followed. In the beginning of the present century, the pulpits which once resounded with the gospel preached by the Mathers, the Eliots, the Shepards, were occupied by men of an alien faith. With a single exception, every old Puritan pulpit in Boston and vicinity was in the possession of men who scorned the evangelical creed. Preaching by the Baptists of the truth, "Ye must be born again," awoke men from the slumbers of spiritual death and dotted New England hills with Baptist churches.

The various sections which bear the Christian name are discriminated by the respective need of human nature to which they specially appeal and for which they specially provide. One appeals to the religious nature; another to the intellectual; another to the spiritual. The question and test of the first is, Do you conform to the religious requirements of the church? Of the second, Do you adhere to the doctrinal confessions and standards? In the third, the first question always asked of applicants for admission to the church or ministry is, Are you regenerate?

ALVAH HOVEY, D. D., LL. D.,
1820-1903.
President of Newton Theological Institution.

CHAPTER II.

The Subjects of Baptism.

BY ALVAH HOVEY, D. D., LL.D.

I may as well begin with a confession of personal faith, which is: That the only proper subjects of Christian baptism are persons who trust in Jesus Christ as their Redeemer and Lord; not believers in Christ, together with their households, including servants; nor believers in Christ, together with their children, of whatever age; nor believers in Christ, with their helpless babes; but solely believers in Christ, who thereby confess their allegiance to him. This is the creed of Baptists in respect to the proper subjects of the first Christian ordinance. And, to the best of my knowledge, they have always held, and do now hold with undiminished confidence, this article of their faith, to be supported, first, by the narrative and expository references to baptism in the New Testament; secondly, by the nature of the Christian religion itself; and, thirdly, by the history of Christendom in so far as it pertains to this subject.

First, then, the narrative and expository references to baptism in the New Testament show that it was administered to persons who repented of sin or believed in Christ; and, in the case of those who heard the gospel, repentance and faith were inseparable; every believer began his life of trust in the Lord Jesus by repentance towards God. Thus on the day of Pentecost the people who "were pierced in their heart," and "received the word of Peter, were baptized." In like manner, when Philip went down to the city of Samaria and preached to them the Christ, those who "believed Philip preaching good tidings concerning the kingdom of God and the name of Jesus Christ were baptized, both men and women." Equally plain is it that Saul of Tarsus was already a believing man, willing to obey the Lord Jesus, who appeared to him on the way to Damascus, before he was baptized by Ananias. The same was also true of Cornelius, the Roman centurion; of Lydia, the seller of purple, and her household; of the Philippian jailer and all his; and of the twelve disciples whom Paul rebaptized at Ephesus, evidently because they had not by their previous baptism confessed their intelligent faith in Christ as the giver of the Holy Spirit and the head of a spiritual kingdom. Indeed, we find no instance of the giving of baptism intentionally to any but persons having faith in Christ. And there is good reason to think that the apostle would not have rebaptized the twelve disciples at Ephesus, if they had heard and understood all that John the Baptist had taught respecting One mightier than himself, who would baptize them in the Holy Spirit.

It will be remembered at the same time that the baptism of John, whatever may have been its relation to that commanded by Christ, was offered by him to none but those who were called to repentance and confession of their sins. Mark says that "they were baptized by him in the river Jordan, confessing their sins." Thus the first use of this significant rite in connection with the new order of things was apparently limited to persons who sought it of their own accord, and by it professed to enter upon a new and inward religious life. And if proselyte baptism was in use before the time of Christ, which is very doubtful, I am not aware of any evidence that it was administered to any class of people, old or young, as a substitute for circumcision. Thus the narrative references to baptism in the New Testament support our conviction that its proper subjects are persons who trust in Jesus Christ as their Redeemer and Lord.

It is true, however, that there are three instances of the baptism of households, or families, mentioned in the New Testament—namely, those of Lydia, of the Philippian jailer, and of Stephanas; but an impartial study of the narratives fails to discover in them the slightest evidence of an infant or unbelieving member in any of these households. It requires a creative imagination, like that of the late distinguished Horace Bushnell, to make such a discovery. A few years ago, the pastor of our church at Newton Centre, Mass., found that it had on its roll of members the names of not less than thirty entire families, all of them having been baptized on profession of faith in Christ. They comprised, in fact, about one-third of the whole church.

The doctrine of believer's baptism is also supported by expository references to this ordinance in the New Testament. Peter's answer to the question of those who were pierced in their heart and said, "Brethren, what shall we do?" was this: "Repent and be baptized, every one of you, in the name of Jesus Christ, unto remission of your sins"—language which certainly gives a leading place to the action of the subjects of baptism in submitting to that ordinance. In striking agreement with this is Paul's account of what Ananias said to him in Damascus: "And now why tarriest thou? Arise, and be baptized, and wash away thy sins, calling on his name." To the same effect is the apostle's word to the Galatians: "For ye are all sons of God through faith in Christ Jesus; for all ye who were baptized into Christ did put on Christ." The ritual and symbolic confession of their union with Christ was as much their own act as was their faith in him. And no less clearly does Peter, in his First Epistle, refer to the moral participation of the subjects of baptism in the act performed. The saving efficacy of baptism is ascribed to its relation to conscience; not the conscience of parents, of sponsors, or of administrators, but the conscience of the persons baptized. In all these and some other passages forgiveness of sins, union with Christ, or being saved, is connected with baptism, either because the new life begins with baptism or because its beginning is normally expressed by baptism, the sign being put for the thing signified. We believe the latter explanation to be correct; for the apostle Paul claims to have been the spiritual father of the Corinthian saints, saying: "I write not these things to shame you, but to admonish you as my beloved children. For if ye have ten thousand tutors in Christ, yet not many fathers; for in Christ Jesus, through the gospel, I begat you." The gospel, not baptism, was the means of their conversion; for Paul, in the first chapter of this very Epistle, disclaims baptizing them, with the exception of a very few, and rejoices in the fact that he had been sent, not to baptize, but to preach the gospel.

Secondly, our conviction that the only proper subjects of Christian baptism are persons who trust in Jesus Christ as their Redeemer and Lord is supported by the nature of the Christian religion. If there is anything which is taught with absolute clearness by the Saviour and his apostles, it is the personal and spiritual nature of our religion. This religion is neither national nor tribal, neither Semitic nor Greek. Pedigree is of no account without faith, and faith is a personal act. The history of Ishmael and Esau, of Absalom and Manasseh, proves that hereditary grace is a fiction. The scientific facts of heredity may, indeed, suggest that religious character is transmissible from parents to children; but the history of mankind disproves the reality of this transmission, and the words of Christ, "Unless a man be born anew he cannot see the kingdom of God," confirm that disproof.

When we think of the gospel as a message of

religious truth to beings of a religious nature, we at once perceive its fitness to arouse thought and feeling, thus leading to action and affecting their spiritual condition. There is no disparity between the means and the end. We assent to the testimony of Paul that the gospel is the power of God unto salvation to every one that believes; but we perceive no such adaptation of means to ends in the baptism of infants. For them the rite has no illuminating or convincing power. Its pictorial and impressive testimony to an inward change, or even to the need of an inward change, is not made or appropriated by them. They are simply passive subjects, unconscious of any spiritual meaning in what is done. If the Spirit of God works at all through the medium of consecrated water, it must work in a merely physical way, utterly foreign to the spiritual character of the Christian religion as this is described in the New Testament.

Thirdly, our conviction, that the only proper subjects of baptism are persons who trust in Jesus Christ as their Redeemer and Lord, is supported by the history of Christendom. This proposition cannot be fully justified in a brief article. A thorough discussion of the events which are believed to justify it would fill more than one respectable volume. But the principle on which the argument for our proposition rests is obvious and sound—namely, that a rule for Christian action in church life, which has been found conducive to purity in that life, is presumably founded on the will of

Christ. And if any important modification of the rule can be shown to have marred the peace or spirituality of that life in its corporate manifestations, this fact will also go to confirm the rule as an expression of the Lord's will.

Now, it may be said, in brief, that the practice of restricting baptism to believers in Christ has always been a protest against the dogma of baptismal regeneration, and, by parity of reason, against the whole theory of sacramental grace. It has also been an obstacle to the union of Church and State and to the use of civil power in support of religion. There were a few Munsterites among the Anabaptists of Germany, but most of the Anabaptists were peaceable citizens, dying for their faith, but not fighting for it. And so it has been everywhere with Christians who have rejected infant baptism. They have been often subject to persecution, but have consistently refused to persecute others. And this has been the logical outcome of their position as to the proper subjects of baptism—a position which puts upon every soul of man the responsibility of deciding for himself concerning the service of God.

It has been truly said that ideas in the long run bear rule, that the beliefs of men determine their conduct. It is, therefore, of the first importance that our belief concerning the proper subjects of baptism should agree, first, with a true conception of the Christian religion; secondly, with a true conception of Christian churches as groups of men and women united together of their own choice for the service of Christ; and, thirdly, with a true conception of the relation of both these to the State, which is entrusted by the will of God with civil authority. And if, as the writer seriously holds, the Baptist position is the only safe and defensible one, it must be maintained with the utmost firmness and charity.

Newton Centre, Mass.

EDGAR YOUNG MULLINS, D. D., LL. D.
1860-1928.
President of Southern Baptist Theological Seminary.

CHAPTER III.

The Case for Immersion at Present.

BY E. Y. MULLINS, D. D., LL.D., PRESIDENT OF THE SOUTHERN BAPTIST THEOLOGICAL SEMINARY, LOUISVILLE, KY.

For one man to shout, "It is!" and another to shout back, "It is not!"—a reiterated affirmation on the one hand and a reiterated denial on the other—is a see-saw of contradiction, rather than a logical process. It must be confessed that the long-drawn baptismal controversy sometimes seems to degenerate into such a contradiction, issuing in little progress towards unanimity, or other fruits of the Spirit. The careful observer, however, will find evidences of an awakening conscience in many quarters on this subject, and it cannot be in vain for Baptists, in all charity, to continue to affirm their strong conviction on a matter which so large a portion of the Christian world seems determined to ignore.

"The Case for Immersion at Present" is the theme assigned to me. An adequate statement of "the case" will require some space, and some patience on the part of the reader.

THE MEANING OF THE WORD.

The case for immersion, as based upon the meaning of the Greek word translated "baptize" in our English Bible, is as convincing as it is possible for evidence to make it. The purposes of this article require a brief presentation of this evidence. Liddell & Scott's Greek Lexicon is a universally accepted standard among scholars. It gives immersion, and immersion only, as the meaning of the Greek word *baptizo*. This applies to classic as well as New Testament Greek. Grimm's Wilke's Lexicon of New Testament Greek says the word means to submerge, to wash by submerging. In the New Testament the word means "an immersion in water, intended as a sign of sins washed away, &c." This lexicon gives no other meaning of the word. Cremer's Lexicon says the word means "submerge," and in the New Testament "submersion for a religious purpose." Thayer's Greek-English Lexicon of the New Testament, which is a translation, revision, and enlargement of Grimm's Wilke's Lexicon, gives an extended definition of *baptizo* in its various New Testament connections, and it is uniformly the same as in the lexicons named above— to submerge, to dip, to plunge. The figurative uses of the word are all based upon the same meaning. Testimony from other lexicons might be given. I will only add that of Professor Sophocles, in his Greek Lexicon of the Roman and Byzantine period, from B. C. 140 to A. D. 1100. He gives the meaning which is found in all the standard lexicons—to dip, plunge, submerge. In addition, he cites Ignatius, Justin Martyr, Gregory, Epiphanius, Origen, Cyril, and others of the earthly fathers, in proof of this meaning. The testimony of the fathers is well-nigh universal in favor of immersion for over 400 years. Modern Greeks regard the translation of the word *baptizo*, "to sprinkle," as absurd. Dr.

Broadus quotes a modern Greek scholar as saying: "The church of the West commits an abuse of words and of ideas in practising baptism by aspersion, the mere statement of which is itself a ridiculous contradiction."

The above position is abundantly sustained on the authority of the reformers of the sixteenth century, as well as by evidence from great numbers of modern scholars. Martin Luther advocated a return to immersion as the New Testament form of baptism. John Calvin admitted that immersion only was the original mode, but that the form was a matter of indifference. Dr. Doellinger, a Roman Catholic scholar of very high standing, has said that, as to the mode of baptism, "the Baptists are, from the Protestant standpoint, unassailable, since for their demand of baptism by submersion they have the clear Bible text." Innumerable modern scholars of all denominations maintain the position that immersion only was the New Testament form of baptism. In Germany, two names of interest are Meyer, the great commentator, and Harnack, the great historian. The latter wrote, some years ago, a very interesting letter to Dr. C. E. W. Dobbs, in reply to questions about the meaning of the Greek word, and especially as to whether a "sacred sense" of the word *baptizein* is ever to be understood, allowing sprinkling instead of immersion. Dr. Harnack wrote, in part, as follows: "*Baptizein* undoubtedly signifies immersion. No proof can be found that it signifies anything else in the New Testament, and in the most ancient Christian literature. The suggestion regarding a sacred sense is out of the question. There is no passage in the New Testament which suggests the supposition that any New Testament author attached to the word any other sense than to immerse." Dr. Harnack wrote the above as a statement on "the present state of opinion among German scholars."

Besides the above, practically all the great names of scholars of the Church of England who have expressed themselves on the point might be quoted in support of the view that immersion, and immersion only, was the form of baptism taught by the New Testament.

In view of the above array of evidence, it would seem that "the case for immersion at present" is closed, if we confine our view to the meaning of the Greek word of which it is the translation.

THE "TEACHING OF THE TWELVE APOSTLES."

The above document revived interest in the baptismal controversy upon its publication, some seventeen years ago. Being a witness raised up out of its grave, so to speak, in the Jerusalem library, and dating from about the middle of the second century, its testimony as to baptism was examined with great eagerness by all parties. Both immersionists and anti-immersionists claimed the document in confirmation of their respective views. Baptists have every reason for the claim that in no degree does the "Teaching of the Twelve" weaken their position as to the teaching of the

New Testament. Its instructions on the subject of baptism are pronounced in favor of immersion. In brief, it directs that baptism shall be "in living water; and if this be not convenient, in other water; and if not in cold water, baptize in warm." Finally, if water in sufficient quantity for immersion be not found, then "pour water thrice upon the head in the name of the Father, Son, and Holy Ghost." It is perfectly clear from the testimony of the "Teaching" that its writer held to immersion as the original and proper mode of baptism. The fact that pouring as an alternative mode in certain contingencies is prescribed does not destroy the force of the teaching as to immersion. The only open question which is left by this document is whether or not the direction about pouring was, in the mind of its author, based upon apostolic example and precept, or upon other considerations. The evidence in favor of the latter view is overwhelming. The following facts shed light on the point. Cyprian (A. D. 200-257) wrote a tract in defence of clinical baptism (i. e., baptism of sick people), against those who denied its validity. It was commonly held about this time that, although in certain cases of sickness pouring was allowable as a substitute for immersion, it was defective baptism and disqualified for the priesthood. Moreover, Schaff says it was probably because Novatian had been baptized by aspersion, when on a sick-bed, that he failed of re-election to the see of Rome, and that this fact became "the occasion of a subsequent schism which attended his name." As to the existence in the age after the apostles of substitutes for immersion, Baptists do not make denial. But the very fact that the substitutes are never adhered to as resting on scriptural authority, and the further fact that they are dealt with and treated as departures from the customary mode, and especially because it was necessary to defend them against many who rejected them, the conclusion is unavoidable that they arose after apostolic times. The adequate cause for their introduction is found in the exaggerated importance attached to baptism, and the supposed peril of unbaptized persons at the point of death. The Greek word employed in "The Teaching" to set forth the three-fold pouring which is admitted as a last resort is a word never once used in the New Testament in connection with baptism.

THE WITNESS OF HISTORY.

Let us glance at the case for immersion as witnessed by Christian history. The briefest survey is all that is possible within the limits of this article. The following are the facts: First of all, there is no shred of evidence that the New Testament form of baptism (immersion) was ever departed from in New Testament times. At an early date, however, clinic baptisms by pouring or sprinkling came into vogue. These clinic baptisms were not the rule, but the exception, and were practised for the benefit of the sick, and were never urged on direct scriptural grounds. Immersion continued to be the usual and the preferred mode for over a thousand years. In the Greek church, immersion has ever been and is still the practice. The longer catechism of the Russian church declares that "trine immersion in water is most essential." Similar witness is borne by Professor Philaret Bapheidos, of the Russian church, and author of a Church History, and many other living writers testify to the same effect. In the Roman church, immersion continued the rule until the thirteenth century. In the Anglican church, there is abundant evidence in favor of immersion as the ancient and biblical form of baptism. In theory, the church of England still holds to immersion, as is evidenced by the Prayer Book and other authorities. In the rubric of the Church of England we read, as to the baptism of infants: "Shall dip the child in water; but, if they certify that the child is weak, it shall suffice to pour water upon it." The witness of Christian history is, therefore, conclusive as to the original mode of baptism. The admission of other forms was due to circumstances and expediency, and not to Scripture teaching. The Protestant world which practices sprinkling, therefore, must maintain it on grounds which are at variance with the fundamental principle of Protestants—the Bible alone the authority in matters of faith and practice.

IMMERSION VIEWED IN ITS RELATIONS.

Baptism, when viewed in its relations, strongly reinforces our contention for immersion as distinguished from all other so-called modes of baptism.

This ordinance is not to be viewed apart from its connections in the Christian system. For one thing, it is related in its very form to most vital Christian doctrine. Death, burial, and resurrection are strikingly symbolized by the act of baptism. A complete purification and cleansing from sin are also thus set forth. A death to the old, a resurrection to a new life, are among the truths which receive graphic portrayal in the baptismal act of obedience to Christ. Rev. William Sandy, D. D., LL. D., author of a very able recent commentary on Romans, says, in connection with Rom. vi. 1-14: "Baptism expresses symbolically a series of acts corresponding to the redeeming acts of Christ: Immersion—death; submersion—burial (the ratification of death); emergence—resurrection." Now, so far from being unimportant because a mere external form, is baptism, its real importance arises from the fact that it is a form. Now, we do not exalt the ordinance of baptism over against the truth of the atonement or other great doctrines, and declare them of equal importance. Such comparisons are unnecessary. To set forms against doctrines, or doctrines against forms, is a thing unwarranted by Scripture. To arrive at an understanding of the importance of a form, we must inquire what use it subserves as a form, and what authority enjoins the form. As to the latter, Christ has spoken. This must suffice for all who accept him as Lord. As to the former, baptism as a symbol must remain unchanged in form. Symbols, in the nature of the case, cannot save. They can only represent pre-existing spiritual life. As a symbol, *form is everything*. This is true because only forms can serve as symbols. Truths cannot be symbolized by other truths. Abstract teachings cannot be symbolized by other abstractions. The fitness of the form to shadow forth truth is the determinative principle in the institution of forms. The ritualistic system of the Old Testament illustrates this at every point. Hence it follows that in symbolics form is all-important. Understand me; I do not say form is all-important in itself, or as compared with doctrine and life, but form, when employed as a means of setting forth truth—form utilized as a symbol—is all-important. This is true because form as a symbol is a "mould of doctrine." The doctrine is contained in the symbol as water is contained in a vessel. To mar the form is to destroy the doctrine, so far as the agency of the form is concerned, just as to break the vessel is to spill the water. Its utility as a symbol is gone the moment you alter its form. Then, too, to change baptism from immersion to sprinkling, when we remember the symbolic uses of the ordinance, is really to make less of doctrine than of form; for it is to make doctrine wait on form, rather than form on doctrine. If doctrine is important in comparison with form, then we should begin with doctrine, and make the symbol conform to the requirements of doctrine. When we alter the form, we compel the doctrine to take its chances for adequate representation in a mutilated form. Doctrine is the jewel, form is the casket. Caskets are made for jewels, not jewels for caskets. Who ever heard of a dealer manufacturing a set of handsome jewelcases, and then casting about for jewels to fit them? Baptists desire that the jewel of doctrine shall abide in its pristine beauty, and that the casket of a symbol shall match it in form, as in the beginning.

Another thought related to the foregoing is that Jesus always viewed things in their totality, and not in fragments. He enjoins truth and its expression. The tree is vindicated by its fruits; words are made good by deeds; life is authenticated by conduct. So, also, faith ripens into expression. The internal and the external are required to complete the Christian act. Baptism is the outward expression of the inward change. Baptism by immersion is not only the fitting expression of the inner life, it is the neccessary complement to the Lord's supper. The two ordinances shadow forth the supreme facts of the gospel. Christ's death is symbolized in the supper, his burial and resurrection in the ordinance of baptism. Thus, in their relations to the Christian system, baptism and the supper occupy a position of unique value. They serve as a medium for the exhibition in striking form of the chief fundamental and vital facts as to Christ and the Christian. Was not this comprehensiveness a part of the design of Christ in instituting the ordinances? Is it not evident that he meant these forms to serve as visible instrumentalities for thus setting forth before the eyes of men a complete gospel? If this completeness of representation was a part of Christ's original design, can we depart from the forms, which are necessary to the symbolic completeness, without violating Christ's will? We must find Christ's point of view in leaving the ordinances to his churches, as well as seek to understand their significance; and, having found his point of view, we must adopt it as our own. The owner of certain grounds desired a landscape gardener's services to lay them out with a view to a given effect from the portico of his residence, which stood on an elevation in the midst of the grounds. The gardener, during an absence of the owner, discovered what he regarded as a better effect from a different point of view, and laid out the grounds accordingly. But he was summarily dismissed upon the owner's return, because of his disobedience, and because his new point of view left out of account the chief item in the owner's plan—viz., the effect from the portico of his residence. The ordinances of baptism and the supper constitute a ceremonial survey of the landscape of Christian fact and doctrine, comprehending the chief vital facts. To break the form of baptism is to eliminate a part of its doctrinal significance. Sprinkling cannot symbolize burial and resurrection. The ordinance is thus left a mere fragmentary representation. Thenceforth the ordinances cease to give the completeness of representation which Christ designed. We thus lose his point of view.

It thus appears that an ordinance even must be viewed in its relations before it can be understood. As a mere form, it is nothing. As a form employed to symbolize vital truth, and as a supplement to another form symbolically setting forth other truth, and as a part of an arrangement for the complete exhibition of a group of truths, prescribed by a supreme will, it is much. A very minute wheel lying on a jeweller's table is an insignificant thing; as a part of the machinery of a watch, it is indispensable; for without the tiny wheel the watch would not run, and would cease to have utility as a timepiece.

THE OTHER SIDE.

Various arguments and objections have been urged against the Baptist position. I can scarcely do more than name some of the more popular of these, and then briefly reply to the more important.

The old claim that the scarcity of water in Jerusalem must have prevented the immersion of 3,000 converts in one day by twelve men is met by the well-known fact that Jerusalem was amply provided with large pools and a water supply which sustained it through numerous sieges of several months duration, and when the supply was exhausted on the outside, it was abundant inside the city; and by the further demonstration, in the immersion of our Telugu converts, of the ability of twelve men to perform the above task. The claim for a "sacred sense" of the word *baptizo* in the Scriptures has never been made out, and is distinctly negatived by the consensus of German scholarship, as represented by Professor Harnack, as well as the great mass of scholars of all Christian nations. The plea for sprinkling, on the ground that immersion is not always "practicable," is met by the explanation that what is "impracticable" is what cannot be done, and that what cannot be done is never commanded. The force of the argument based on the rigors of the colder climates is neutralized by the fact that in cold England immersion continued much longer than in Spain and some of the warmer climates of the south. The fact that many learned and good men have believed in sprinkling, which is a solace to some, should not stand a moment as an excuse for personal investigation on the part of all, and personal obedience to the commands of Christ. Few of the errors of Christian history in doctrine and life are without learned and good men as their advocates. It was often thus that they originated. Over against this fact is another, far more significant— viz., that there is an increasing demand for immersion on the part of the common people, with their English Bible in their hands. This demand is witnessed to a greater or less extent in every Protestant community. It has reached such proportions in the Church of England that more than 100 baptisteries, according to The Freeman, have been erected in recent years for the baptism of adults, and others are in process of construction. The truth is that, although the word "baptize" is not a translation, but a transference of the Greek original—thus obscuring its meaning—nevertheless, the act of baptism as described in the English Bible, and as expounded especially in the Epistles, is convincing in itself as to mode. The passages describing the baptism of Jesus in Jordan and the baptism of the Ethiopian, as well as other Scriptures, leave no escape for the plain reader from the conclusion that immersion is the baptism commanded in the New Testament.

There are two really important arguments against our position—important not in themselves, but in their prevalence and power over men. The first is that the church has the power to alter the form of baptism. This is the view of Roman Catholics. I need not delay to reply to it in detail. It raises the larger question as to the authority of the church. Baptists can never admit that any church is co-ordinate in authority with Christ himself. The Protestant world is guilty of a gross inconsistency whenever it admits the principle for a moment. The Bible, and the Bible only, as Christ's revealed will, is authority for Protestants in matters of religion. Hence the clear-cut deliverance of Dr. Doellinger, as given earlier in this article. Roman Catholics grasp this vital distinction better than some who claim to oppose them.

The second of these important arguments is that based on Christian liberty. Among the scholars and the well-informed laity of to-day in all denominations which do not practise immersion this is the final and sufficient ground, consciously or unconsciously held, for adherence to another mode. The case for immersion as the original New Testament teaching and practice has been so completely made out that another position has become necessary. "If you retain the *essence*," they say, "you are not obliged to do more in matters of form; Christian liberty relieves you from slavish obedience in externals." The sufficient Baptist reply is not far to seek. In the first place, Christian liberty never admits of departure from positive commands which are of permanent obligation. In the application of general principles to specific cases which may arise, it is true that Christian liberty sometimes allows room for variation in conduct. But not in definite, positive commands. Now, those who practise sprinkling maintain that baptism is an ordinance of permanent obligation, and binding because commanded by Christ. As a symbol it sets forth certain doctrines. To retain the "essence" of the symbol, we must retain its form, as has already been shown. To alter the form so as to deprive it of power to symbolize death, burial, and resurrection, is to rob it of a part of its "essence" as a symbol. If Christian liberty is to be pleaded in the case, the Quakers alone represent the consistent position; for liberty to alter a form implies liberty to reject it entirely. Indeed, in this case, to alter is to reject in part, because to alter the form is in part to destroy the meaning. To reject in part involves liberty to reject altogether. The Quakers do this. If to the Quaker it should seem allowable, in the name of liberty, to reject baptism as a symbol of purification, burial, and resurrection, why should it seem allowable for a Methodist in the name of liberty to *retain* it as a symbol of purification, and *reject* it as a symbol of burial and resurrection? Why split the ordinance into parts, and deal with one part on the principle of obedience, and with the other on the principle of liberty? There is no middle ground between Baptists and Romanists on the issue as to the relative authority of the Scriptures and the church, and there is no middle ground between Baptists and Quakers on the issue as to the principle of Christian liberty in the matter of baptism.

Our survey of "the case for immersion at present" brings us to the following conclusion: That, in view of the classical and New Testament meaning of the Greek word for baptize, as learned from standard lexicons; in view of the testimony of the Christian fathers of the early centuries; in view of the "Teaching of the Twelve Apostles"; in view of the testimony of Christian history; in view of the symbolic significance of baptism and the relation of its form to truth, to the Lord's supper, to the will of Christ; and in view of the authoritativeness of the Bible, and of any proper interpretation of Christian liberty, the case for immersion seems abundantly proved.

Reader, have you obeyed your Lord in his appointed ordinance? Have you the witness of a conscience void of offence in this matter? Do you know the joy of obedience, which is vouchsafed to all who take up their cross and follow their Lord into the experience which he knew as he entered the waters of Jordan, saying, "Thus it becometh us to fulfil all righteousness"?

HOWARD L. OSGOOD, D. D., LL. D.
1831-1911.
Professor of Oriental Languages, Rochester Theological Seminary.

CHAPTER IV.

Archaeology of Baptism—The Bath, under the Old Testament.

BY HOWARD OSGOOD, ROCHESTER, N. Y.

Bread and wine, the symbols of the support of life, were brought forth by Melchizedeck to greet Abraham; they were constant symbols on the golden table in the tent and temples, and the invariable accompaniment of the Passover feast. These simplest of all symbols were filled with deeper meaning than they had ever borne when Christ made them the memorials of his broken body and his blood poured out. The custom of dipping the person in water, common from the earliest times in Israel as a religious rite of impressive and spiritual import, was made by God the witness of Christ in his all-comprehending life and death and resurrection for us.

One of the unexpected revelations of the countless Egyptian monuments, by their inscriptions and pictures, is that for at least a thousand years before Moses, they were a people of excessive and minute cleanliness, especially with regard to religious services.

The laws concerning cleansing, given by God through Moses, were not something far off from the thought of that age. These laws are far stricter in this matter of cleanliness than any of our present codes. Cleanliness of person, of dress of house, of furniture, of utensils, of habits, of food, was prescribed with minute insistence. The Israelite who from the heart strove to be true to the teaching of God was, in consequence, an excessively clean man. No priest and no others could take part in the sacrifices and services of the temple or even in the Passover with any uncleanness upon him, under the penalty of being cut off from his people. There were less and greater uncleannesses. Some of these rendered unclean for a day only. Others could only be put away by ceremonies continued through a week. The greater bodily uncleannesses were contracted by being in the house of a dead person, touching any dead body or a bone of a man or a grave, by leprosy, etc. Of course, these were typical, and the cleansing was merely "unto the cleanness of the flesh," for the greatest of all uncleannesses, that which by the teaching of God defiled soul and body with utter abomination, was turning from the heart worship of the only God to serve idols, the work of men's hands. That is the uncleanness that sends its poison through every nerve and vein.

The lesser uncleannesses were put away by washing the clothes and bathing, immersing the body in water. But the greater uncleannesses could be put away only by ceremonies continued through a whole week. That which concluded them all was the immersion of the body in water, the bath, which immediately preceded the sacrifice offered on the eighth day.

From the very numerous causes of defilement, seen and unseen, no Israelite could be sure of his being ceremonially clean. And hence the bath was a constant religious necessity, frequently repeated, and always taken before offering sacrifice. Its high importance in the service of the temple is marked on the greatest of all the high days of Israel, the day of atonement, when the high priest, though he had bathed before, was required during those supreme services to "bathe his flesh in water" when he exchanged his usual dress for the holy linen garments, and again when he put off the holy linen to take his usual dress.

What the form of this washing (bath) was, how it was clearly understood in Western Asia, is plain from Elisha's direction to Naaman the Syrian, "Go and wash in the Jordan seven times." "Then went he down and dipped himself seven times in the Jordan, according to the saying of the man of God." The New Testament terms these various washings, baths, "various dippings," "baptisms" (Heb. ix. 10). And when Pedobaptist Hebrew scholars of the first class, like the Lutheran Delitzsch, and Salkinson, translate the New Testament into its corresponding Hebrew, they must use for baptism and these various washings the Old Testament terms signifying washing, dipping. The authoritative Jewish writings on these subjects from New Testament days teach that these ceremonial washings were complete immersions. The great Christian writers for five centuries after Christ use the terms "washing" and "bath" for baptism quite as often as they use the specific New Testament term. And in this they are only following the example of the New Testament. Acts xxii. 16; 1 Cor. vi. 11; Eph. v. 26; Tit. iii. 5; Heb. ix. 10; x. 22.

That this ritual washing, dipping, bath, was understood in its spiritual typical import by spiritually-minded men under the Old Testament is shown by the cry out of the depths from Israel's king returning from his long and foul uncleannesses: "Wash me thoroughly from mine iniquity and cleanse me from my sin." And, referring especially to the cleansing from the greater uncleanness by sprinkling from a bunch of hyssop twigs the ashes of the red heifer (Num. xix. 18, 19): "Cleanse me with hyssop, and I shall be clean; wash me, and I shall be whiter than snow." The presumptuous are warned away by God: "Wash you, make you clean," for Zion's dawn shall not appear till "the filth of her daughters has been washed away."

Our eyes and our thoughts have been so far restricted to the one word "baptism" and its significance after Christ that we have overlooked the same fact under another term, "washing," "bathe," with its spiritual significance under the Old Testament. But the New Testament does not overlook it. The Epistle to the Hebrews applies that older ceremony in both its parts with vivid realism to the new condition: "Let us draw near with a true heart in fulness of faith, having our hearts sprinkled from an evil conscience and our body washed with pure water." To the Corinthians, befouled with all the uncleannesses of heathenism, Paul says: "Such were some of you, but ye washed yourselves, but ye were sanctified," etc. And, in the Epistles to the Ephesians and to Titus, Paul uses the term "bath" with plain reference to the custom of the Old Testament applied to the New; and still further in that beautiful word painting of Christ's bringing the church to himself (the washing and renewing of the garments was always prescribed with the bath): "As Christ loved the church and gave himself up for it; that he might sanctify it, having cleansed it by the bath of water with the word, that he might present the church to himself a glorious church, not having spot or wrinkle or any such thing; but that it should be holy and without blemish."

It has been assumed, against the facts, that there was no ceremony ordained by the law of God for the reception of proselytes from the heathen. But the law certainly provided for the reception of slaves purchased from the heathen, as well as for captives by war. And the Pentateuch tells us of one foreigner who became eminent in Israel, Caleb the son of Jephunneh the Kenizzite. The succeeding books tell us of Rahab the Canaanitess, the Hivites who became servants of the house of God, Othniel the son of Kenaz, Heber a Midianite, the lovely Moabitess Ruth, and others. Was the only rite of reception for men? Was there no ceremony for the reception of Rahab and Ruth?

The mistake in assuming that the law did not provide for the reception of converts from the heathen has arisen from a forgetfulness of the reiterated statute of the law, that there shall be one and the same law for the homeborn Israelite and for the alien who would come near to sacrifice to God. Ex. xii. 49; Lev. xvii. 16; xxiv. 22; Num. ix. 14; xv. 14-16, 29-31; xix. 10. The Israelite could be cleansed from the greater uncleannesses only by certain ceremonies. The alien coming to take refuge under the wings of Jehovah could be cleansed from his uncleannesses just as Israel was from his. The bath and the sacrifice, the bath and the sacrifice—these were the two rites that stood out most prominently in their reception. It is to these ceremonies of cleansing, the sprinkling of the ashes of the red heifer, to be followed by the bath and the sacrifice, that God himself refers when, in his glowing prophecy of bringing back his people from all the uncleannesses of their idolatry in Babylon, he says: "I will sprinkle clean water upon you, and ye shall be clean; from all your filthiness and from all your idols will I cleanse you." Ezek. xxxvi. 25. As is so frequent in the Bible, a part of the week's ceremony is here put for the whole. If Israel—that was said by God to be more defiled by idolatry than Sodom or Assyria or Egypt—could be so cleansed, surely those with lesser uncleannesses upon them could be cleansed in like manner.

Until the appearance of John the Baptist, the dipping of the person in water was the absolute prerequisite under the law for every man and woman who would enter the inner court to take part in the worship. It was as common as sacrifice. Its spiritual meaning was known and felt by every one taught by the Spirit—as David, the prophets, Joseph and Mary, Zacharias and Elizabeth, Simeon and Anna, and all who "were looking for the redemption of Jerusalem."

It is not at all surprising, therefore, that, when John came dipping, baptizing in living, running water, there should be no query by the Jews as to the well-known custom. Their only query was as to John himself: "Who art thou? Art thou the Christ? Art thou Elijah? Art thou the prophet?"

The great sacrifice, "once for all time," was about to take place, and it was in exact accordance with the law and the promise that those who repented of their sins should be dipped, baptized, "unto remission of sins"; that is, that they might enter in and have part in that final really-atoning sacrifice. "John baptized with the baptism of repentance, saying unto the people that they should believe on him who should come after him; that is, on Jesus." They were baptized in expectation and hope of that sacrifice. We are baptized because we know it has taken place and we trust in it.

That the baptism (dipping) enjoined in the New Testament was a complete immersion is now so fully acknowledged and taught by those most familiar with the language, customs, and history of that time that it is not needful to add to this discussion.

BAPTISM AFTER THE TIME OF CHRIST.

From Justin Martyr (A. D. 150) onwards for 700 years there is the united testimony of literature and art that baptism was a dipping, immersion of the candidate. There are a few minor councils that, with Cyprian of Carthage, advocated a sprinkling of the body of a dying man, in case he had not received baptism; but none of the great authors or the numerous rituals or the great councils acknowledged this exception, even in the case of the dying. With united voice they teach that immersion, most frequently repeated thrice—that is, at each name of the Trinity—is the only baptism, and anathematize all who would teach differently. The Egyptian ritual, A. D. 200-300; the Roman ritual, A. D. 250; the Apostolic Constitutions, A. D. 350-400; the church of Palestine, A. D. 386; the Milanese church, A. D. 397; Chrysostom, the Gregories, Augustine, about A. D. 400; Dionysius, A. D. 450, and many lesser authorities, all agree that all around the Mediterranean, in Europe, Asia, and Africa, there was but one baptism, trine immersion. But for *trine* immersion there is no warrant in the New Testament.

What the "washing" of the Jews at this date was we know from the twelve treatises on purification in the heart of the Talmud, the Mishna. Every one, even with any of the lesser uncleannesses upon him, must dip his body wholly under water, and the least quantity of water sufficient for this purpose was put at eighty gallons. No exception is allowed to this requirement. That the Jewish washing and Christian baptism were the same in form is proved by Tertullian's (A. D. 220) argument that the difference consisted in the secret power of God conveyed in baptism.

From A. D. 450 there is a long series of pictorial representations of baptism, found in churches, catacombs, manuscripts, etc., etc. They all follow closely one type—the baptism of Jesus by John in the Jordan. The Saviour stands in the water, John stands on the bank and extends his hand over the head of Jesus. There are no representations for 800 years after Christ of the baptizer being in the water with the candidate, and the literature on this point is very decided—the baptizer is outside the baptistery.

What, then, was the action of the baptizer and of the candidate? Here the literature, Christian and Jewish, comes in to confirm the uniform representation in art. The candidate entered the baptistery, either alone or attended by a friend, the minister placed his hand upon the head of the candidate, pronouncing the words, and the candidate bowed his head forward beneath the water. In this, literature and rituals agree. There can be no doubt that this was the usual, though not exclusive, action in New Testament times and for hundreds of years afterwards. To baptize one's self and to be baptized are expressions found in the New Testament, and more frequently in Christian writers of the following centuries. For instance, in Acts xxii. 16,

Ananias says to Paul, "Arise and baptize, immerse thyself" (though it is wrongly put in the old and new versions, "be baptized"). So in 1 Cor. vi. 11, "Ye washed yourselves" (in the old and new versions, "Ye are, were washed").

The following witnesses, among many others, show the custom in their days:

The Christian church in Rome (A. D. 250) observed the following custom: "Then the candidate descends into the water, but the elder ('who stands above the water') places his hand upon his head and asks him in these words: Dost thou believe in God the Father almighty? The candidate answers: I believe. Then for the first time he is immersed in the water. Again he asks him in these words: Dost thou believe in Jesus Christ, the Son of God, whom the virgin bore by the Holy Spirit, who came to save men, who was crucified for us under Pontius Pilate, who died and arose from the dead on the third day and ascended to heaven and sits at the right hand of the Father, and will come to judge the living and the dead? He answers: I believe; and the second time he is immersed in the water. He is asked the third time: Dost thou believe in the Holy Spirit, the Comforter, proceeding from the Father and the Son. He answers: I believe; and the third time he is immersed in the water. At each of these times he (the elder) says: I baptize thee in the name of the Father, and of the Son, and of the Holy Spirit." Canons of Hippolytus. sections 123-133. And in accord with this,

Hippolytus, in his "Divine Theophany," tells us: "Christ bowed his head to be baptized by John."

Gregory Thaumaturgus (A. D. 270) sets before us his idea of the hesitation of John to touch the head of Jesus to baptize him. "How shall I dare to touch thine immaculate head? How shall I extend my servant fingers over thy divine head?" And Jesus is said to reply: "Lend me, O Baptizer, thy right hand for the present dispensation. Touch my head. Baptize me." "The Baptizer obeyed the divine command, and, stretching out his gently trembling and rejoicing right hand, he baptized the Lord."

Cyril of Jerusalem (A. D. 386): "Even Simon Magus dipped his body in water." Gregory Nyssen (A. D. 395): "Coming to the water, we hide ourselves in it."

Ambrose of Milan (A. D. 397): "Thou wast asked, Dost thou believe in God the Father Omnipotent? Thou saidst, I believe, and thou didst dip thyself; that is, wast buried. Again thou wast asked, Dost thou believe in our Lord Jesus Christ and in his cross? Thou saidst, I believe, and thou didst dip thyself; and so thou wast buried with Christ. The third time thou wast asked, Dost thou believe in the Holy Spirit? Thou saidst, I believe; and the third time thou didst dip thyself."

Chrysostom (A. D.) 407: "For when we immerse our heads," etc. "It is easy for us to dip and lift our heads again." Augustine (A. D. 407):

"After you promised to believe, we thrice dipped your heads in the sacred fountain."

It is this custom of standing in the water and bowing the head beneath the water that explains the peculiar usage of the Syrians in their very early translation of the New Testament and in their literature, where "to stand," "standing," is always the translation of "to baptize," "baptism," etc. The candidate stood up to confess Christ, and his baptism was standing up for Christ.

Baptism, then, was not merely the dipping of the head beneath the water, but the dipping of the head at the same time that the minister laid his hand upon the head and pronounced the words of baptism.

That this custom in baptism—standing and bowing the head, while the baptizer placed his hand upon the head of the candidate and pronounced the words of baptism—was the universal custom of early Christianity, is the united testimony of ritual, literature, and art. It is simple, dignified, safe. The present custom generally observed in our churches is the invention of very recent centuries.

To the apostle of Burma, Adoniram Judson, who returned to the ancient custom of baptism, and who united the refinement and fire of Greek Christian culture with absorbing gratitude and love to Christ his Saviour, we are indebted for the noble lines with which I close this paper.

"Come, Holy Spirit, Dove divine,
 On these baptismal waters shine;

And teach our hearts in highest strain
To praise the Lamb for sinners slain.

"We love thy name, we love thy laws,
And joyfully embrace thy cause;
We love thy cross, the shame, the pain,
O Lamb of God, for sinners slain.

"We sink beneath thy mystic flood:
O bathe us in thy cleansing blood!
We die to sin and seek a grave
With thee beneath the yielding wave.

"And as we rise, with thee to live,
Oh, let the Holy Spirit give
The sealing unction from above—
The breath of life, the fire of love."

FRANKLIN JOHNSON, D. D., LL. D.
1836-1916.
Professor of Church History, University of Chicago.

CHAPTER V.

Baptism the Door to the Lord's Supper.

BY FRANKLIN JOHNSON, D. D., LL.D., OF THE UNIVERSITY OF CHICAGO.

It is my purpose to consider in this paper the proposition that all Christians ought to be baptized before they come to the Lord's supper. Since baptism is the immersion of a believer "into the name of the Father, and of the Son, and of the Holy Ghost," the proposition may take another verbal form, and affirm that all Christians ought to be immersed before they come to the Lord's supper. Some of my brethren proceed further, and teach that, not only immersion, but membership in a Baptist church, is prerequisite. Some proceed even further than this, and require membership in the particular Baptist church by which the supper is announced. To consider all these propositions would demand more space than I have at my disposal, and hence I limit myself to the first. This, after all, is the decisive one. If it is left in doubt, the others must fall; if it is established, they will occasion but little difficulty, and will be treated as questions of administration, to be decided in the affirmative or in the negative without affecting the essential principle that baptism should precede the Lord's supper. Dr. Norman Fox has given me an additional reason for the limitation of my study to the one proposition in his recent statement ("The

Invitation to the Breaking of Bread," page 13) that "it has never really been discussed among Baptists," by whom "it has been thought sufficient to say, 'All other churches hold this view.'"

THE NATURE OF THE EVIDENCE.

If I say that the evidence in favor of the proposition is inferential, I do not disparage it. Inferential evidence is often of the strongest kind; it is that circumstantial evidence upon which the gravest cases in our courts of law are decided. Many great truths of our religion are known to us only by inference. The Christian Sabbath, as distinguished from the Mosaic, is known to us only by inference. The doctrine of the Trinity is proved only by inference. The argument of our Lord against divorce (Matt. xix. 3-6) is purely inferential. So, also, is his proof of the resurrection (Matt. xii. 26, 27). That there should be a Lord's supper at all, as distinguished from the common meal, is proved only by inference.

The Baptist is not alone when he consults inferential evidence to ascertain who may properly partake of the Lord's supper; he has the entire Christian world with him, as all denominations appeal exclusively to this evidence. If we shall make any proposition whatsoever concerning the terms of admission, we shall be compelled to support it solely by inferential evidence, for there is no other that can be produced. Three pastors—one a Baptist, another a Presbyterian, and the third a Methodist—

once conversed on this subject somewhat as follows:

Presbyterian to Baptist—"What passage of Scripture commands you to limit your invitation to the supper to baptized believers?"

Baptist—"There is no explicit command."

Presbyterian—"I do not think that there should be any limitation for which a 'Thus saith the Lord' cannot be adduced."

Methodist to Presbyterian—"I quite agree with you."

Baptist to Presbyterian—"What invitation do you give?"

Presbyterian—"I invite all members of evangelical churches."

Baptist—"And where do you find 'Thus saith the Lord' for that?"

Methodist, after a moment of silence—"But I invite all who love Christ, whether they are members of evangelical churches or not."

Baptist—"And where do you find a 'Thus saith the Lord' for that?"

Baptist, after some moments of silence—"It appears that each of you establishes a limitation, and that neither of you can find an express warrant in Scripture for the limitation which he establishes. If either of you should attempt to support his limitation, his argument would be inferential. It is the same with the Baptist, except that his inferential evidence is cogent, while that which could be adduced for either of the limitations you have mentioned would be feeble and easily set aside."

This parable may suffice to convey my thought concerning the nature of the arguments with which I shall support the proposition that all Christians ought to be baptized before they come to the Lord's table.

THE ARGUMENT FROM THE IMPORTANCE OF BAPTISM.

If baptism were an ordinance of small importance, it might not be worth while to maintain its position as a prerequisite to the Lord's supper. Granting that it appears in this honorable station in the New Testament, this might have been the result of chance, or of temporary convenience, or of some conception peculiar to the apostolic age, and of no permanent value. But when we observe the vast importance which the New Testament attaches to baptism, and the vast importance of the function of baptism in the history of the individual soul, and hence of the church, we perceive at once that the position of precedence assigned to it in the New Testament cannot be the result of accident or of passing circumstances.

Our Lord was baptized at the very beginning of his ministry, and at the very close of his ministry he left a formal command to baptize every disciple; and thus he interwove the ordinance with his solemn inauguration as the suffering Messiah, and again with his solemn inauguration as the reigning Messiah. The heavens were opened to approve his baptism, and immediately after his proclamation of the law of baptism they were opened again to receive him up into glory, thus making his last words more impressive than any others. When the Holy Spirit distinguished the day of Pentecost with the overwhelming display of his regenerating grace, all those who repented under his influence were baptized, and the work of the Spirit began, as the work of Christ had begun, in the observance of this rite. The New Testament often speaks of baptism in such an emphatic manner as almost to identify it with the work of God in the soul, of which it is a symbol; that is, with spiritual washing, with death to sin and resurrection from it, and with the removal of guilt by pardon. "Verily, verily, I say unto thee, except a man be born of water and of the Spirit, he cannot enter into the kingdom of God (Jno. iii. 5). "Arise, and be baptized, and wash away thy sins" (Acts xxii. 16). "He saved us through the washing of regeneration and renewing of the Holy Ghost" (Titus iii. 5). "Which also after a true likeness doth now save you, even baptism, not the putting away of the filth of the flesh, but the interrogation of a good conscience toward God, through the resurrection of Jesus Christ" (1 Pet. iii. 21). If we find any difficulty with these expressions, is it not because we have accustomed ourselves to regard baptism as a mere ceremony, a vague emblem, setting forth certain indefinite phases of the divine life, but not ministering nourishment to it?

Thus in every way the New Testament affirms the importance of baptism, and does so even at the risk of creating the impression in some minds that the rite contains an occult spiritual power to save the soul, a danger which the Holy Spirit of inspiration evidently deemed less hurtful than that of undervaluing the ordinance.

It is sometimes said that the apostle Paul esteemed baptism lightly, and his statement to the Corinthians (1 Cor. i. 17) that "God sent him to preach, and not to baptize," is offered in evidence. This opinion is always heard, when it is heard at all, from persons who belong to denominations which have reduced baptism to a drop of water applied to the forehead of an infant as a symbol of the desire of the parents and friends that it may be saved. As these persons reduce baptism to a rite without much meaning or utility, it is natural for them to attribute their low estimate of it to the apostle, whose bodily infirmities may well have compelled him to arrange that it should be administered by his assistants. Christ himself baptized by the hands of his disciples, and yet, as we have seen, he assigned to the ordinance a lofty position in his example and his instructions to his church; and if the apostle Paul, under the compulsion of infirmity, had baptism administered by his assistants, he thought as little as did his Master of disparaging the holy ordinance. The apostle does not say that those to whom he wrote had not been baptized; indeed, the contrary is implied; and he merely expresses his gratification that, as events had turned out, the ordinance had been administered by others, lest some of the Christians at

Corinth, in the heat of partisan strife, should declare that he had baptized into his own name. So far is the apostle Paul from depreciating baptism, that he exalts it as few other writers of the New Testament do. "Are ye ignorant that all we who were baptized into Christ Jesus were baptized into his death? We were buried, therefore, with him through baptism into death; that, like as Christ was raised from the dead through the glory of the Father, so we also might walk in newness of life" (Rom. vi. 3, 4). "Having been buried with him in baptism, wherein ye were also raised with him through faith in the working of God, who raised him from the dead" (Col. ii. 12). It will be observed that in these passages the apostle, who is supposed to think lightly of baptism, associates it not only with the greatest truths of the gospel, the death and resurrection of Christ, but also with the greatest duty of the believer, to live in a manner worthy of his holy calling.

But why is baptism exalted in the Scriptures to this lofty position? God is infinite reason, and he has not done this thing arbitrarily. He is infinite love, and his reasons for this act have reference to the salvation of men.

The lofty position conferred upon baptism by Christ and his apostles and by the Spirit of inspiration is explained when we consider the functions of the ordinance in the history of the individual soul, and hence of the church.

1. As a means of publishing the gospel to the

world, it is excelled only by the living preacher. Wherever it is administered, it proclaims the great central truths of our religion. First, in an emotional picture, in an action of incomparable appropriateness and beauty, it sets forth the Saviour of mankind in the two moments around which thought and feeling chiefly cluster; in the moment of his burial, deserted by his disciples, and rescued from nameless indignities only by the intervention of one who had not been numbered with them, and in the moment of his resurrection—the first a moment the contemplation of which plunges us into tears, the second a moment the contemplation of which exalts us to a heaven of joy and triumph. But, next, the ordinance sets forth the death of the soul to sin and its resurrection to a new life of holiness. If the first truth is the greatest of all concerning Christ, the second is the greatest of all concerning the Christian. But, still further, the ordinance sets forth our assurance of a future resurrection after death has done its worst against us. If the first and second truths are the greatest concerning Christ and the Christian, the third is the greatest of which we can think in connection with our destiny after our earthly career is closed. Now, these are the central truths of our religion. They are mighty when they are proclaimed by a faithful ministry, but they receive additional might when they are illustrated in the graphic action of baptism. Hence many thousands of happy Christians attribute their first favorable impressions of

Christianity to the overwhelming influence of baptism, as they have witnessed its administration to others.

2. Not only the world, but also the church, has need of this preaching. Sometimes her living teachers err. They may lay the chief emphasis upon the incarnation of Christ and remand his cross to a secondary position. They may deny the reality of his resurrection. They may deny the essential sinfulness of the soul and its need of a radical change in regeneration. They may deny the future resurrection of the body. But baptism, where it is faithfully preserved and administered, continues to proclaim these great central truths, and to admonish those who forget them by its silent, but impressive, witness. Hence any perversion of it is a calamity. The church which substitutes effusion for it rules out of court a volume of testimony to the chief doctrines of the gospel which Christ himself has produced, and thus renders the task of its misleaders far more easy.

3. Baptism is of inestimable value to the disciple just born again and just entering upon a new course of life. His old habits of thought and feeling and action are broken, but not destroyed. He has within him a celestial life, but it is only pushing its shoots above the soil, and is exposed to drought and frost and the trampling of herds, and it needs nourishment and shelter. At the beginning of any new and trying course of life, a moving ceremony, which surrounds the opening of the

pathway with strong and attractive associations, which can never be forgotten, is a ministering angel. Every student of the mind recognizes the wisdom of making the greatest possible impression upon it when it forsakes some evil and determines to practice some virtue hitherto untried. Thus Bain ("The Emotions and the Will," page 453) says: "If we can only strike a blow with such power as to seize possession of a man's entire thoughts and voluntary dispositions for a certain length of time, we may succeed in launching him on a new career, and in keeping him in that course until there is time for habits to commence, and until a force is arrayed in favor of the present state of things able to cope with the tendencies and growth of the former life." James ("Psychology," I., 123) refers to this passage, and adds: "We must take care to launch ourselves with as strong and decided an initiative as possible. Accumulate all the possible circumstances which shall reinforce the right motives; put yourself assiduously in conditions that encourage the new way; make engagements incompatible with the old; take a public pledge, if the case allows; in short, develop your resolution by every aid you know."

If this teaching of the psychologists needs any further confirmation, let us consider that we are accustomed to start men on new and trying courses of life with solemn ceremonies. Thus we have an inaugural ceremony when a civil officer assumes his new position, and we cannot doubt that kings and presidents and judges are often aided to bear faithfully their heavy burdens and to live above the temptations which plead with them to swerve from the highway of honor, at least a little and in secret, by calling to mind the oath which they swore in the beginning and the assembled multitudes of spectators who witnessed it. Nor can we doubt that the care which we lavish upon the marriage ceremony aids the young husband and wife, but partially adapted to each other, and but partially fitted for their new duties and responsibilities, to have patience, and to acquire those habits of yielding and unselfishness which the home demands. They look back at the marriage service, and picture the faces of friends gathered together to hear their vows of love and fidelity, and grow ashamed of the petty and exacting tempers which might mar their peace or destroy it altogether. Our Saviour, who created the soul and knows it perfectly, did his first miracle to aid in rendering a marriage service successful. As he began his ministry by putting the supreme seal of his approval on the ceremony of baptism, so he began his miracles by putting the supreme seal of his approval on the ceremony of marriage. He performed this divine act in order to approve the married life and the home. But let us not pause when we have said this. The most obvious feature of the act was the solicitude of Christ to bless the ceremony itself and to make it complete, so that his young friends, when they should remember it in after years, should not associate it with distress and humiliation, but should find in it a source of joy and a sweet constraint to all the domestic virtues. We are following Christ when we make the ceremony of marriage impressive and helpful. Let us imagine a society in which it should be reduced to a few cold words or should be wholly abolished. Such a society would be either angelic, and in no need of aid to overcome sin, or else bestial, incapable of gentleness, and unrestrained by love or conscience from the indulgence of all base passions.

We are now prepared to understand in some small measure the divine utility of holy baptism. In saving the soul, God works both directly and indirectly, both by the immediate contact of the Holy Spirit and by mediate external agencies. Hence we speak not only of the sovereignty of grace, but also of the means of grace. Were the means of grace unimportant, we might dispense with preaching, with the study of the Bible, with the counsels of Christian friends, and with the hallowed associations of the church. Now, baptism, a powerful depiction of the burial and resurrection of Christ, of the death and resurrection of the soul, and of our future blessed resurrection, standing at the very beginning of the new life, is a most precious means of grace. Its picturesqueness, its mighty appeal to the intelligence, to the imagination, to the emotions, and thus to the will, render it most effectual in producing the greatest possible initial impression, which, the psychologists tell us, is so necessary at the beginning of a new course. To apply it in unconscious infancy, or to alter its form and thus to blot out its testimony concerning the great central truths of Christianity, is to render it nugatory.

4. But more than this should be said. Baptism is a much-needed aid to the disciple, not merely because it is a moving ceremony. It is an act of faith on his part, "the interrogation of a good conscience toward God." Now, every act of faith leads to a gracious manifestation of God to the soul. The highest acts of faith—like those of the martyrs, for example—often lead to overwhelming manifestations of God to the soul, and hence many Christians who have "given their bodies to be burned" have broken forth into singing in the midst of the flames. Among the most decisive acts of faith we must reckon this holy ordinance, in which the new disciple puts on Christ before an assembled world. It is common, therefore, for new disciples to receive in it a vast influx of spiritual power. The Holy Spirit responds to faith and communicates abundance of peace and joy and power, testifying of cleansing and pardon, of the gracious smiles of the Heavenly Father, and of the inheritance of glory, and giving unusual influence to the words and deeds with which the soldier of the cross, but just enlisted in the service, seeks "to destroy the works of the devil."

So common is this experience that, when I was a pastor, I counted upon it as one of my most valuable auxiliaries, and never in vain. In every community there are good, but discouraged, Christian people who, humbly conscious of their faults, hesitate to enter the church as members. All who know them hold them to be Christians, though of the timid and shrinking class, but they themselves stand in doubt, "waiting for the waters to be moved," with some emotional assurance that they are accepted. I was accustomed to promise these excellent and modest children of God that they would receive the light for which they longed, if they would obey Christ and be baptized; I led many of them into the church, and I never knew my prediction to fail. Their act of faith was met by the Holy Spirit with a corresponding act of grace.

Let no one misrepresent this view by calling it sacramentarianism. It is as far from sacramentarianism as the east is from the west. Sacramentarianism affirms that the sacraments are channels of grace; but I affirm that faith is the sole channel of grace. Sacramentarianism affirms that, since the sacraments are channels of grace, the reception of them is the usual condition upon which grace is conferred; but I affirm that faith is the sole condition upon which grace is conferred. After having guarded myself in this manner, I may surely insist, without being misunderstood, that baptism is an act of faith, and hence a means of grace, and that, as it was appointed for all his followers by the Son of God, the Spirit of God honors it by conferring light and comfort and strength on those who receive it in faith.

These are some of the effects of baptism in the economy of grace. To the Baptists chiefly has been granted the honor of restoring this holy ordinance to the Christian world. Were it a mere form, it would not matter whether it was placed before or after the Lord's supper. But it is an agency of infinite practical value in launching the new disciple upon his new way, and its place of utility is at the beginning of his discipleship; and, since infinite wisdom has assigned it this position, the Baptists should keep it there. Nor should they recognize as baptism the christening of infants, or sprinkling or pouring administered to older persons—ceremonies containing nothing of the significance and power of the Christian ordinance. But unrestricted communion is a recognition of these ceremonies as baptism, and a recognition in action, which is far more decisive and impressive than any words. It would be vain for the Baptists to hope to bring baptism back to the place from which these ceremonies have thrust it, if they should practise unrestricted communion. In spite of all verbal protests, they would be understood to recognize infant christening and sprinkling and pouring as valid baptism, and in the end they themselves would come to feel that these ceremonies are in some sense valid. This would not be a misfortune if baptism were a light thing; but, since the New Testament has charged it with the weightiest meanings and appointed it to the weightiest functions, the Baptists have no right to pursue a course which would silence its voice and smite its beneficent power with paralysis.

CHAPTER VI.

Baptism the Door to the Lord's Supper.

BY FRANKLIN JOHNSON, D. D., LL.D.

THE ARGUMENT FROM THE IMPORTANCE OF THE LORD'S SUPPER.

Some of those who teach that baptism need not precede the Lord's supper do so because they hold a view of the Lord's supper quite different from that of the New Testament. Thus Professor Seeley (in his "Ecce Homo") has told us that our Lord instituted a sort of "club dinner," in which his friends were asked to remember him. The theory requires us to forget much that our Lord said at the last supper—as, for example, "This is my body," and "This is my blood"; but Professor Seeley found no serious difficulty here. Many other writers join him in presenting the Lord's supper in this secular light. In order to do so, they trim away some of our Lord's expressions recorded in the Gospels as not genuine—that is, as not convenient—and pronounce some expressions of the other books of the New Testament later accretions, of no authority for us. Now, if I believed that our Lord intended to institute a mere club dinner, I should not regard baptism as prerequisite to it. The chief prerequisites to a club dinner are those social qualities which render a person "clubable," and a good appetite.

Dr. Norman Fox (in his two booklets, "Christ in the Daily Meal" and "The Invitation to the Breaking of Bread"; so, also, McGiffert, "The Apostolic Age," pages 69, 70) is an able representative of the view that our Lord, at the last supper, intended to make all meals commemorative of his person and his death, and not to institute a special commemorative meal. Dr. Fox infers from this premise that baptism cannot be a prerequisite to the Lord's supper, for every meal, partaken in a proper spirit, is to him the Lord's supper. The conclusion may be granted if the premise is proven, for it is difficult to think of our Lord as wishing to make baptism a prerequisite to every meal. Had he done so, it would be necessary to compel every convert to fast until baptism could be administered. But the premise does not appear to me to rest on any solid support.

It is the purpose of Dr. Fox to bring all meals up to the level of the Lord's supper, and not to depress the Lord's supper to the ordinary level of the present daily meal. But this is impossible. The mind is so constituted that it seeks to attend to certain definite things at certain definite seasons, and we cannot force it to attend to all things at all seasons. The holiest mind distinguishes the common and the uncommon, the secular and the religious, the material and the spiritual, in our duties and observances. If a man should try to make every day a commemoration of the Declaration of Independence, he would end by having no Independence Day. If a man should try to make every day a New Year's Day, he would end by having no New Year's Day. It has been proposed to abolish the Sabbath by making every day a Sabbath; but no one has ever succeeded in carrying the proposition into practice, and the effort, were it made, would result only in the secularization of the Sabbath, and not in the sanctification of the other days of the week. A poet has sung that "every place is holy ground"; but we cannot make every place holy in the sense in which Galilee and Jerusalem and Calvary are holy, except as we cease to think of them as holy. Even so, the effort to make all our meals suppers of the Lord would leave us without any Lord's supper.

Moreover, the New Testament clearly gives us a special meal in the Lord's supper. Our Lord instituted it, not at a common meal, but at the paschal supper, a very uncommon meal. He has suggested to us thus the analogy between the paschal supper and the Lord's supper, the one pointing forward to "the Lamb slain from the foundation of the world," and the other pointing back to "the Lamb of God that taketh away the sin of the world," and both meeting in harmony "in the night in which he was betrayed." Moreover, the apostle Paul distinguishes sharply between the common meal and the Lord's supper: "What! have ye not houses to eat and to drink in?" "If any man is hungry, let him eat at home."

But many, who do not agree with Professor Seeley or Dr. Norman Fox, deem the Lord's supper of relatively slight importance, and regard it as "a mere ceremony," "a mere emblem." I think that a large share of the sentiment in favor of unrestricted communion springs from the feeling that the communion, after all, is not of very great consequence. Thousands of good Christians have recoiled from the papal doctrine of transubstantiation and the awe with which the Roman Catholic beholds the wafer, to the opposite extreme of easy apathy in the presence of the holy bread and wine.

In answer to these three typical views, which tend to unrestricted communion, I present the Lord's supper, as I have presented baptism, as a ceremony, but not "a mere ceremony"; as an emblem, but not "a mere emblem." Between these inadequate views and sacramentarianism, which I abhor, there is a wide continent of rich truth, which we should by no means overlook. I, therefore, present the Lord's supper as containing elements of spiritual truth and power similar to those which I found in baptism. 1. It preaches the cross: "Ye proclaim the Lord's death." 2. It offers to the believer a touching memorial of the entire person and work of Christ, and especially of his sacrificial atonement: "Do this in remembrance of me." "This is my blood of the new covenant, which is shed for many unto the remission of sins." 3. It is a symbol of God's covenant with his people: "This is my blood of the new covenant." 4. It presents Christ as the nourishment and life of the soul: "Eat all ye of it"; "Drink all ye of it." 5. It is a prediction of the second coming: "Ye proclaim the Lord's death till he come." 6. It is a prediction of our future glory with Christ: "I will not drink henceforth of this fruit of the vine until that day when I drink it new with you in my Father's kingdom." 7. It is a symbol of the fraternal unity of those who partake of it: "We, who are many, are one bread, one body; for we all partake of the one bread." This ordinance, therefore, contains a precious freightage of Christian truth.

Moreover, in partaking of the Lord's supper, the Christian performs an act of faith and receives a refreshing of his faith, a brighter manifestation of God to his soul, since God always manifests himself to men in proportion to their faith. As I said of baptism, so I say of the Lord's supper—that, while it is neither a channel of grace nor a condition of grace, it is a means of grace. Faith is the only channel of grace and the only condition of grace; but faith leads to action, and all acts of faith are means of grace. Nor do I deem it unreasonable to suppose that Christ makes a special and abundant manifestation of himself to those who partake of his supper in faith. Is it not natural to expect that he will honor with a special display of his presence the memorial meal which he founded, and at which he is the host and his people the guests?

There is a doctrine of "the real presence" which the Baptist may hold, because it sets forth his personal experience. The phrase "the real presence" has been used to affirm the real presence of the flesh and blood cf Christ in the bread and wine. But there is no reason for limiting its use in this manner. The Baptist, who rejects with loathing the doctrine of the physical presence of Christ in the supper, knows of his spiritual presence; and that, after all, is the only "real presence" for which he is concerned. There are two kinds of spiritual presence of Christ of which the Scriptures speak. First, there is his omnipresence as God, his immanence in his universe, so that he is in every place, even where we forget him and see him not. But, again, there is a presence of manifestation. He is everywhere; but often, like Jacob, we awake from some carnal slumber and say: "Surely Jehovah is in this place, and I knew it not." At other times he is so manifest that "our hearts burn within us." It is for this presence of manifestation that we pray when we ask him to be with us. It is this that he has promised his assembled people: "Where two or three are gathered together in my name, there am I in the midst of them." It is of this that the disciple is conscious at the Lord's supper:

> "How sweet and awful is the place
> With Christ within the doors,
> Where everlasting love displays
> The choicest of her stores."

The disciple, therefore, need only consult his own experience to find an answer to those who plead for unrestricted communion on the ground that the Lord's supper is a mere club dinner, a mere daily meal, or a mere vague emblem.

THE ARGUMENT FROM THE NATURAL RELATION OF THE TWO ORDINANCES TO ONE ANOTHER.

Dr. Norman Fox, deeming every daily meal the Lord's supper, not unnaturally denies that baptism logically precedes it: "Is there in fact any logical relation between baptism and the memorial eating? The breaking of bread is in order to—an assistance towards—a remembrance of Christ. Like kneeling in prayer or lifting the voice in praise, it is a physical act to assist the spiritual exercise. Now, if it be proper for an unbaptized person to remember Christ, why should he not break bread to assist such remembrance? Why should lack of baptism forbid one's breaking bread in order to remembrance of Christ, any more than it would forbid his kneeling in prayer or his playing on a harp to assist his soul to praise? Baptism has no logical antecedence to the breaking of bread, any more than to kneeling or singing." If I believed the premise which Dr. Fox urges—that Christ intended to institute no memorial meal other than the daily meal, and that he intended it to do nothing more than to bring him to the thoughts of his disciples—I should conclude that "baptism has no logical antecedence to the breaking of bread, any more than to kneeling or singing."

But we have already found in the Lord's supper

special characteristics which set it apart from the daily meal and elevate it into the class of Christian ordinances. Now, things which belong together as members of a class are related in thought to the other members of the same class as they cannot be to objects belonging to other classes. Jupiter is related in thought to Mercury as it is not to the Sultan of Turkey or to Mount Hood. The Capitol at Washington is related in thought to the houses of Parliament as it is not to a pine tree or a bottle of rose-water. The President of the United States is related in thought to the President of France as he is not to the Atlantic Ocean or the Alhambra. If we should try never so earnestly to follow Dr. Norman Fox in his effort to give baptism only such a relation to the Lord's supper as that which it sustains to preaching, to praying, and to singing, we should succeed only as he has succeeded, by forgetting the unique character of the ordinances as ordinances, or else by blinding ourselves to a necessary law of classification. We should probably not succeed at all. The moment we should classify the two as ordinances and as forming a group by themselves, we should see that baptism necessarily sustains a relation to the Lord's supper which it does not sustain to preaching, praying, and singing; and having determined this point, we should readily perceive that the logical relation of baptism to the Lord's supper is that of precedence.

We have found already that the two ordinances

have a large body of meaning in common, while yet each presents some special phases of truth, and also presents the truth common to both in a light of its own. In general, baptism sets forth the beginning of the Christian life, and the Lord's supper its sustenance. The key thought of baptism, so far as it relates to the recipient, is a burial to sin and a resurrection to holiness; the key thought of the Lord's supper, so far as it relates to the recipient, is the perpetuation of the Christian life by feeding on "the Bread of Heaven." As Dr. Alvah Hovey well says: "The former speaks of change from one spiritual condition to another, from moral pollution to moral purity, while the other speaks of growth, progress, power, in a present condition. 'For as many of you as have been baptized into Christ have put on Christ.' 'As often as ye eat this bread and drink this cup, ye proclaim the Lord's death till he come.'"

Hence, in the New Testament, baptism is administered to each disciple but once, while the Lord's supper is administered many times; for life begins but once, while it requires many reinforcements of food for its furtherance.

Hence, also, in the New Testament, baptism is linked to faith as the first formal and ceremonial expression of it, while the Lord's supper never has this position. Thus in the great commission we are directed to "make disciples of all the nations, baptizing them." Observe here the intimate association of discipleship with baptism as the confession of discipleship. The practice of the disciples was strictly in keeping with this feature of the commission, and they always administered baptism as the first formal symbolical act of the believer, while the Lord's supper followed it. On the day of Pentecost, "they that gladly received his word were baptized." Afterwards "they continued steadfastly in the apostles' teaching and fellowship, in the breaking of bread, and the prayers." The people of Samaria, "when they believed Philip preaching good tidings, were baptized, both men and women." Such was the universal rule, exemplified in the case of Cornelius, of Saul of Tarsus, of Lydia and her household, of the jailer and his household, of Crispus and his household, and of "many of the Corinthians" who believed with him; when these persons believed, they were baptized. The rule has no exceptions. We do not read that any persons believed and received the Lord's supper. To quote the words of Dr. A. N. Arnold ("The Scriptural Terms of Admission to the Lord's Supper"): "In no case is it said, 'Then they that gladly received the word came together to break bread'; or, 'Who can forbid bread and wine, that these should not eat the Lord's supper, who have received the Holy Ghost as well as we?' or, 'Believing in God with all his house, he sat down at the table of the Lord, he and all his straightway'; or, 'Repent and receive the Lord's supper, every one of you'; or, 'When they believed the preaching concerning the kingdom of God, they broke bread, both men and women.'

In no case are they described as receiving the Lord's supper immediately after their conversion, or as receiving the Lord's supper first and baptism afterwards."

If this precedence of baptism to the Lord's supper were a mere accident or an adjustment of practice to local and temporary circumstances, it would not necessarily be a guide to us. But it is based upon a profound reason. It is based upon the significance of baptism as related to the significance of the Lord's supper. For us to reverse the divine order would be to reverse the meaning of one ordinance or of both. We might do it lightly, if we regarded baptism as the mere dedication of a babe by means of a drop of water, or a mere initiation of an older person into the church by the same means. We might do it lightly, if we regarded the Lord's supper as a mere club dinner, or a mere daily meal, or a mere vague religious emblem, with no special message for the observers or the participants. But so long as we recognize in baptism and the Lord's supper that which the Scriptures find in them, we shall not willingly change the order of precedence which the Scriptures establish.

It may be said, in answer to these biblical proofs of a definite order of precedence, that the eleven apostles who were present at the last supper may have been unbaptized, since the Gospels contain no express record of their baptism. To grant this would not disturb my argument. Baptism must have been instituted by some unbaptized man or men. It must have had a beginning. The apostles were appointed for the express purpose of laying the foundations of Christianity, "Jesus Christ himself being the chief corner-stone." If, therefore, it could be shown that they were unbaptized, because baptism did not yet exist, and that they were the divinely commissioned administrators of both baptism and the Lord's supper, this would render only more remarkable the fact that they themselves established and maintained the logical and reasonable order of the ordinances, and always placed baptism at the beginning of the new Christian life, and the Lord's supper after it, because the one is the symbol of the beginning of the new life, and the other of its sustenance.

But it is not probable that they were unbaptized. Two of them, at least, had been disciples of John the Baptist, and probably all the rest came from his school. He was sent to prepare a people for the fuller revelation and the greater demands to be made by the Messiah, and when we observe the alacrity with which they left all and followed the new Teacher, we cannot avoid the inference that their souls had been thus prepared. But John baptized his disciples, and also pointed them to Him who was to come. Christ himself was baptized by John, "in order to fulfil all righteousness," and it is in the highest degree probable that he would instruct them to follow his example, if they had not been baptized already. Moreover, he had them baptize his own disciples, and this would render it reasonable to suppose that they had been baptized. The words of Peter, in which he describes the man to be chosen in the place of Judas, are quite in accordance with these indications: "Of the men, therefore, which have companied with us all the time that the Lord Jesus went in and out among us, beginning from the baptism of John, unto the day that he was received up from us, of these must one become a witness with us of his resurrection."

CHAPTER VII.

Baptism the Door to the Lord's Supper.

BY FRANKLIN JOHNSON, D. D., LL.D.

THE ARGUMENT FROM THE GENERAL UNDERSTANDING OF CHRISTIANS.

With but very few exceptions, all Christians have understood the New Testament to teach that baptism should precede the Lord's supper. In the "Teaching of the Twelve Apostles," possibly the earliest Christian writing after the apostolic age, we read this direction: "Let no one eat of your eucharist except those baptized into the name of the Lord." Similar to this is the testimony of Justin Martyr, who died about 160: "This food is called by us the eucharist, of which it is not lawful for any one to partake but such as believe the things taught by us, and have been baptized." From those earliest times to the present the limitation has been maintained by almost all denominations. If it is relaxed to-day by a few in the Baptist and the evangelical Pedobaptist denominations, it is still maintained with practical unanimity by the Christian world. This is admitted by all, and by none more clearly than by Dr. Norman Fox, who says: "Pedobaptists will not invite to the table one who has been neither immersed, sprinkled, nor poured upon; they declare that only baptized persons should be admitted. When, therefore, they claim that a Baptist church should admit them, they demand that Baptists shall recognize them as baptized persons." Again: "The Pedobaptists stoutly maintain that baptism is an essential prerequisite to the breaking of bread. In a review of 'Christ in the Daily Meal,' the Evangelist, of New York, which is by no means the most unprogressive of Presbyterian papers, criticised the book for its doctrine that the unbaptized should be invited to the church supper. While among Pedobaptists there could doubtless be found individual ministers who would consent to admit the unbaptized to the table, it would certainly be impossible to carry through the Presbyterian General Assembly or the Congregational National Council or the Methodist General Conference a declaration that it is proper to invite to the church supper all true believers, irrespective of baptism."

I might establish this well-known fact by a thousand testimonies from the highest Pedobaptist sources, were further evidence necessary.

Dr. Fox supposes that this unanimity of the Christian world grows out of the doctrine of baptismal regeneration, from the effects of which, according to him, even the Baptists have not freed themselves. He urges, therefore, that the Baptists cast off this last vestige of a great error, and invite all Christians, whether baptized or not. He is somewhat severe towards those Baptists who would invite Pedobaptists and yet believe that baptism should precede the communion, and towards those Pedobaptists who wish the Baptists to admit that they are baptized by inviting them; and he would solve the entire difficulty by denying that baptism has any logical relation to the Lord's supper, and by inviting all the unbaptized as unbaptized.

I quite agree with him that the only tenable ground of unrestricted communion, other than the validity of sprinkling and pouring, is the denial that baptism has any logical relation to the Lord's supper. But we have seen that the denial itself has no ground upon which to stand.

Moreover, I do not suppose that we should advance in the good opinion of our Pedobaptist brethren, if we should make them clearly understand that we invited them as unbaptized. Nor should we ourselves be able to rest in the opinion, should we adopt it, for the evidences against it are too cogent.

Some of these we have already examined. But another, which well deserves to be weighed, is precisely this general understanding of the Christian world which Dr. Fox sets forth so clearly. It is possible for the Christian world to go astray and to persist in error for centuries. But this was easier when no dissent was permitted. The present division of the Christian world into many denominations, each interested more or less in the discovery of truth and the abandonment of mere tradition, renders unanimity in a gross error exceedingly improbable. Moreover, all denominations deny that they are influenced by tradition in making baptism a prerequisite to the Lord's supper, and affirm that they are influenced solely by the teaching of the New Testament. I present this unanimous judgment of the Christian world as an argument worthy of respect.

THE ARGUMENT FROM PROFIT AND LOSS.

The opponent of these views often tells us that they hinder the growth of our denomination. It is true that they have cost us the adherence of some noble ministers, whom we should have been glad and proud to retain. It is true, also, that they have kept many from coming to us. We regret all this, and shall ever continue to love those who thus refuse to walk with us.

But let us suppose that the loss were even far more serious than it is. Would that prove our position wrong, or justify us in abandoning it? On the contrary, it is our duty to accept and teach the truth in love, without too much selfish care for our own growth. Are we doing good by our teaching? Are we saving other denominations from superstition, from sacramentarianism, from the greater abuses of infant baptism, and hence from spiritual weakness? These are some of the questions that should give us concern. If we can answer them in the affirmative, we should rejoice and press on our way, even if we were reduced to numerical insignificance by our fidelity to the truth.

Now, no one can become acquainted with the history of the Baptists in England and America without recognizing the mighty influence they have wielded against infant baptism and in favor of the spirituality of the church, of the separation of Church and State, and of religious liberty. No one can examine the work they are doing to-day on the continent of Europe without perceiving that it is a most beneficent leaven there, as it is in England and this country. The larger part of the Christian world, though profoundly affected by its views, is still reluctant to admit their justice, and its mission is not yet at an end. What if it were a small and despised denomination, with such a record of usefulness, and such a field of action?

But, after all, our maintenance of restricted communion seems to have ministered to our numerical strength, rather than to have diminished it. It appears to have brought to us a multitude of adherents for every one whom it has repelled. About 1820, Robert Hall, the famous English Baptist preacher and writer, attacked restricted communion, and attributed the slow growth of the English Baptists to it. His influence, combined with other causes, led the majority of them to abandon it. The result has not been favorable. They have pursued a wavering course, and their increase has been meagre. Their practice of unrestricted communion has led them necessarily to low views of baptism. Dr. A. N. Arnold thus sketches the effects of the movement from which Robert Hall anticipated so much: "The administration of believer's baptism on a week-day evening, to avoid giving offence to the Pedobaptist members of the church; the reception, without baptism, of persons who have renounced their belief that the ceremony performed upon them in infancy was valid; the manifest disposition to give up baptism as non-essential, where the cause of peace and union is supposed to demand this sacrifice; the banishment of scriptural teaching on this subject from the pulpit, and even from the private conversation of the minister with his people, as a stipulated condition of the continuance of the pastoral relation; the discipline and exclusion of members for the offence of propagating Baptist sentiments; the relaxation of all scriptural church discipline; and, after all, unpleasant collisions with Pedobaptist churches—these legitimate logical consequences and certified actual results of mixed communion are more than enough to stamp it as a practice at war with truth, purity, liberty, and union." With such a lack of denominational spirit, there could not be a rapid denominational growth. The influence of the denomination upon other denominations has been relatively feeble, and the denomination has shown a constant tendency to melt away and dissolve.

We have only to look at the Baptists of this country to perceive the beneficial effects of restricted communion in creating denominational self-respect and vigor, in making us courteously aggressive, in building up our numbers, and in attracting to all our views the keen attention of the Christians about us. The Baptist who studies this contrast attentively will not ask that his denomination adopt the practice of unrestricted communion as a means of growth in numbers.

A similar conclusion will be reached by those who study the Free Baptists, who practise unrestricted communion, and yet achieve but little increase.

THE ARGUMENT FROM CHRISTIAN LOVE.

There are Pedobaptists who say to the Baptists: "I grant that we, like you, require baptism as a prerequisite to the Lord's supper. But we have a practical advantage over you. As our definition of baptism is broader than yours, we are able to invite to the supper all who will probably care for our invitation, and thus to satisfy the cravings of Christian love. You cannot do this. Your logic is without fault, but it brings you into an embarrassment which we escape. Moreover, the majority of men and women deem us more charitable than you, for they care little for the argument on either side, and judge mainly by the practice. Perhaps they would not understand your argument, if it were presented to them; but they understand your practice." In a measure this is true.

There are Baptists who may be tempted to judge the question at issue in the same manner. They may say: "We grant that your logic is sound. But we do not care much for the logic of the head. The heart has a logic of its own. Christian love, as well as abstract reason, has its rights. Your argument seems to us cold, remote from the heart, a sort of mathematical demonstration. But Christianity is not one of the exact sciences; it is love. We refuse to be moved by your reasons, and we do not care even to try to answer them."

Perhaps there are few Baptist ministers to whom this antagonism of reason and love has not suggested itself at one time or another. It is true that our practice is in some sense a cross, and I do not envy the man who can carry it jauntily and boastfully. But are Christian reason and Christian love ever really opposed to each other? Over against this attitude of mind, which in fact is chiefly one of Christian sentimentality, rather than Christian sentiment, I place my appeal to a reasonable Christian love.

1. The Baptist ought to love his brethren of other denominations very warmly. He ought to esteem them very highly for their works' sake. He ought to manifest his affection for them, and to seek their friendship, that they may learn to love him in return. Fortunately, there are a thousand ways in which he can do this, not only without coming into conflict with reason, but according to the most earnest urgings of reason. He need not leave his heart hungry for Christian fellowship with any part of the Christian world.

2. Love to Christ, as well as to his people, should be consulted in this matter. Christ has made known his will concerning the holy ordinance of baptism. The Baptist has been led to know and to respect that will. Others have not yet made the

discovery of it. The Baptist does not judge them; he loves them and judges himself. His love for Christ should lead him to a high regard for the will of Christ, which he has learned, and should debar him from doing anything which might tend to make that will ineffectual. Over against a sentimental love for the Christian I place a profound and obedient love for the Lord of the Christian.

3. Is there, then, a conflict between love for Christ and a proper love for his people? There should be none. Nor should there ever be a conflict between Christian love and Christian duty. But there is a short-sighted love, which may be brought into conflict with the best and holiest sentiments of the soul and the best and holiest determinations of the will. Short-sighted love in a mother may bring her into violent conflict with the dictates of a wise love, of good sense, of duty, and may lead to the injury of the child. Short-sighted love always works mischief. No love which acts at variance with reason is far-sighted or is worthy the name by which it calls itself. Now, a prudent love for the Christian world will lead the Baptist to see what a calamity infant christening is, and how great a blessing the restoration of baptism would be. In proportion to his wise love for his fellow-Christians will be his longing to give them this added power; and he will recoil from any course which could hinder him from bestowing it upon them. How great the blessing would be the Baptist will see, if he will pause a moment to consider

the evils of infant christening. These have been well presented by Dr. Alvah Hovey, under the following heads: 1. Infant christening takes away from the Christian ordinance the larger part of its meaning by making it no longer a confession of faith, but, on one hand, a regenerating rite, or, on the other, a mere vague ceremony; and, still further, by altering its form from immersion to sprinkling or pouring, thus divesting it of its power to preach Christ crucified and risen. 2. Infant christening ascribes to the ordinance an imaginary virtue, keeps alive in the greatest denominations the fatal delusion of baptismal regeneration, and in some others a vague conviction that God will be more favorable to infants which have been baptized, should they die. 3. Infant christening mars the constitution of the church by introducing unconverted persons into it. 4. Infant christening facilitates the union of Church and State, with all its terrible results. 5. Infant christening divides the followers of Christ. The mission to which the Baptist denomination is called is high and holy. The happiness and the success of the Christian world are bound up with it. A prudent love, a far-sighted love, should lead the Baptist to firm fidelity to the truth committed to him.

4. Yet further. His love for other denominations should not make the Baptist inattentive to the claims of love for his own. Was he brought up under Baptist influences? Then he owes his spiritual life to the Baptist denomination, and he should

not be ungrateful. Was he brought up under Pedobaptist influences? Then he was guided and enlightened by the Baptist denomination, or he would not have entered it, and he should not be ungrateful. Is he one of its ministers? Then he was educated largely by the Baptist denomination, and was entrusted by it with its dearest interests and called to its highest honors, and he should not be ungrateful. But it is committed to the practice of restricted communion, and the agitator, who admits the conclusive cogency of its argument and yet rends it asunder on the plea of Christian love, has but little of the love which he pleads.

THE OBLIGATION IMPOSED ON THE BAPTISTS BY THIS RESTRICTION.

The sole purpose of Christ in establishing his religion among men was to implant and to nourish Christian character. Every constituent element of Christianity is of use in the production of Christian character, and the loss of any constituent element is a loss to the forces which produce Christian character. Our restriction of the Lord's supper to baptized believers is based on the truth that baptism was instituted to render service in the production of Christian character, and that, in fact, it does render this service, where it is preserved in its integrity. But does it render this service to us who have received it? That is what the Christian world asks of the Baptist, when he teaches the doctrine of Christian baptism. The Baptist must answer by pointing to its observed effects. "By their fruits ye shall know them." These effects should be exhibited in his own character and in his own denomination. The Baptist should be able to point to his denomination as an object lesson, and to prove three things by it: 1. That baptism, where it is observed faithfully, tends to produce the most complete Christian character known—stronger to resist temptation, more thoughtful for others, more brave, more courteous, more sympathetic, more wisely helpful. 2. That it tends to produce a wide variety of admirable Christian characters of the types most esteemed and most efficient, and is not operative within a single narrow range of qualities. It must produce a better type of wifehood, of motherhood, of fatherhood, of childhood, of magistrates, of soldiers, of merchants, of teachers, of lawyers, of physicians, of employers, and of the employed. It must adapt itself to various natural dispositions, and produce a meditative piety in some, an active piety in others, an emotional piety in some, and a merely military and obedient piety in others. 3. That, since it tends to produce such effects as these, it also tends to produce men and women more successful than others in winning the world to Christ and in building up the kingdom of God in the world. Such is the obligation. It will not do for the Baptist to pride himself on the mere observance of a prescribed rite, without regard to its meaning and power; that is what the Pharisees did. The Baptist must be able to show that his obedience has done something for his character.

And since the Baptists are compelled by their consciences to preserve Christian baptism to the Christian world at the cost of a restriction not in itself agreeable, they should give much of their energies to the Christian culture of those who come to them for guidance. They have not been insensible to this obligation. They have paid great attention to evangelization, on the one hand, and to education, on the other. They are now organizing their young people for the express purpose of cultivating them in knowledge and in varied usefulness. But "there remaineth very much land to be possessed." Do we give a disproportionate emphasis to conversion, and too little emphasis to growth? Do we employ a great variety of means to nurture the souls committed to us, so that all kinds of disposition and temperament find help from us? Or do we have a single mould in which we place all alike, misshaping many and repelling many? Do we ask reverent souls to come to us, and then shock them by irreverence? Do we ask shrinking souls to come to us, and then force them into a publicity from which their finest instincts recoil? Do we ask the imaginative, the esthetic, the poetic, to come to us, and then wound them by inexcusable crudenesses? We have broad fields of toil out in the glare of the sun; have we any shade for the weary, the wounded, the sick, the despondent, the fearful? Or are we courting the rich, the educated, the refined, and forgetting the poor, the ignorant, and the crude, among whom the Redeemer passed his earthly life, and for whom our fathers labored most earnestly? If in any of these respects we are lacking, the remedy is not to be found in the abandonment of baptism as the door of the Lord's house, but in such a care of the house as shall render it befitting the majestic entrance which the Lord has provided and committed to the care of his people.

BENJAMIN O. TRUE, D. D.
1845-1902.
Professor of Church History, Rochester Theological Seminary.

CHAPTER VIII.

Baptists and Religious Liberty.

BY BENJAMIN O. TRUE, D. D., PROFESSOR OF CHURCH HISTORY IN ROCHESTER THEOLOGICAL SEMINARY.

The struggle of Baptists for religious liberty is a long and a complicated story. The details cannot be recounted in a brief article, but there are certain features of the conflict which are of fundamental importance. These have found place on the continent of Europe, in England, and in America, where three phases of a common struggle have been enacted.

From the fourth to the sixteenth century, civil rulers, generally in alliance with ecclesiastical officials, assumed authority to dictate to their subjects forms of doctrine, polity, and worship, and to enforce uniformity of creeds, rites, and liturgies. The civil magistrate and the church official, one or both, practically exercised this power from the time of Constantine the Great until the historic protests of Luther, Zwingli, and Calvin. These reformers appealed from the Pope, from councils, and the Roman church, to the Scriptures as the final and supreme authority in matters of religious faith and practice. But not one of these great men, or the movements which they directed, consistently recognized the proper separation of Church and State, the rightful autonomy of the church, or the complete rights of the individual conscience. All these leaders strenuously advocated the continued union of Church and State. They desired to supplant the religious influence of the mediæval emperor and civil rulers by the authority of local princes in Germany, of the council at Zurich, and of magistrates at Geneva. Leading types of Protestantism—Lutheran, Zwinglian, Calvinian, and Anglican—agreed in the repudiation of papal authority, but all retained a State church, without adequate provision for the permanent freedom of the church from secular control, or for the sacred and inalienable rights of the individual conscience.

The supreme authority of the Scriptures was declared to be the formal principle of the Protestant Reformation, but Protestants disagreed in the application of this principle. Some held that customary forms of worship, not expressly forbidden by the Scriptures, might properly be retained; others strenuously held that many practices of the old church were superfluous and misleading, and that nothing in the constitution or worship of the church ought to be inculcated which is not explicitly authorized by the Scriptures.

To those who believed in the final and supreme authority of the Scriptures their authoritative interpretation became "a question of urgency." On this subject there were three conceivable positions.

The organized church might be regarded as the proper interpreter of the Scriptures, through its councils and higher officials, priests, bishops, and theologians, and, by those who held to the papal primacy, through the Pope, as the visible head of the church.

The prerogative of interpreting the Scriptures might be attributed to the State, through its legislators and magistrates, or through the expressed will of local rulers. The effort was actually made among the numerous States of Germany, when the conflict between Romanists and Protestants was intense, to have the religion of every State determined by its civil ruler. It was soon found, however, that the prince could decide only what religion should be established by law. He could not compel intelligent subjects by force or convince them against their will. Thus dissenters might easily outnumber the cordial adherents of the State church. Moreover, the interpretations of Scripture by either civil or ecclesiastical officers in different States were variant and discordant. Often they were manifestly modifications, rather than expositions or applications of the Scripture—the mere expression of personal preferences or partisan prejudice.

The natural and inevitable tendency of Protestantism increasingly favored the interpretation of the Scriptures by the individual believer. This was the right of private interpretation, and it involved an obligation commensurate with the privilege. It was, indeed, desirable that all believers should be intelligent and conscientious, but in the last analysis it was felt that every man must have personal dealings with the Almighty. Whoever held to this right of private judgment could not consistently permit either civil magistrates or ecclesiastical officials to dictate or control his personal religious convictions or practices.

Out of these two principles—the supreme authority of the Scriptures in matters of religion and the right of private judgment—have arisen the historic and repeated protests which have been made in continental Europe, England, and America against unscriptural creeds, polity, and rites, and against the unwarranted assumption of religious authority over other men's consciences by either priests or civil rulers.

Scarcely had Luther and Zwingli denied the validity of papal indulgences before men in Germany and Switzerland, and a little later in the Low Countries, declared that infant baptism was not supported by Scriptures, and that the inability of the infant to exercise personal faith rendered such an act priestly, or at best parental, and therefore invalid because it was not the personal and voluntary act of the subject. It therefore had no place in the Christian dispensation and was not an indication of the personal faith of the child. Zwingli was at first disposed to accept this view. Melancthon was greatly troubled to explain the consistency of infant baptism with justification by faith, the material principle of the Reformation. But Zwingli had been called to Zurich by the civic council. He had never known a church separate from the State. When he realized that the rejection of infant baptism involved the restriction of church membership to professed believers and the organization of churches without State support, he drew back from such consequences, and insisted upon the continued practice of infant baptism. He soon withdrew all sympathy with antipedobaptists, and became one of their most bitter and persistent persecutors. Largely through his influence, multitudes who discarded infant baptism were imprisoned and banished. Not less than six antipedobaptists were put to death by the Reformed at Zurich.

Meanwhile, numerous churches of professed believers who rejected infant baptism came into existence, while refugees of the same faith carried their views to remote parts of Europe. Among the continental antipedobaptists of his time, no one was more notable or more worthy of remembrance than Balthasar Hubmaier. He was born at Friedburg, banished from Zurich after painful imprisonment, and finally burned at the stake by Romanists at Vienna, March 10, 1528. In his tractate, "Concerning Heretics and Those Who Burn Them," written about 1524, Hubmaier made one of the most emphatic early protests against the prevalent infringement of religious liberty. "A Turk or a heretic," he wrote, "is not to be overcome by fire or sword, but by patience and instruction. The burning of heretics is an apparent confession, but an actual denial of Christ."

The Mennonites of the Low Countries, like the

so-called Anabaptists of Germany and Switzerland, suffered severely for their repudiation of infant baptism. They have been denounced for refusing to serve as magistrates, but as a body they were pure and peaceable men, and utterly repudiated the fanatical lawlessness which prevailed at Munster. When we remember that civil magistrates were called to execute laws and edicts which banished, imprisoned, and even put to death, godly citizens for their fidelity to their consciences, it is manifest that refusal to serve as magistrates did not necessarily imply opposition to magistracy or civil order. Men like Felix Mantz, Balthasar Hubmaier, and Menno Simons were not anarchists, but good citizens, faithful to God and true to their fellow-men. They insisted that Christian faith is a personal matter; that every man sustains direct personal relations to God; and that private judgment is a natural and an inalienable right. They denied the right of the State through its magistrates, or of any organized church by its priests, to intervene between the believer and his Lord, and thus assume to compel religious opinions or worship. They held that true religion cannot be compulsory, but must be voluntary, and in this contention they were undoubtedly right.

It is understood that the early English Baptists, either in their native country or during their banishment to Holland, early in the seventeenth century, were led to adopt the views of the Dutch antipedobaptists. During the reign of James I., in 1612,

Edward Wightman rejected infant baptism, and was burned as a heretic. He was the last person who suffered capital punishment in England for his religious opinions. During that same reign, many from London and the north of England fled to Holland, as exiles, where some boldly advocated religious liberty. John Smyth, in his famous confession, written a year before Wightman's death, declares that "the magistrate is not to meddle with religion or matters of conscience, nor to compel men to this or that form of religion, because Christ is the King and Lawgiver of the conscience."

In 1614, Leonard Busher wrote a noble work, far in advance of the prevalent views of his countrymen, entitled, "Religious Peace; or, A Plea for Liberty of Conscience." In it he pleads for the rights of Jews and Romanists, not only to speak, but to write and to print any views of religion for which scriptural authority may be claimed. "It is not only unmerciful, but unnatural and abominable—yea, monstrous—for one Christian to vex and destroy another for difference and questions of religion."

The confession of the seven Baptist churches in London, issued in 1643, is the first complete and comprehensive statement of religious liberty adopted by associated churches. It declares: "We cannot do anything contrary to our understanding and consciences, neither can we forbear the doing of that which our understanding and consciences bind us to do." From this time on, in treatises and confessions, English Baptists have urged religious liberty and the restriction of the magistrate's functions to their legitimate sphere.

It is abundantly manifest that, when Roger Williams declared to the Puritans of Massachusetts Bay that the civil magistrate had no right to punish men for the violation of the first table—that is, the first four commandments of the Decalogue—he advanced a principle which had been held more than a hundred years earlier by Hubmaier and had been urged by his own countrymen when Williams was a mere youth. Yet to Roger Williams, without doubt, belongs the distinguished honor, accorded to him by Judge Story, of having established a State in whose "code of laws we read, for the first time since Christianity ascended the throne of the Cæsars, that conscience should be free and men should not be punished for worshipping God as they were persuaded he required."

Apart from the Quakers in Pennsylvania, no other colonial government in America adopted and retained such generous provision for civil and religious liberty as did Rhode Island, and it should be remembered that the early English Quakers were historically connected with those same early English Baptists, who, as we have seen, were powerfully influenced by Dutch antipedobaptists. "We are compelled," says Barclay, in his "Inner History of the Religious Societies of the Commonwealth," "to view George Fox as the unconscious exponent of the doctrine, practice, and discipline of the ancient and stricter party of the Dutch Mennonites."

The long and painful struggle for religious liberty in the Puritan colonies of New England did not cease in Connecticut until the new Constitution was adopted, in 1818, and religious equality was not attained in Massachusetts until 1834. In Virginia, the Episcopalian church was disestablished and practical religious liberty was secured, largely through the determined efforts of the Baptists, soon after the American Revolution, after a period of prolonged, provoking, and at times cruelly severe persecution. It seems strange that the Puritan founders of Massachusetts, who sought for themselves an asylum from the persecution which they despaired of escaping in the Old World, should have failed to recognize that to worship God according to the dictates of conscience is an inherent and an inalienable right—a right as valuable to others as to themselves.

It seems strange that men who counted not their lives dear in their determined effort to secure their own religious freedom should have refused to grant to others that which they so highly prized for themselves. Their descendants were slow to learn the lesson which the fathers failed to understand; but we may confidently hope that this fundamental principle of Protestantism has at last, in this country at least, been well learned. Dr. Lyman Beecher says, in his "Autobiography," of the agitation which resulted in the adoption of the new Constitution in Connecticut in 1818, with its article in favor of religious liberty, that he "suffered what no tongue can tell' for what he afterwards came to regard as "the best thing that ever happened to the State of Connecticut."

Thanks to the vigilant foresight of Virginia Baptists, the first amendment to the Constitution prohibits, we may hope forever, any establishment of a national religion in the United States. Writing of "the establishment of the American principle of the non-interference of the State with religion and the equality of all religious communions before the law," Dr. Leonard Woolsey Bacon, in his "History of American Christianity" (page 221), says: "So far as this was a work of intelligent conviction and religious faith, the chief honor of it must be given to the Baptists. Other sects, notably the Presbyterians, had been energetic and efficient in demanding their own liberties; the Friends and the Baptists agreed in demanding liberty of conscience and worship and equality before the law for all alike. But the active labor in this cause was mainly done by the Baptists. It is to their consistency and constancy in the warfare against the privileges of the powerful "Standing Order" of New England, and of the moribund establishments of the South, that we are chiefly indebted for the final triumph in this country of that principle of the separation of Church from State which is one of the largest contributions of the New World to civilization and to the church universal."

We have seen that the early English Baptists, like many who repudiated infant baptism on the Continent, were earnest advocates of religious liberty. There have been repeated acknowledgments of this service by writers not themselves Baptists—such as Dr. John Stoughton, Professor David Masson, and Principal A. N. Fairbairn.

In the Old World, the rapid growth of the democratic spirit has greatly modified, though it has not altogether removed, the injustice which is always involved in the establishment of a religion by the State. The logic of Protestantism tends irresistibly to favor civil and religious liberty, but every form of hierarchy demands priestly rule in the church and is naturally allied to an oligarchical or a monarchical rule in the State. Therefore, it is idle to claim that the Roman Catholic church has been or can be favorable to real democracy or to genuine religious liberty.

Probably that church is to-day the most complete organization and can wield the most masterful worldly power of any organized agency on earth. Those greatly err who suppose that the loss of temporal power in Italy restricted the Roman church to the performance of strictly spiritual functions. Her social, economic, and political influence is still manifold and far-reaching. It is almost alike potent in monarchies and republics, in Protestant Germany and Roman Catholic Austria, in the republic of France and in portions of the United States. This unequalled organization is historically the product of imperial sacerdotalism, a combination of the methods and polity of the old Roman empire, the greatest secular power of the ancient world, and of sacerdotalism, partly Jewish and partly pagan. The child, like each of its parents, is the historic and mortal enemy of true historic freedom. The votaries of the Roman organization boast that their church does not change; that it is everywhere and always the same. The two forces from which it sprung, imperialism and sacerdotalism, are foreign to the spirit of the New Testament. Like the singularly strong organization which they produced, they antagonize the inherent rights of men.

Roman imperialism held that man exists for the State, not the State for man. It pitilessly destroyed the happiness and needlessly sacrificed the lives of multitudes in order to extend the limits of the empire and increase the glory of the State. Sacerdotalism obtrudes a class of functionaries between the ordinary man and his Maker. A distinctive mediatorial priesthood assumes to monopolize the application of saving and efficient grace, and so denies every man's fundamental right and duty to have direct personal dealings with the Almighty.

The Roman church magnifies the externals of religion, and, by the most cruel persecution and inquisitorial torture, it has attempted to enforce outward uniformity of doctrine, worship, and polity. Between this system of imperial sacerdotalism and the demand of the New Testament that every man shall sustain direct personal relation to a personal God there is wide divergence. Every branch of Christendom and every intelligent Christian man is called to choose between these opposing systems, whose antagonism is radical and irreconcilable. Every young man who enters upon the work of the Christian ministry must decide whether he will be a priest or a preacher; whether he will assume to be a distinctive channel of saving and efficient grace or will strive to hold forth "the word of life" as a teacher sent of God to his fellowmen.

JAMES BRUTON GAMBRELL, D. D.
1841-1921.

Editor of The Baptist Standard, Dallas, Texas
and President of the Southern Baptist Convention.

CHAPTER IX.

Obligations of Baptists to Teach Their Pinciples.

BY REV. J. B. GAMBRELL, D. D.

Speaking of a Christian, an able writer says: "It is by the truths of the divine word that he is to expand and strengthen his intellect; it is these which he is to convert into principles, that are to form the substratum and basis of his character; that are to purify his heart and regulate his conduct."

These apt and forceful words furnish a good text for a discourse on the importance of exegetical preaching. It is the design of the Scriptures to furnish truths which will, if received, expand the intellect, enrich the heart, formulate doctrines, settle the foundations of life, regulate the conduct, and mould the character. Character is the end of the process, the ripe fruit of all teaching and all grace. It is a powerful proof of the divinity of the Bible that, amid the conflicts of the ages, even with all the indifferent handling of priests and partisans, it has steadily advanced every people who have given it a chance to elevate and guide them. The Bible is to-day the very core of the highest civilization the world knows. It is the fountain-head of all that is best in literature, in art, in song, in law, in sociology, in human life, whether in the palace or the cottage. It holds the same place in civilization given it by Burns in that noblest of all the poems in the English tongue, "The Cotter's Saturday Night."

The burden of revelation is Jesus Christ. From the fall onward, the pages of the Bible are illuminated with promises, all pointing to the coming of the Restorer of all things. The scheme of restoration, evolved with more and more clearness through the ages, contemplates the elevation of man to kinship with God. This elevation was to come through the acceptance of truth, which is the world's only liberator. But truth was to be evermore connected, not with the intellect only, but with the spirit also. God seeketh such to worship him as worship in spirit and truth. Not spirit alone, not truth alone, but both together, binding heart and mind to God.

A proper study of this divine method of delivering the race from the slavery of error into real liberty must deeply impress us with the necessity of spiritual preaching, as well as of the transcendant importance of doctrinal preaching. In some quarters there has grown up a strong and hindering prejudice against the preaching of "dry doctrine." The trouble does not lie in the doctrine, but in the dry preaching of it. Dry preachers have turned the very bread of heaven into stones, and not a few have found no better use for the stones after they are made than to cast at their theological adversaries. Much of the doctrinal preaching is not only distastefully dry, but distressingly gritty. We can scarcely wonder that hungry souls turn away from a ministry which preaches predestination without pathos, election without grace, baptism without its sublime spiritual meaning, communion without sensibility, and all duty without beauty.

A DEPLORABLE REACTION.

The reaction from what has just been described is no better, possibly some degrees worse. There be many who discredit doctrine entirely. They have gone away into the mists of mere sentimentalism. Feeling is everything, teaching nothing. This notion is at the bottom of modern revivalism of the sensational order. It abounds in clap-trap, and after a community has been swept by it, by-and-by, when the revivalist has gone, nothing substantial remains. There is no substratum of truth upon which the converts can stand. I do not undervalue evangelism. The true evangelist is a gift from Christ, and two signs go with him—he preaches in the Spirit and he preaches God's revealed truth. By these signs he may be known with infallible certainty. The cure for both evils named is a return to biblical preaching, both as to spirit and substance. And this it behooves Baptists to do, even more than other people; for Baptists are nothing without the Bible, and will go to nothing, if they have not the unifying and guiding power of the Spirit among them. They are committed unreservedly to the voluntary principle in religion. They have no human authority over them. Their only hope of unity is in the spirit and the truth.

Leading up to the main features of the discussion in hand, as a kind of background for what is to follow, I here enter a plea for doctrinal preaching in the spirit of Christ and the apostles. Perhaps it would be well to enter a plea for a *return* to such preaching, for many pulpits have followed the drivel of the age a long way from the solid teaching of the New Testament. In the first place, there needs to be created in many Baptist churches a spiritual hospitality for doctrinal teaching. There is in not a few churches a truce with surroundings. Alliances with peoples of defective and alien doctrinal views have become a real hindrance to honest, thorough-going New Testament teaching on doctrines about which there are differences of opinion. It has come to pass that some preachers are following public opinion, rather than teaching and leading it. There is scarcely a sorrier spectacle in the world than a man, with a commission from the King Eternal to herald his everlasting truth, secretly taking counsel of Mrs. Grundy as to what he shall say. It is pre-eminently the function of the pulpit to mould and lead thought, so that the thoughts of the people shall be God's thoughts. Until people think right, they will not act right. As Baptist principles are peculiar to Baptists, every Baptist church, with all its appointments, from preacher to Sunday-school teacher, ought to stand, in the community where it holds forth the word, for something different from any other congregation. When a Baptist church thinks of itself as just one of the churches in a community, with no mission above others, it has become a very weak affair.

We may invigorate our faith and renew our courage by reflecting that divine power has always attended the preaching of doctrine, when done in the true spirit of preaching. Great revivals have accompanied the heroic preaching of the doctrines of grace, predestination, election, and that whole lofty mountain range of doctrines upon which Jehovah sits enthroned, sovereign in grace as in all things else. God honors the preaching that honors him. There is entirely too much milk-sop preaching nowadays, trying to cajole sinners to enter upon a truce with their Maker, quit sinning, and join the church. The situation does not call for a truce, but for a surrender. Let us bring out the heavy artillery of heaven, and thunder away at this stuck-up age as Whitfield, Edwards, Spurgeon, and Paul did, and there will be many slain of the Lord raised up to walk in newness of life.

People, after all, want to hear preaching with substance in it. The truth was made for human hearts as certainly as bread was made for human mouths. A ministry strong and tender, true to the Word of God, will never be a slighted ministry. I am deeply convinced that there should be a return to doctrinal preaching, taking care to keep clear of the faults of the professional religious pugilist.

This is true with respect to doctrine in general; it is specially true of doctrines which Baptists are peculiarly bound to hold aloft before the world.

TRUTH A TRUST.

Truth is a trust. Whoever has it has it, not for himself simply, but for the world. Paul regarded himself a trustee of the gospel. The whole world were beneficiaries of the trust. From his day till now there has been a succession in the trusteeship. The apostle, with a spiritual thrift and economy taught him by the Spirit of God, committed the truth to faithful men, with instructions for them, in their turn, to do likewise, that the truth might never fail among men to the end of time. Baptists are peculiarly in the succession of trusteeship. When they were few and despised, without papers, colleges, or even the common rights of men, they felt the solemn obligations of trusteeship. They saw, under the gloom of spiritual ignorance surrounding them, certain great principles taught in the Word of God, held them aloft amid the dust and smoke of mighty spiritual conflicts, and sealed their devotion to them in martyr fires. These principles spring out of the New Testament, and are for the guidance of the race to the highest destiny fixed in the mind of God.

All real progress in the world is along the line of these principles. They are intended and are suited to develop the highest type of manhood. They greaten the individual by forming his character after that of Jesus Christ, who was the world's one complete man, its most perfect gentleman, its truest and best citizen. Great States cannot be constructed of little people. A little man, narrow in his views of human rights and possibilities, narrow in his sympathies, without noble thoughts, can never make a great anything. And an aggregation of such people will make a State no better than the average of them. Herein lies the explanation of the differences between Catholic and Protestant countries. Nations have progressed as they have given hospitality to the great principles for which Baptists stand. That is only another way of saying that nations have risen in proportion as they have become genuinely Christian, and they have become Christian as they have accepted the teachings of the New Testament.

RAPID PROGRESS.

Within the last hundred years the world has made more progress than in 1,000 before. The century just closing has been pre-eminently a Baptist century. During this time, the principles for which they stand have had something like fair play, and have been widely, and in many cases unconsciously, accepted. They have, like leaven, worked a change in the thought of all the leading nations of the earth. They have emancipated the minds of men and opened the door of knowledge to all mankind. They have put out the martyr fires over nearly the whole world. Those who do not yet accept them in full feel the passion of their power as they work their way to the seat of power everywhere—the conscience of the masses. That was a splendid tribute to the power of the masses, enlightened and blessed by the Word of God, the London Times inadvertently paid when it opposed taking President Kruger a prisoner. This exponent of public opinion and Tory politics said: "The Non-conformist conscience of England would revolt at the picture of President Kruger a prisoner, sitting with the Bible open on his knee." Keeping clear of the political aspects of the case, the Times is to be congratulated on its clearness of vision. That open Bible is properly associated with the whole history of human freedom. Before Luther or Calvin or Knox, before modern Protestantism was born, Baptists stood for the right of a man to have a Bible open on his knee, and for the further right to read it, and, looking to God for guidance, walk in its commandments, as he understood them. The right to read the Scriptures, the right to interpret them, the right to obey them, Baptists have always held to be inalienable rights, belonging to every human being alike. This doctrine lies at the fountain-head of all modern enlightenment and progress. It correlates with the principle of individualism in religion, and this principle has its application in many directions. It finds expression in the Constitution of the United States, which guarantees religious liberty to every one. It goes to the very foundations of the vast superstructure of proxy religion, and is rapidly working the destruction of the whole vicious system. Individualism means that every one must read, think, and act for himself. Sponsors are passing away, with many other inventions of Rome. Infant baptism must and will go down before the great principle of individualism taught in the New Testament and held by Baptists; for, if it is the believer's duty to be baptized, it is not somebody's business to have him baptized, *nolens volens*, when he knows nothing. With the destruction of infant baptism, the corner-stone of popery disappears, and the religious life of humanity is rid of an enormous incubus.

INDIVIDUALISM AND THE PRIESTHOOD OF BELIEVERS.

Individualism correlates with the priesthood of all believers. Let it be known that every man may for himself, at all times, anywhere, come to a throne of grace and find pardon, peace, and life eternal, and the whole vast system of priestcraft receives its death blow. Freedom to read God's Word, freedom to worship God as he feels he should, freedom to act for himself in religious matters, freedom to go to God for himself for wisdom and all spiritual blessing without the intervention of a human priest or preacher, complete the disenthralment of the man and put him in the shining way of all blessings.

The value of these principles goes further. The disappearance of the priest makes way for the preacher, whose business is to open the Scriptures to the minds and hearts of men. His work is to educate the conscience and move the heart to obey the commands of God. The preacher is the mightiest human force in the world. He is the forerunner of civilization. He is the most effective reformer known to men. His power lies in his message. The word of God, which is quick and powerful, he lays on the hearts of the people. When the priest, with all his flummery, retires, the preacher has an open field for his great work, and the priest has nothing to do, when the doctrine of individualism is accepted.

I will not go into other phases of the subject at any great length. The all-sufficiency of the Scriptures as a guide in religion is a cardinal principle with Baptists. This eliminates the authority of councils, popes, synods, conferences, bishops, etc. It gives no place to history as a supplement to the teaching of the Bible. It shuts the world up to take the law from the mouth of God. Here we stand, and on this principle will settle all questions. Baptists are immersionists, not for the sake of immersion, but because it is a command. They are close communionists, not because they do not love other people, but because the Scriptures fix the place and order of the table. They are congregationalists, because the Scriptures fix the nature and order of New Testament churches.

The world wants and sorely needs a centre of unity. That centre is the Word of God. The more it is preached in its fulness, the quicker will Christian union be realized.

I must not prolong the discussion. Our obligations to teach the principles long held by Baptists grow out of our obligation to God, and also to men. God has put his highest glory among men in his word. The first purpose of the gospel is to glorify God. The angels first sang "Glory to God in the highest." Every principle of the gospel reflects the glory of its author. If we would honor God, we must stand for his truth. As trustees of his truth, we are under every obligation known to the redeemed to see that the truth is faithfully preached.

Our obligations are to men, also. Their highest good is wrapped up in the principles of the gospel. The more truth one has, the richer he is. The more he walks in the truth, the happier and more useful he is. Error is not good enough for any one. We bless the world in proportion as we disseminate sound principles. To fail in this is to default in a trust.

The marvellous progress of Baptist principles during the last 100 years ought to inspire us to renewed faithfulness in proclaiming them. They have been largely accepted by other denominations, though they still maintain a separate line of policy, but with ever-increasing weakness. Few Methodists now will defend some of the early teachings of Wesley. The conservative Presbyterians repudiate some of Calvin's doctrines. Infant baptism is gradually passing away. The Romish reason for it, though strong traces of it are found in Pedobaptist standards, is now generally reprobated.

The great Baptist principle of religious liberty is taking the world, and its correlative, separation of Church and State, is following in its wake. Individualism in religion has made wonderful progress even in Catholic countries and in the Catholic communion, while it has nearly completed its conquest in some Protestant communions.

The work, so encouraging to-day, ought to be pressed to a finish. We live in tremendous times. The truth never had so fair a field for conquest. Baptists were never so well equipped to wage an aggressive campaign. In the language of another, "with malice toward none, with charity for all," let us complete the work we are in and fulfil our solemn obligations to God and to men.

"We may now announce, in order, the distinctive Baptist principles. FIRST, THE NEW TESTAMENT -- THE LAW OF CHRISTIANITY. Doubtless many of my fellow Christians of other denominations may be disposed to smile at the announcement of this as a distinctive Baptist principle. But let us not smile too soon. Patiently await the development of the thought . . . All the New Testament is the Law of Christianity. The New Testament is all the Law of Christianity. The New Testament will always be all the Law of Christianity. This does not deny the inspiration or profit of the Old Testament, nor that the New Testament is a development of the Old. It affirms, however, that the Old Testament, as a typical, educational, and transitory system was fulfilled in Christ, and as a standard of law and way of life was nailed to the cross of Christ and so taken out of the way. The principle teaches that we should not go to the Old Testament to find Christian law or Christian institutions. Not there do we find the true idea of the Christian church, or its members, or its ordinances, or its government, or its officers, or its sacrifices, or its worship, or its mission, or its ritual, or its priesthood. Now, when we consider the fact that the overwhelming majority of Christendom today, whether Greek, Romanist or Protestant, borrow from the Old Testament so much of their doctrine of the church, including its members, officers, ritual, ordinances, government, liturgy, and mission, we may well call this a distinctive Baptist principle. This is not a question of what is the Bible. If it were, Baptists would not be distinguished from many Protestants in rejecting the apocryphal additions incorporated by Romanists in their Old Testament. Nor is it a question of a stand with Chillingworth on the proposition, 'The Bible, and the Bible alone, is the religion of Protestants.' If it were, Baptists would not be distinguished from many Protestants in rejecting the equal authority of tradition as held by the Romanists. But when Baptists say that the New Testament is the only law for Christian institutions they part company, if not theoretically at least practically, with most of the Protestant world, as well as from the Greeks and Romanists. We believe that the church, with all that pertains to it, is strictly a New Testament institution. We do not deny that there was an Old Testament ecclesia, but do deny its identity with the New Testament *ecclesia*. We do not deny the circumcision of infants under the Old Testament law, but do deny their baptism under New Testament law . . .

The New Testament is the law of Christianity. All the New Testament is the law of Christianity. The New Testament is all the law of Christianity. The New Testament always will be all the law of Christianity. Avaunt ye types and shadows! Avaunt Apochrypha! Avaunt O Synagogue! Avaunt Tradition, thou hoary-headed liar! Hush! Be still and listen! All through the Christian ages -- from dark and noisome dungeons, from the lone wanderings of banishment and expatriation, from the roarings and sickening conflagrations of martyr fires -- there comes a voice -- shouted here, whispered there, sighed, sobbed, or gasped elsewhere -- a Baptist voice, clearer than a silver trumpet and sweeter than the chime of bells, a voice that freights and glorifies the breeze or gale that bear it. O Earth, hearken to it -- *The New Testament is the law of Christianity!* Let the disciples of Zoroaster, Brahma, Confucius, Zeno, and Epicurus hear it. And when Mahomet comes with his Koran, or Joe Smith with his book of Mormon, or Swedenborg with his new revelations, or spirit-rappers, wizards, witches, and necromancers with their impostures, confront each in turn with the all-sufficient revelation of this book, and when science -- falsely so called (properly speculative philosophy) -- would hold up the book as moribound, effete, or obsolete, may the Baptist voice rebuke it. Christ himself set up His kingdom. Christ himself established His church. Christ Himself gave us Christian law. And the men whom He inspired furnish us the only reliable record of these institutions. They had no successors in inspiration. The record is complete. Prophecy and vision have ceased. The canon of revelation and the period of legislation are closed. Let no man dare to add to it or take from it, or dilute it, or substitute for it. It is written. It is finished."

B. H. CARROLL
Distinctive Baptist Principles.
(Dallas, TX: The Pastor's Conference, 1903).

PART III.

What Baptist Principles Are Worth to the World,
A. E. Dickinson, D. D., Editor of the Religious Herald, Richmond, Va.

Why I Became a Baptist,
Madison C. Peters, D. D., of New York.

Candid Scholarship,
W. R. L. Smith, D. D., of Richmond, Va.

Sunday Observance and Religious Liberty,
R. H. Pitt, D. D., Editor of the Religious Herald, Richmond, Va.

One Hundred Years Ago,
B. H. Carroll, D. D., of Texas.

ALFRED ELIJAH DICKINSON, D. D.
1830-1906.
Editor of the Religious Herald, Richmond, VA
and Trustee of Richmond College.

What Baptist Principles Are Worth to the World.

BY A. E. DICKINSON, D. D., EDITOR OF THE RELIGIOUS HERALD, RICHMOND, VA.

The subject chosen is by no means trivial. It is worthy of the candid and prayerful study of all Christians of every name and denomination. It is as much every other person's duty to ascertain what is true about these matters as it is yours and mine.

I shall not put forward unwarranted and exaggerated claims for the Baptists, nor underestimate what other Christian people have done. In speaking of what Baptists have done, and of what their principles are worth, I hope not to use a word to which any of God's dear children not of this fold can rightly take exception. May great grace rest upon all who love our Lord Jesus Christ in sincerity, here and everywhere, now and evermore!

In the very beginning, I must frankly confess that Baptists have accomplished for the human family scarcely a tithe of what they might have done and ought to have done. We are summoned to the profoundest humiliation in reviewing the failures and follies which have almost everywhere and always marred the force and beauty of our principles. Many a time have these blunders brought us into disrepute among great masses of good people. You know that the worst enemies to any good cause are those who profess to be its champions, and yet, in their teaching and living, misrepresent its spirit and aims.

Whenever the Spirit of Christ departs from a Baptist church, whenever such a church turns from its God-given mission, it dies—dies surely, dies completely, and often dies speedily. The bones of such a church soon become as "exceeding dry" as were those of which Ezekiel had a vision "in the open valley." No amount of excited breath expended in Baptist brag and brazen boastings, no fierce indictments of other Christian denominations, no iron bands of organization—nothing can keep alive a Baptist church which turns its eyes from its high and holy mission and fixes them upon low and grovelling aims and purposes. Such a church soon wastes away and gives up the ghost, and the sooner it does this the better.

CARICATURING OUR VIEWS.

Whenever Baptists give their chief and almost exclusive attention to emphasizing the points of difference between them and others, they place their denomination at a frightful disadvantage. Multitudes, who might be won to our faith but for this distorted view, because of it are driven into organized and unrelenting opposition to us, and they in turn make thousands more our enemies, who might as well have been our friends. While this unwise advocacy of our views—this caricature of them, I might better say—has often damaged us immensely in the eyes of other good people and the world at large, such so-called Baptist champions have often not stopped there, but have turned their guns upon their own citadel. Not content with the ruin inflicted upon their own denomination by their unwise methods in attacking others, they have too often found additional vent for their pugnacious impulses in keeping up a lively fight at home within their own lines. There is nothing such Baptists like so well as hot water—the hotter, the better for them. If necessary, to make things lively, they will invent new tests of Baptist orthodoxy, of which our Baptist fathers never so much as dreamed. Anything is to their liking, if it serves to foster and forment dissensions and distract and destroy feeble churches, which, but for some unworthy leadership, might soon become great and glorious exponents of the true Baptist faith.

Had Baptists been as loyal to the command to go into all the world and disciple all nations as they have been to keeping the ordinances as they were delivered, long before this all Christendom might have accepted the truth as we hold it, and the kingdoms of this world might have been brought into loving subjection to Him whose we are and whom we serve.

In other particulars, also, we have often, in antagonizing unscriptural views and practices. gone too far in the opposite direction. If others have had too much machinery, often we have had too little. Their cast-iron polity, their wheels within wheels, should not have deterred us from having all the wheels we really need that are in keeping with the necessities laid upon us for doing our work and in line with Scripture teaching. In exalting our New Testament doctrine of church independency, putting the supreme power and authority in the local church, where they belong, it is not necessary that we let our great resources run to waste. That doctrine does not hinder, but rather calls for such combination and concentration of these little Christian republics as may be for the good of each and all.

If others have sought too exclusively the patronage of the more influential classes, have we not too often satisfied ourselves with evangelizing the neglected masses, while overlooking others, whose wealth, learning, and position we might have brought into active co-operation with us in the defence and diffusion of our denominational views? If knowledge is power in other directions, is it any less so here? Had we been wiser, we might more diligently and generously have fostered institutions of learning and have led others, instead of being led by them, in this and in many more great Christian movements. Because of these and many more Baptist blunders (which, with becoming humility, let us all now confess and deplore), Baptist principles have not had a fair chance in the world. The victories they have gained have been won largely in spite of their advocates.

It is not the fault of the Baptist idea that it has

not been worth a thousand times more to the world. It is not the fault of good seed that they fail to produce a good harvest, when they are not properly planted and wisely cultivated. A medicine may be ever so good, but it may fail of producing the desired effects, when diluted or improperly administered. McCormick's best reapers fail to gather the waving harvests, if those in charge do not know how to use them. Baptist principles are not responsible for Baptist follies. As we become wiser and learn better how to wield this old Jerusalem blade, we shall secure results which will fill us with wonder and rejoicing. We shall then probaby accomplish as much in a year as we now do in a century.

Even now we see, here and there, how mightily the wise use of our resources tells. Often you will find one single Baptist accomplishing as much as dozens of his brethren, all told, equally gifted in many respects with himself. Such an one may chance to go into a community where there are no Baptists, and where the tide is all against them, and yet, in a year or two, by a wise and loving presentation of our views, he will capture almost the entire population. Under his leadership, men, women, and children, with all they have, in head and heart and purse, turn joyfully to the Baptists. Indeed, there is nothing under heaven which unprejudiced people take to so readily and hold to so firmly as to Baptist principles, when they are rightly put before them in the voice and life. The chief, if not the only reason, why Baptist principles have not long ago gained a thousand-fold stronger hold upon Christendom is to be found in Baptist blunders. Not Pedobaptist logic, but Baptist living, has kept us in the background.

With these preliminary remarks, I come now to consider

WHAT BAPTIST PRINCIPLES ARE WORTH TO THE WORLD.

And, first, it may be well to indicate what are Baptist principles. Baptists hold to certain views and practices which are distinctive and peculiar, and are held by no others on earth. They regard these as immensely important—worth living for and worth dying for. And hence, when it is proposed in the name of Christian union to merge all denominations into one general organization, it seems to us but idle talk. Such a union may suit those who have nothing in particular to stand for; but it does not commend itself to us, who have great doctrines which can be maintained only by our continued separate existence. None desire more than we that all God's people may be really and truly one in faith and practice. We pray daily for the coming of the time when all who love Christ shall be one, even as he and the Father are one. But, starting out with the principle that the New Testament is our ultimate and only authority as to church order and church action, the question of church organization is settled for us for all time. The inspired Epistles emphasize the importance of holding firmly to gospel order, leaving nothing to the caprice and ever-changing whims of poor, fickle mortals.

The inspired volume does not contain a line which indicates that anything will do for baptism; that if you think a thing is right, it is right to you. You search the Book of God in vain to find that baptism means this, that, or the other thing, or nothing, just as one may choose to have it. You will find no line there which so much as remotely intimates that this ordinance is for any but penitent believers. Nor will you find anything there which could give the faintest idea that the supper was ever to come before baptism. The india-rubber system of our Pedobaptist brethren has millions of advocates in this world, but no whisper is heard in its behalf in the Book of God.,

That those who can so readily set aside inspired command and example should keep up their own separate ecclesiastical organizations, is something we do not understand. Surely nothing less than the demands of conscience, enlightened and guided by the Word of God, can justify the continued separation of Christian denominations. If it is a mere question of church government, for example, between two ecclesiastical bodies, neither of which tries to find a scriptural basis for its polity, then such bodies ought to coalesce, and as soon as possible. Unity is desirable—unity of form as well as unity of spirit; and hence every denomination of Christians is perpetually challenged for the reason of its existence. If it has no distinctive principles, it has no right to live, nor does it deserve to live if its principles are comparatively valueless. Without a "Thus saith the Lord" for what is peculiar in its teachings, as its Christian basis, a religious denomination has no right to exist, and the sooner it disbands and unites with a denomination which has such authority for its existence, the better for all parties. Continued separation from other Christian workers, under such circumstances, is schismatic, injurious, and un-Christian.

We are not disposed to avoid the issue here raised. We will not be disloyal to our convictions by asking that the Baptists be relieved from the test herein involved. Baptists are not exempt from the application of these principles. They have no right to maintain a separate existence, unless they stand for great New Testament doctrines which are peculiar and distinctive. Ordinarily, we have not been slow to accept this challenge.

THE BAPTIST MONOPOLY.

There are certain things in Christian doctrine and practice of which we have a monopoly. No one else is manifesting any special concern about these views and practices of ours, except to oppose them, and, if possible, to banish them from the world. This is the sect now, as it has ever been, everywhere spoken against. However our brethren of other persuasions may differ among themselves, they are solidly one in opposing Baptist principles; and hence it is manifest that there is something peculiar, as well as provoking, in our position and principles. And yet to all charges of creating schism and division Baptists may lift their hands to heaven and cry: "These hands are clean!" We simply stand by the old rules—as old as the New Testament. If others come in with new rules, upon them must rest the responsibiltiy which comes with warring sects. From the peace which is bought at the expense of truth, may the good Lord deliver us! One particle of truth, in God's sight, is more precious than all earth's glittering treasures. Union in the truth is the only union worth the name.

Baptists, from the days of John the Baptist, have given the most emphatic testimony to their conception of the value of their denominational tenets. In maintaining them, they have accepted imprisonment, stripes, and death itself. If the noble army of Baptist martyrs, who joyfully welcomed all the ills that earth could inflict rather than abandon their advocacy of Baptist views, were not greatly deceived, there is something wrapped up in this Baptist idea of priceless value. Roger Williams knew what he was doing when he plunged into the wilderness, and for days went without bread or water (he says, "For fourteen weeks I knew not what bed or bread did mean"), in his zeal for soul liberty, which was then as peculiar and distinctive a Baptist principle as believers' baptism is now. But Roger Williams was only one of a great multitude—we might almost say a multitude which no man can number—who proved their appreciation of what Baptist principles are worth by enduring fierce persecution in their behalf. It might quicken the zeal of Baptists for them to recall the sufferings endured by their fathers, to bear in mind at what cost this liberty they now enjoy was obtained, and how joyfully their fathers paid that price in the dungeon and at the whipping-post. They counted life itself a thing of no value, when called to abandon Baptist principles. The man who does not see anything worth living for or dying for in Baptist doctrines is a man immensely unlike Obadiah Holmes, who, after a term in jail, was tied to a public whipping-post, his clothes stripped off, and received thirty lashes, "the executioner striking with all his might, and spitting upon his hands three times, that he might do his utmost. His flesh was so torn and cut that for weeks afterward he could only rest upon his hands and knees, even in his bed." It was his profound conviction of the value of Baptist principles which cheered and sustained him through it all. He calmly accepted the situation, believing that the coming ages would prove that his sufferings were wisely endured. And so thought the old Virginia Baptists, who laid the foundation of our faith in this old Commonwealth, as their songs of praise to God rang out from many an old jail.

Adoniram Judson and Luther Rice did not stop to count the cost when, far from home and friends, in a heathen land, they gave up their only guaranteed support, as soon as they discovered that Baptist principles were simply New Testament principles, and cast their lot in with the Baptists. They did not stop to ask as to the social position or the wealth and worldly influence of the Baptists. They did not once raise such inquiries. As soon as they discovered that the Baptists had Scripture authority for the points on which they differ from others, Judson and Rice were ready, at any and every sacrifice, to espouse their cause. What a rebuke to all who desert the old Baptist banner because their lot happens to be cast in a community where it is not popular to be a Baptist, or because they happen to be associated with those who would be pleased to have them abandon these principles!

NO ROOM FOR COMPROMISE.

If nothing is ever settled until it is settled right, loyalty to conscience and to the Word of God must always rank higher than any mere sentimental desire for the union of Baptists with other denominations. There is no room for compromise left us. It is not a mode of baptism that Baptists plead for, but the thing itself. No immersion, no baptism. Nor do we put baptism above other commands and teachings of Christ. Underlying our denominational position on all these questions there is one great cardinal, basal principle, the bed-rock of Baptist faith and practice. That principle is that the sacred Scriptures are the only and the absolute authority in religion. We object to the phrase "paramount authority," and we are not quite satisfied with the phrase "all-sufficient." The Word of God is the sovereign, and this sovereign has no parliament and no prime minister. It is a matter of no earthly interest to us, as modifying in any way our beliefs, what councils, popes, cardinals, bishops, canons or deans, or even district associations, may proclaim. The Word of God—what does that teach? is the only question which concerns a true Baptist.

Along this line Baptists have been working through the centuries, and their labors have not been in vain. Baptists have been worth something to the world. They have stood for soul liberty, for converted church membership, for loyalty to Christ as the only King in Zion. They have kept the ordinances as they were delivered. With them there is one Lord, one faith, and one baptism. No one has a right to say two or three; God excludes all but his own "one." He has a right to dictate as to his own gospel and its ordinances, and we have no more right to undertake to change them than we have to change the physical laws which he has appointed to govern the material universe. There would be no more presumption in attempting to abolish the law of gravitation than the law of baptism. We read: "Teaching them to observe all things whatsoever I have commanded you." Again: "If there come any unto you and bring not this doctrine, receive him not." And yet again: "Though we or an angel from heaven preach any other gospel unto you, let him be accursed." "Behold! to obey is better than sacrifice."

No, friends, it is not that we are bigots—not that we are lacking in love for you and in appreciation of all the good that is in your heart and life; but because we dare not be disloyal to Him who has loved us and given himself for us. If he counts the immersion of the penitent believer baptism, then nothing else in the universe is baptism. If he has put baptism before the supper, no one in earth, heaven, or hell, should dare to change that order. If he has put the governing power in the local church, you have no right to put it anywhere else.

BAPTISM NOT THE CHIEF DOCTRINE.

After all that has been said about Baptists unduly magnifying baptism, we do not hesitate to affirm that baptism is far from being the chief doctrine of the Baptists. If the other so-called modes of baptism could be shown to have scriptural authority, we would not hesitate to adopt them. The very principle which makes us immerse would, in that case, make us conform to scriptural precept and precedent, whatever that might be shown to be. The reason for the existence of Baptist churches would scarcely be weakened by so startling and improbable a discovery. They might have to change their practice, but their controlling principle would remain intact. We count as the small dust in the balance any question of much water or little water. Whether a goblet or a gulf, would make little difference to a Baptist, who understands that the ground of separation lies much deeper than that.

There are great differences between Baptists and all other denominations apart from the ordinances. We differ as to the first principles. They have one idea of the constitution of a Christian church, and we have quite a different idea. They start out with the old Abrahamic idea, and they say the church is for our children as much as for us, their parents; the Baptist begins with asserting that every human being that is born into the world is dead in sin—conceived in sin, born dead—and that nothing but the Almighty Spirit of God can infuse life into that dead soul, and that until that is done it is the supremest folly to think of bringing it into the church. Only those who have received Jesus, and to whom he has given the privilege of becoming sons of God, "who are born, not of blood, nor of the will of the flesh, nor of the will of man, but of God," have, according to our principles, any right to the church and its ordinances. Thus, if all others were to adopt immersion as baptism, and stop there, they and we would be as far apart as the poles.

In holding to immersion in water as essential to the act of baptism, the Baptists have saved to the world one of the only two great symbolic ordinances instituted by the Head of the church, and the other they have kept just where the New Testament placed it. We have also made prominent the principle of unquestioned obedience to the Word of God, placing it not only above, but infinitely above, all questions of custom or conscience, all decisions of ecclesiastical courts and councils; so that these latter are not thought of as having any authority whatever.

Baptism symbolizes some of the most precious truths of our holy religion. It tells us that we are dead and buried and raised to a new life—that our sins have been washed away—buried out of sight.

It points to a blissful resurrection and a glorious immortality. It assures us that, having been planted in the likeness of his death, we shall also partake of the likeness of his resurrection. Baptism proclaims what no tongue can speak. One may in the most eloquent language explain what the Lord has done for him, but his words are cold and lifeless compared with the pathos and power which accompany the silent submission to this symbolic ordinance. We have seen vast crowds melted to tears as they gazed upon this expressive and beautiful picture—God's own picture—and we have known men converted by the sight, when all else had failed to move them.

As long as Baptists hold to their baptism, so long they will secure to the world this precious symbol, rich in soul-saving truth. As long as our baptism stands as an expression of obedience to Christ (and it grows more absolutely clear every day that it is), we exalt the Word of God, and everything that exalts God's Word and authority is something that the world needs. "The Bible, the Bible alone, the religion of the Protestants," was the famous dictum of Chillingworth. But it is lamentably true that the most serious and insidious—serious because insidious—attacks upon the Bible have, in recent years, come from Protestants. The few Baptists who have shared in this unholy crusade have found themselves quickly and surely shorn of all influence. The great Baptist body has had sufficient spiritual health to dispose of them effectually and promptly, without the slow and factitious aid of ecclesiastic courts. The principle which expresses itself in our baptism and communion and church polity has made this possible. This literalism, for which we are often mercilessly criticised, has done the world good service, and will render far more service in the future, unless we misread the signs of the times.

Baptists not only cleave to the act of baptism, as given in the sacred Scriptures, but they also adhere to the Scripture authority as to the subjects of the ordinance. We baptize none but such as make a personal confession of faith. Here, as elsewhere, we maintain not only the supremacy, but the absolute sovereignty of the sacred Scriptures. The failure of others to do this, the abolition of the scriptural prerequisite for baptism, has as a matter of history led, and does as a matter of fact lead, and will as a matter of logic continue to lead, in the direction of the union of Church and State.

INFANT REGENERATION.

Many who practise infant baptism affirm that infants are "regenerated, made members of the mystical body of Christ, and inheritors of the kingdom of heaven." This rite gives Romanists an unanswerable argument against Protestants. A Roman Catholic catechism asks: "Can Protestants prove to Baptists that the baptism of infants is good and useful?" "No," replies the same catechism, "they cannot, because, according to Protestant principles, such baptism is useless." An eminent Romanist recently said to a Baptist: "Either your people or mine are right. You are at one end of the line, we are at the other. Infant baptism, if anything, is all we claim for it."

Infant baptism lays the foundation for national hierarchies, and, where universally practised, surely and speedily abolishes all distinction between the church and the world. For the legitimate fruits of any such practice we must look where that practice has had ample scope for working out its results, and not where it is hedged in by opposing influences. If you would know what are the inherent tendencies of this "part and pillar of popery," inquire in the countries where for ages it has had uninterrupted and complete sway. There you will find great hierarchies crushing out the spirit and teachings of the gospel of Christ, and, with their imposing ritual and numberless and meaningless rites and ceremonies, ruling with despotic power over the bodies as well as the souls of its subjects, the partner and the patron of Cæsar.

This ghostly delusion of the papacy has in it the germ of persecution. The infant is not consulted. His baptism is a question of mere physical force, rather than of religious faith. If he is the child of Pedobaptists, and, upon coming to years of responsibility, wishes to be immersed, but desires to hold his membership in the church of his parents, it cannot be done. The act performed on him without his consent has logically, though most unjustly, robbed him of the right of choice. It is easy to see how the State naturally comes at last to take the place of church and parent.

Infant baptism is the egg out of which all this confusion and perversion of God's truth are hatched. It removes and abolishes the line of separation which God designed should ever stand between the church and the world, paves the way for a union of Church and State, and of this adulterous union a numerous progeny is born—persecution lighting its lurid fires through the dark centuries, the church hunting rather than comforting, multiplying rather than dividing the sorrows of humanity, killing when it ought to have been saving. And whence came all this? It grew, as all the world knows, though all the world may not acknowledge it, out of this union of Church and State, against which Baptists have always and everywhere protested. They stand to-day, as they have ever stood, the natural enemies of every principle which would enslave the soul.

NO MERE ACCIDENT.

Baptists did not stumble upon religious liberty. It is no mere accident that wherever Baptist views have prevailed, and to the extent to which they have prevailed, men have been left to worship God according to the dictates of their own conscience, with none to molest or to make them afraid. Soul freedom as surely comes with the adoption of Baptist principles as day comes with the rising sun. It is the inevitable, logical outgrowth of the doctrine that each must hear for himself, repent for himself, believe for himself, confess Christ for himself, and be baptized for himself—that as we come one by one into the world, so we must go to Christ one by one for mercy, and at last go one by one out of the world, to be judged according to the deeds done in the body. The doctrine of regenerated church membership, with its basis in the written Word, like the light of the sun, goes everywhere, and everywhere opens the way for the highest civil and religious liberty.

Our form of church government has been of unspeakable value to the world. With us the function of the local church, our only ecclesiastical authority, being exceedingly simple and its authority very limited, there is room for the development of liberty of thought and speech, while the very basis of the organization being in the Scripture model, that fact supplies all needful restraint. If Baptists have ever failed to be in line with all movements looking to human freedom and progress, then in every such case they have gone counter to their own foundation principles. In their own ecclesiastical organization (the local church) there is a decided and perpetual protest against every form of tyranny in religious matters, and in the equality among its membership there is a suggestion of that civic freedom which is beginning in some measure to be realized. If it be the true theory of the republic that "that community is governed best which is governed least," then it is a truth which finds striking exemplification in our simple, but effective—and effective because simple—church polity.

In emphasizing what Baptists have done for the world, often sufficient attention has not been given to this free-and-easy church polity of ours. More and more men of strong episcopal church governments are looking on with amazement at the organized power of these thousands of Baptist churches in America. They do not see how we manage to combine and concentrate the power of the denomination as we do in great philanthropic movements; nor can they see how it is that so easily and quietly we rid ourselves of the heretics and impostors who spring up among us.

We have only to answer that all this proves that the great Head of the church made no mistake in laying down the church polity to which the Baptists cling. Some one has said that "it is no discredit to a Christian organization that it cannot succeed without Christianity." As the Baptists obtain more of the spirit of Christ and more Christian education, as they grow in grace and in knowledge, this church polity will work so well that all the world will see that it is of God, and, abandoning their great ecclesiastical church governments, they will adopt this, which has no machinery to drive—no great driving-wheels which will keep the concern rolling on when Christian love and holy zeal have departed from it. A Baptist church dies when there is no more consecration of heart and life left to it—of course, it dies then; there's nothing to keep it going a day longer.

But these strong aristocratic churches run on centuries after the Spirit of God has left them. Their machinery—wheels within wheels—drives them on long after the divine power has left them.

BAPTIST INFLUENCE ON PEDOBAPTISTS.

In estimating the value of Baptist principles, we must not fail to take into the account their influences upon other Christian denominations—how they hold back Pedobaptists from the ruinous extremes to which they would inevitably go but for such restraining power. Nothing hinders the baptism and church membership of every infant except the Baptists. But for them, every babe would as surely come into the church as it comes into the world.

Wherever Baptists are not found, there infant baptism goes unchallenged among Protestants and Roman Catholics, and is universally practised. You have only to turn your eyes to Europe, Mexico, and South America to see what sad work it does when left to do its worst. Even over the lands where Martin Luther's Reformation won its brilliant victories this evil has spread desolation and ruin. Baptists are now reforming Luther's work, by taking from it the fatal error of birthright church membership. Where will you find a spot on the map of this earth where Christianity has anything more than a name, if on that spot infant baptism has not been held in check by the Baptist protest? That rite, as our friends call it, carries with it a dead formalism, which, as surely as an effect follows its cause, works evil, and only evil, and that continually. The reason it does not work out such results in this country is to be found in the prevalence of opposing influences. Baptists here keep Pedobaptist errors from running to seed; or, to change the figure, we put down the brakes and hold back the Pedobaptist car from the frightful precipices over which it would plunge, if left to itself.

Every godly Pedobaptist minister is doing far greater good because of the Baptist influence upon him and upon his people. He and they may not be conscious of it—indeed, they may be very unfriendly to us—but that does not alter the fact that Pedobaptists are a thousand times more useful because of the Baptists. And hence, before you can tell what Baptist principles are worth to the world, you will have to work upon this problem. You will have to ascertain what pedobaptism would be if its position as to the order of ordinances of the gospel were everywhere as fully accepted and practised among us as they are in some other countries, before you can tell what Baptist principles are worth. Close these Baptist churches, silence these Baptist pulpits, cast aside all our Baptist agencies for spreading our principles, and what then? In a few decades you could not find in all this broad land an unbaptized infant. They would all be in the church, and once there they would remain there in the same enclosure with their parents, and as truly church members as they. With such a universal acceptance of this "rite," surely and speedily all distinction between the church and world would vanish, and pedobaptism would be left to do for our fair land what it has done for every other land where it has had full and undisputed sway. We say these things in no boastful spirit, and certainly with no desire to misrepresent our Pedobaptist brethren. This is no time for self-admiration among Baptists. Nor is it a time—nor can there ever come a time—for placing our brethren of opposing creeds at a disadvantage. God knows that I love with a full heart Christians who do not wear the Baptist name. If feet-washing were now in vogue among us as a religious ceremony, I should desire no higher honor than to wash the feet of some of the very men who most bitterly oppose our views. They may not love us, but they love Christ, our Master, and I hope and pray that in time they may come to love our Baptist principles. Learned theologians of all faiths seem to be more favorable to us than formerly, and there is among Protestants a constant approximation to our views. Positions that a hundred years ago were distinctly and peculiarly Baptist, and for which thousands of our people suffered stripes and imprisonment, are now firmly held by millions who do not wear the Baptist name.

LEAVENING THE LUMP.

Thank God, Baptist leaven is spreading throughout the whole lump in this, our "Baptist America," and we are mercifully saved from that dead formalism which otherwise would rest like a nightmare upon us. "The Goddess of Liberty" stands upon our shores, and with uplifted torch is "enlightening the world." With the blessing of God, Baptist principles will more and more prevail in this, our loved land, and they will be preached and adopted in all lands. Some day in the coming years—God hasten that day!—the sun in his journey will not look down upon any section of this globe of ours unblessed by these principles.

Baptist principles, when rightly held, lead to a life of consecration to God's service and to a worldwide philanthropy. One cannot take this Baptist idea into his heart without taking with it all else that is good. He is false to his burial with Christ, if there is in him no resurrection to a new life. He must feel, as Paul felt, that this world has been put upon his shoulders, that he may lift it up to God; that every human being has a claim upon his best energies; that his commission is to each and every being on earth. Nothing less than such a consecrated life does the Baptist idea demand, and nothing less will it accept.

And here let me say that, as a matter of fact, Baptists have led in agencies for the world's redemption. Were not Carey and Thomas, the pioneers in foreign missions, Baptists? Was not the first Foreign Mission Society of modern times formed by English Baptists in 1792? Were not Adoniram Judson and Luther Rice among the first to go from America to the heathen? Were not the first Christian churches organized in India and Burmah, and China and Siam, Baptist churches? And are not more than one-third of all the converts from heathenism Baptists? And have not the Baptists ever been the true and fast friends of education? Have they not sought everywhere to enlighten the masses, reaching down to the lowest and up to the highest? Who but Baptists made the earliest translations of God's Word into heathen tongues? Was not the first Bible Society called into being under the leadership of Joseph Hughes, a Baptist minister? And does not a Baptist deacon share with Robert Raikes the honor of originating the Sunday school? In every great movement for the evangelization of the world Baptists have held no mean place. Nor is this strange. The very principles underlying our system bind us to go into all the world and preach the gospel to every creature. That Baptist would better never have been born into the world who refuses to do all in his power to save the world, and that Baptist church which knows nothing of this sense of responsibility to save the perishing nations of earth can do for the Baptist name no nobler service than to lay that name aside and wear it no more.

No word of mine can do the subject justice. I cannot tell—no man living can tell—what Baptist principles are worth to this poor, sin- what Baptist principles are worth to this poor, sinning sorrowing world of ours. The world is bad enough as it is, but who can tell how much worse it would be but for these principles? Who can tell what this uplifting of the word and authority of God has been worth to humanity? Who knows what a calamity it would have been, had the ordinances of the gospel been lost to the world, and these two great monumental pillars in the house of our God been torn to pieces and forever cast aside? Where is there under the blue arch of heaven a man who has more than the faintest conception of what religious liberty is worth to the world? Who can tell how much of the good done by other Christian denominations comes from the influence, direct or indirect, of this Baptist idea upon their heads and hearts?

No, brethren, I beg to be excused. You might as well ask me to tell you what the shining sun in mid-heavens is worth. It cannot be done; life is too short to tell it all. A greater calamity than the overthrow of Baptist principles one can scarcely conceive. If any are seeking to bring this to pass, they know not what they do. To succeed would be to wreck and forever overthrow the beautiful and symmetrical system as given by Christ and his apostles, and snatch from a perishing world its brightest—I might almost say its only—hope.

BEST OF ALL, GOD IS WITH US.

But, brethren, you need not fear any such catastrophe. The God of providence is our God. He has often turned the bitterest enemies of the Baptists into their most helpful friends. Many of the greatest names in Baptist history are names that have come to us from other denominations. How often, in searching for arguments against us, have men and women found that the Baptists have a "Thus saith the Lord, and gone forth frankly confessing that our position must stand while the inspired record stands.

If Baptists could have been overthrown, it would have been done long ago. Almost every weapon has been tried against them, and with what result? Since our Lord bade us go into all the world and disciple all nations, baptizing them into the name of the Father, Son, and Holy Ghost, there has never dawned a day when the prospect for the Baptists was brighter than it is this day, and the morrow will be for them brighter still. These principles of ours are yet to be laurel-crowned. To use the words of a celebrated Baptist martyr: "Divine truth is immortal. It may be scourged, crucified, and for a season entombed, but on the third day it will rise again victorious, and rule triumphant forever." That Baptist martyr did not overstate the great fact; for back of these Baptist principles is the Almighty throne, and it is pledged to their complete triumph. If there were but one Baptist on the earth, he might throw his banner to the breeze with a full and unquestioning faith that it will surely and completely win in the great coming struggle.

"Every plant which my Heavely Father hath not planted shall be rooted up." Multitudes in other denominations believe as we do, and the number of such increases daily. Their preachers may preach some other baptism, but more and more their people are practising ours, and daily they are seeing more clearly that infant baptism is without divine authority.

Let us gird ourselves for the conflict. To-day one of the chief points of attack is the integrity of the inspired Word. The enemies of Christianity are gathering at this point as never before, and the very atmosphere around us seems to be laden with skepticism. The mission of the Baptists is hardly yet begun. Theirs is the post of honor in the conflict for God's Word. Clad in God's armor, they must more than ever stand in serried phalanx where the fight is hottest. It is a most comforting paradox that as we defend the Bible it furnishes us with weapons, defensive and offensive.

THE BRIGHTER DAYS.

If God has wrought so mightily through the Baptists in the past, with all their lack of faith, and zeal, and tact, and toil, what may we not hope for in the better days that are ahead of us, when we shall realize as never before the weighty responsibilities which press upon us—in the coming days, when we shall see that having more truth than others devolves upon us the solemn obligation to live a more holy, a more consecrated life? We are Christ's witnesses, and his only witnesses, for the great distinctive principles he has committed to us. Shall he look in vain to us to witness aright for him?

There can be but one issue of the struggle, unequal as it is, with all the mighty forces arrayed against us. He who is for us is mightier than they who are against us. "As we have received Christ Jesus the Lord, so let us walk in him." Let us teach these Baptist principles to all the people, and in doing that let us not forget our own children. And let us cultivate fraternal relations with other Christian denominations. Let us give them full credit for all the good they are doing, and rejoice with them in it all. Often their holy zeal and Christian endurance will put us to the blush, and cause impartial observers to say that, while Baptists have the doctrine, others have the practice. Let us seek to profit by all this, and then, at last, when the crowning day shall come, it will appear to all that not only have Baptist principles been valuable to the world, but invaluable.

Madison Clinton Peters, D. D.
1859-1918.
Pastor of Immanuel Baptist Church, Baltimore, MD.

Why I Became a Baptist.

BY MADISON C. PETERS, D. D., OF NEW YORK.

[In the year 1900, Dr. Madison C. Peters, of New York, one of the most popular and prominent Pedobaptist preachers in that great city, resigned his flourishing pastorate and announced his purpose to unite with the Baptists. This he promptly did, and was duly baptized by Dr. R. S. MacArthur. Shortly afterwards, a representative of the Religious Herald sought him out and secured from him the following interview, which was printed in the Herald of June 7, 1900. As setting forth the views and opinions of a trained Pedobaptist preacher on whom the light has broken, the paper is of unique and remarkable value.—R. H. Pitt.]

Question: How long were you in the Presbyterian and Reformed ministry?

Answer: I entered the ministry of the Reformed church in Indiana when twenty years of age, preaching in both the English and German languages. After two years, I concluded that I could be more useful if I gave myself to preaching to an entirely English congregation. I determined, therefore, to leave a church of over 1,000 members, and entered the Presbyterian ministry at Terre Haute, Ind., starting a new enterprise in an abandoned Methodist church. I may say that going from the Reformed to the Presbyterian church can hardly be called a denominational change, as in all matters of faith and practice they are essentially one, and ministers transfer from one to the other as though they were one and the same. In about six months we had perfected an organization, known as the Greenwood Presbyterian church, now known as the Washington Avenue Presbyterian church. I came to this church as a "supply," and when the organization was complete and the church ready to call a minister, feeling that I might be more useful somewhere else, Rev. Thomas Parry, now of Pittsburg, called my attention to the Presbyterian church at Ottawa, Ill., a church which had been closed for several years, and which had long been considered a forlorn hope. The very desperateness of the condition attracted me. There were just twenty-seven people left in the membership, and these seemed only too glad to give me a chance. I shall never forget the look on Mr. S. S. Scott's face, the elder of the church, and one of the leading merchants of the city. My enthusiasm seemed to take his breath away. I began to preach, after the steps of the church, which had rotted away, were repaired. The city had a population of about 10,000. I at once began a systematic canvass of the town, and before long I had shaken hands with nearly all the men and women in the town, and was on good terms with the babies. The audiences began to gather, and during the fifteen months of my ministry 143 joined the church. One of my printed sermons fell into the hands of an old minister in Philadelphia, who handed it to one of the elders of the old First Northern Liberties Presbyterian church, Philadelphia. An invitation to preach followed. A call was extended. This old down-town church had long been given up as a forlorn hope. Hotels, boarding-houses, schools, and colleges abounded in the neighborhood. I studied by day and visited by night. The crowds began to gather, and before long I was compelled to preach to overflowing meetings in the basement. Five hundred joined the church in five years. At twenty-nine, I received a call to the Bloomingdale Reformed church, Broadway and Sixty-eighth street, New York. This church had been in the slough of despond. A congregational meeting was called to elect a minister. Eleven gathered, and I am pleased to say that I received all the eleven votes. Inherited wealth enabled a small congregation to build one of the handsomest church edifices in this city, with a fifty-feet-front parsonage adjoining on Broadway.

Question: What was the character of the congregation you gathered in New York?

Answer: The Reformed church in New York has a small constituency. She has enormous wealth in what is known as the Collegiate church. I found, after a thorough canvass of my section of the city, that there were not more than two or three families who were Dutch Reformed, either by birth or education. To build up a church along denominational lines was, therefore, out of the question. Beginning with sixty-four members, composed of various denominations, a congregation of less than 100, and a Sunday school of twenty-one, I had at the time of my resignation a communicant membership of 600, a Sunday school of 650, and a congregation crowding our large auditorium. For no one thing am I more grateful than that I was permitted to bring God's truth to such various minds and souls as constantly gathered to hear me. My membership was composed of eleven different denominations of Protestants, while scores of Jews and Catholics were in constant attendance upon my ministry.

Question: What led you to become interested in the matter of "infant baptism"?

Answer: The superstitious regard with which Pedobaptists hold infant baptism was always repulsive to me. That repulsiveness grew until I became filled with insufferable disgust. In eleven years in New York, I never preached on baptism, and practised infant baptism in public once only. I never did—and I know very few Presbyterian ministers who do—use the prescribed form, which declares that baptism is not only a "sign," but a "seal of ingrafting into Christ, of regeneration, of remission of sins." The Reformed church declares that the christened baby is "sanctified in Christ."

Question: What is the basis of the remark sometimes made that there are many ministers, not Baptists, who do not believe in infant baptism?

Answer: For fully three months before I became a Baptist I talked with scores of my brethren on infant baptism, and nearly all of them declared that they looked upon it as a dedication, a consecration of both the child and the parents. I believe that the majority of baby-sprinklers do not in their hearts consider it baptism; very few, except the Episcopalians, use the prescribed form.

Question: Is infant baptism lessening its hold on the minds of persons not connected with Baptist churches?

Answer: Infant baptism is undoubtedly dying out among intelligent Christians. It is now practised almost exclusively by the ignorant and superstitious. I have had women to drag their weary frames to my house hundreds of times, with babes from ten to fourteen days old, "to get them christened," for "fear they wouldn't have any luck." It may not be known that "baby-christening" is a source of revenue. Many German preachers derive a large part of their income from "infant baptism." It may be that Pedobaptist preachers fight so hard against "infant baptism" dying out because "it pays."

Question: Did you have any experiences in connection with infant baptism which produced a crisis in your attitude towards it?

Answer: About two years ago, one of my Episcopalian parishioners asked me to "baptize" her baby, and requested that I use the Episcopal service. When I got to that part in the Book of Common Prayer which reads, "Seeing now, dearly beloved brethren, that this child is regenerate and grafted into the body of Christ's church," I began to sweat. I stood condemned a hypocrite and liar. I knew different; every sensible man does. I was handed a splendid fee for the performance of the "rite," as is the custom. I went home feeling that the whole thing was a farce, a fraud perpetrated on an innocent babe. Infant baptism got its death knell with me on that day.

Question: Why did it take so long for you to reach your present convictions?

Answer: There is a difference between a man having a conviction and the conviction having the man.

Question: What does it cost a man in his feelings and prospects and ideals to make such a change?

Answer: I can assure you it is not a comfortable position to take, in which you not only confess to thousands, who have for eleven years believed all you told them about divine things, that you have been wrong all your life, and also pronounce thereby an unwilling judgment upon others, who remain where you have been. I had a happy pastorate—a people whose kindly counsel and generous support made my work among them delightful. It was a position of power and influence, and, taken all in all, one which ought to have filled the cup of any man's ambition. I had a life position, a palatial home, a good salary, and perquisites galore. For months I passed sleepless nights, debating whether I should stand by people who for eleven years had stood by me, and go on smothering my convictions, or be an honest man and preach what I could practise and practise what I could preach, and, though the saddest day of my life, it was the happiest, when I made answer of "a good conscience toward God," resigned my church, and went down into the baptismal waters and was baptized in Christ's appointed way. And now at forty, I start life over again, ready to begin once more at the bottom.

Question: What were the Scripture reasons for rejecting "infant baptism"?

Answer: I am glad you say "Scripture reasons" for "rejecting," as there are none for practising "infant baptism." Our Lord baptized disciples. He blessed babies. The Lord's great commission enjoins baptism only on those who believe. Peter baptized those who "gladly received his word." The Samaritans were baptized "when they believed." It was when the Ethiopian could say that he "believed in Christ with all his heart" that he was baptized. Not until Paul had been "filled with the Holy Ghost" was he baptized. It was not until they were "taught" and "believed" and "received the Holy Ghost" that Cornelius and his friends were baptized. It was when Crispus and his house "believed in the Lord" that they were baptized. Paul tells us that those only are fit subjects for baptism who are ready to bury the old sinful life and lead a new and holy life. Peter tells us that baptism is "the answer of a good conscience towards God." On all occasions in the New Testament the apostles required repentance before baptism. There is not a single instance in the New Testament but baptism was a matter of choice by those who were baptized.

Question: How do you get around the households mentioned in Scripture as having been baptized?

Answer: 1. That of the Philippian jailer; but to his household the word was first spoken, and all of them, we are told, were believing in God. 2. That of Stephanus, of whose household it is said that they "addicted themselves to the ministry of the saints." 3. That of Lydia. To prove infant baptism by Lydia and her household, you must prove three things: (1) That Lydia had a husband; (2) that she had children; (3) that the children were babies. It would seem from the story that Lydia was a single woman at the head of a household, and her household were her servants, who helped her in the dyeing business. I rejected infant baptism because it was unscriptural, because it implies a libel on God—it implies that baptism is a saving ordinance, and most people who have their babies baptized, if they do not believe in the horrible doctrine of infant damnation, yet secretly fear that without "baptism" their darling babe might be lost. "Infant baptism" nourishes the idea in people that something has been performed towards their salvation, and that somehow they will be saved because they are within the church.

W. R. L. SMITH, D. D.
1846-1935.
Pastor of Second Baptist Church, Richmond, VA.

Candid Scholarship.

BY W. R. L. SMITH, D. D., RICHMOND, VA.

It is safe to say that Hastings' "Dictionary of the Bible" and "The International Critical Commentary on the Holy Scriptures," when completed, are likely to contain the finest body of biblical learning in the English-speaking world. While these works are not radical, they do candidly accept many of the decisions of recent critical research. Their spirit is perfectly loyal and reverent, while their method is constructive, and not destructive. Of course, they must be read with care and caution. Having on our shelves two instalments of the first work and five of the latter, we have naturally sought to discover their quality of scholarly fairness by examination of their treatment of New Testament baptism. The inspection has been of the most gratifying and assuring character. Controversial evasions, shifts, and dodges are abjured as irreverent and contemptible in its eyes. The calm, dispassionate, impartial spirit of scientific inquiry has at last seemed to enter victoriously into the realm of biblical study.

It will be useful and interesting to set in order, briefly, their learned testimonies on the subject of baptism.

HASTINGS.

"The simple verb 'baptein' in the Old and New

Testaments is frequent in the sense of 'dip' or 'immerse.'"

"The verb is sometimes followed by a preposition, indicating either the element into which or in which the immersion takes place."

Speaking of proselyte baptism, it is said: "His sponsors took him to a pool, in which he stood up to his neck in water; and he plunged beneath the water, taking care to be entirely submerged."

Again: "Scripture tells us that repentance and faith are requisite for baptism." "Not only is there no mention of the baptism of infants, but there is no text from which such baptism can be securely inferred." Yet, strange to say, right in the face of these brave admissions, the writer goes on to make the usual impotent pleas for infant baptism—such as the silence of Scripture, household baptisms, the naturalness of it, &c. But it is the witness of his scholarship in the revealed word that concerns us, and not his confessedly unwarranted conjectures.

Coming to the great Commentary, let us take

GOULD ON MARK.

Mark 1. 4.—The baptism of repentance: "This rite of immersion in water signified the complete inward purification of the subject."

PLUMMER ON LUKE.

"*Baptizo* is intensive from *bapto*. *Bapto*, 'I dip'; *baptizo*, 'I immerse.'" "It is only when baptism is administered by immersion that its full significance is seen."

SANDAY ON ROMANS.

"Baptism expresses symbolically a series of acts corresponding to the redeeming acts of Christ.

Immersion—Death.
Submersion—Burial.
Emergence—Resurrection."

Commenting on Romans vi. 4, he says: "When we descended into the baptismal water, that meant that we died with Christ—to sin. When the water closed over our heads, that meant that we lay buried with him, in proof that our death to sin, like his death, was real."

Thus these men, learned, reverent, and conscientious, speak of our Lord's sacred institution. They are all Pedobaptists, and yet not one of them seems to have heard that any man ever tried to fix "affusion" or "sprinkling" as a definition of *bapto*, or *baptizo*. The candor of these scholars on this long belabored and stubbornly contested doctrine has given us a delightfully comfortable confidence in their intellectual honesty. This is a great point gained, and alas for the teacher or writer who fails to inspire it!

BEYSCHLAG'S TESTIMONY.

This profound and illustrious German theologian has the following in his recent book on New Testament Theology: "It is the symbolism of baptism, of immersion and burial in the water, that causes

Paul, in Rom. vi. and Col. ii., to connect the being dead with Christ with baptism rather than with faith." "There is no mention in his (Paul's) writings, or in any part of the New Testament, of a baptism of children." "All that has been read into the Acts of the Apostles about the baptism of children is pure fancy."

Here is the unequivocal, unqualified statement of another great Pedobaptist scholar. It is a good sign. There has never been a time when biblical learning was nearly so masterful or so fearlessly honest as it is to-day. Its massive intelligence impatiently overwhelms the tiresome and outworn discussions of "pouring" and "sprinkling." Real learning knows nothing, *absolutely* nothing, of either in the New Testament. And yet a great and reputable body of American Christians solemnly stated, not long ago, to an intelligent world, that immersion is not Christian baptism! It was a courageous thing to do, but it does not enhance respect for the intellectual powers of the human race. It is a terrible thing to have the Bible against you.

R. H. PITT, D. D.
1853-1937.
Editor of The Religious Herald, Richmond, VA.

Sunday Observance and Religious Liberty.

BY R. H. PITT, D. D., EDITOR OF THE RELIGIOUS HERALD, RICHMOND VA.

[The following paper, omitting certain local and occasional matter, which has been for obvious reasons edited out, was prepared by me, at the request of Drs. J. B. Hawthorne, Thomas S. Dunaway, and J. B. Hutson, and Rev. M. Ashby Jones, who served with me on a committee of the Baptist Ministers' Conference of Richmond and Vicinity, and later was adopted unanimously by the Conference. It is printed here out of deference to the, perhaps, too partial judgment of my brethren, who deem it worthy of permanent preservation. If it has any merit, it is in the fact that it discusses briefly, and, I venture to hope, with some discrimination, the application of the doctrine of religious liberty to a very practical question. We have much valuable literature telling of the struggle for the establishment of this doctrine, but scarcely any showing its application to the practical questions which are continually arising.—R. H. Pitt.]

We feel constrained to put on record our cordial and steadfast belief that the State has no right to legislate concerning Sunday as a holy or religious day, and that, when the civil arm is invoked for the protection of that day, it must not be on the ground that the day is a Christian institution, but on the ground that certain physical and economic laws, which have been disclosed and verified by the experience of mankind, render cessation from ordinary labor necessary one day in seven, and it falls in with the convenience of the public, for obvious reasons, to fix the first day in the week as that period. If the State is to protect the day as a religious day, as an institution of the Christian religion, then why limit legislation to the mere matter of cessation from ordinary labor? As a Christian institution, the duties of worship and of active Christian work are not less obligatory on that day than the duty of rest. Indeed, it may be safely maintained that, in passing from the old Sabbath to the new Lord's-day, the emphasis was changed. Rest was the main idea of the seventh, worship and Christian work are the chief features of the first day. It would be singular, indeed, to appeal for protective legislation for the day as a Christian institution, and yet neglect in such legislation the chief Christian features of the day—to enforce the Jewish idea of rest and ignore the Christian ideas of religious work and worship! And this, too, while the ground on which such legislation is urged is that the day is a Christian institution, and ours is a Christian nation.

The emphasis which has been laid upon this statement, that "we are a Christian nation," and the insistent assertion that we have therefore the right to enact general Christian legislation, to discriminate in favor of the Christian religion as against any other, though not to discriminate in favor of any special sect of Christians, seems to make it necessary to travel over somewhat familiar ground and to restate some fundamental principles.

We *are* a Christian people, in the sense that the great majority of our people are either actively or nominally sympathetic with some form of the Christian religion; we *are not* a Christian nation, in the sense that we have a right to impose by law distinctively Christian duties upon others. The ethical principles which Christianity presents in their most complete form, and which are reflected to a gratifying degree in our laws, are not true because they are taught by Christ and his inspired followers. Christ taught them because they were true, and they would have been true if he had never taught them. They are eternally and unchangeably true. For this reason, and not because Christ taught them, are they inwrought in our laws. Of course, this by no means implies that Christianity has not put added emphasis on many of these principles and made it possible to give them full recognition in the laws of the State. That the State depends for its safety and stability upon the prevalence of pure religion among its constituents is certainly true; that the State cannot properly administer in religion is equally true.

We can easily test for ourselves the validity of the new and modified doctrine of the separation of Church and State, which, we regret to say, has gained currency recently, and against which we earnestly protest. If ours is "a Christian nation," in the sense that we may properly invoke State support for Christianity or for its institutions, then why for one Christian institution and not for another? Why for Christian Sunday, and not for Christian baptism? If for Sunday, which commemorates the resurrection, why not for Good Friday, which a large portion—indeed, a large majority—of the Christian world holds peculiarly sacred as the anniversary of the crucifixion?

It is somewhat vaguely set out that, while the State may not discriminate among the various sects of Christians so as to favor one at the expense of another, it may enact a sort of general Christian legislation. But the moment the State undertakes to support and protect distinctively Christian institutions by law, because they *are* Christian, it is surely guilty of unjust discrimination in two directions. First, and most obvious, is the discrimination againt non-Christians. They are compelled at once to the extent of this protective legislation to support the institutions of a religion in which they do not believe. This is utterly subversive of personal liberty and abhorrent to the foundation principles of the Christian religion, which never proposes to get itself established or propagated by the sword or the civil arm. But, supposing that the unbelievers are for one reason or another a negligible quantity, there is inevitable discrimination among believers; for, if the State undertakes to support a Christian institution as such, it must define it, it must interpret it. And when it begins its work of definition and interpretation, it will be confronted with an embarrassment of riches. Whose definition shall be regarded as orthodox? In the most conservative community, the prevalent views of the Lord's-day, of its relation to the Jewish Sabbath and the fourth commandment, of how far the restrictions surrounding the old apply to the new day, are as various as the individuals who hold them. Whose views shall prevail? Shall we settle these matters of religion by a majority vote? Besides, what would we do with that small, but devoted, body of Christians who hold that the *ancient* Sabbath remains, and that it is their sacred duty to observe it?

Over against all this crudity and confusion we may put a few sentences from the immortal "Memorial and Remonstrance" drawn by James Madison, and submitted to the Virginia General Assembly in 1785. The occasion was the anticipated consideration of the "General Assessment Bill," which had been introduced at a previous session. This was not a bill to establish any one sect as against others, but to establish "provision for the teachers of the Christian religion," of whatever name—just the sort of legislation which, we are now told, we have a right as a "Christian nation" to enact. Against this bill the famous remonstrance was written. Here are some of its sentiments: "The religion, then, of every man must be left to the conviction and conscience of every man, and it is the right of every man to exercise it as these may dictate. This right is, by its nature, an unalienable right." * * * "We maintain, therefore, that in matters of religion no man's right is abridged by the institution of civil society, and that religion is wholly exempt from its cognizance." * * * "The bill implies either that the civil magistrate is a competent judge of religious truths or that he may employ religion as an engine of civil policy. The first is an arrogant pretention, falsified by the extraordinary opinion of rulers in all ages and throughout the world; the second, an unhallowed perversion of the means of salvation."

This "Memorial" argues that such legislation as was proposed corrupted Christianity, was unnecessary for the support of the civil government, "departed from the generous policy which" offered "an asylum to the persecuted and oppressed," destroyed the "moderation and harmony" which prevailed then among the sects, was "adverse to the diffusion of Christianity," and finally that this invasion of an inalienable right imperilled all other civil liberties, which had been won at such frightful cost. It need not be added that the General Assessment Bill never saw the light. It died in committee.

We are at pains to quote thus freely for two reasons: First, these views of Madison were fully shared by Thomas Jefferson and George Mason. The former drew the "Act to Establish Religious Freedom," which, offered by Mr. Madison, was adopted by the General Assembly of Virginia, December 16, 1785, and which provided "That no man shall be compelled to frequent or support any religious worship, place, or ministry whatsoever; nor shall be enforced, restrained, molested, or burthened in his body or goods, nor shall otherwise suffer on account of his religious opinions or belief; but that all men shall be free to profess and by argument to maintain their opinions in matters of religion, and that the same shall in no wise diminish, enlarge, or affect their civil capacities." The latter (Mr. Mason) was the author of the Virginia Bill of Rights, while James Madison himself moved the adoption of the first amendment to the Constitution of the United States, which declares that "Congress shall make no law respecting an establishment of religion or prohibiting the free exercise thereof." Hence Mr. Madison's "Remonstrance" helps us—if, indeed, we need any help—to interpret his amendment. And Mr. Jefferson's and Mr. Mason's sympathy with Mr. Madison shed light on the significance of the "Act to Establish Religious Liberty" and the Bill of Rights, of which they were respectively the authors.

But we are giving attention to this matter for another reason. The principle with whose advocacy Baptists are historically and doctrinally identified is on trial in various ways. We are told that the courts have decided against it. As a fact, the decisions of the courts have varied touching this, as they have concerning all other questions, but the tendency of the decisions has been toward the full recognition of the principle. And, if we were careful to quote human authorities, it might be said, in answer to any decisions that looked in the other direction, that Congress has in recent years had the whole question of the relation of the State to religion exhaustively debated, with the result that by an overwhelming majority appropriations to sectarian schools in the Indian Territory have been abandoned, and on the distinct ground that these appropriations were in support of religion. But, as Baptists maintained this principle when courts, legislatures, and popular opinion were all against it, it would be strange indeed if an occasional court decision seemingly out of sympathy with it should break their allegiance. It goes without saying that courts and legislatures have frequently invaded the principle and perverted the doctrine of separation of Church and State. Some of the customs and traditions which prevailed in the days of the Establishment still linger among us. They are not of great importance, but we hope to see the day when every trace of the old and hateful tyranny has disappeared.

The principle is on trial, too, in Cuba and the Philippines. Among the many perplexing questions arising in connection with our new colonial policy is this constantly recurring one of Church and State. It is not the time to palter with this great doctrine of the separation of the two. If our fathers, speaking through Mr. Madison, could "take alarm at the first experiment upon their liberties," surely we, who know how hardly the battle was won, and who know from how many unexpected directions it has been and is being assailed, ought now to be ceaselessly vigilant.

Benajah Harvey Carroll, D. D., LL. D.
1843-1914.
Principal of Southwestern Baptist Theological Seminary.

One Hundred Years Ago.

CONDENSED FROM HOT SPRINGS CENTENNIAL ADDRESS, BY B. H. CARROLL, D. D., OF TEXAS.

It is next to the impossible to draw a realistic picture of times prior to one's own experience, observation, and recollection. It is quite impossible to find distinct lines of cleavage at any century mile-stone. Concerning any great thought or movement of time, who can put his finger on date and place, and confidently say, "This is when and where it started?" Past, present, and coming events are mingled and related like the waves of the sea. Centuries are not divided from each other by mountain ranges, oceans, rivers, or chasms. History, like nature, has no leaps. If we go back 100 years, we must go beyond, or find ourselves reading the middle volume of a serial. It is equally impossible for me to turn my back on the present, like a Chinaman, and worship ancestors. Habitual dwelling among reminiscences indicates death at the top. Yet sometimes

> " 'Tis greatly wise to talk with our past hours
> And ask them what report they bore to heaven."

With this purpose, let us now for one hour turn back the shadow on the dial-plate of time 100 years; turn it back until we are boys again—back until we become our own fathers; yet back until we are become our grandfathers. The process reverses Rip Van Winkle's dream and loses us with strange identity in a strange world, experiencing the sensations of Mark Twain's Yankee at King Arthur's court.

The time is January 1, 1800. The place is Philadelphia, both capital and metropolis of the United States, and nearly as large as Dallas, Texas. The Alien and Sedition laws are in force. John Adams is President, with fast fading power, prestige, and popularity, and this very year he will be overwhelmingly beaten by Thomas Jefferson, who will be inaugurated next March at the new capital on the Potomac. George Washington has been dead about two weeks. Philadelphia itself is in mourning on account of a malignant fever prevalent here for some years. The old Philadelphia Association, which for nearly a century rarely convened out of this city, has been kept out now for three years in succession by this awful plague. Since 1797, they have been praying, fasting, and resolving concerning this dreadful visitation, and for at least seven years to come each annual minute will record that Philadelphia has been selected as the place of the next meeting; *provided* there be no recurrence of the malignant and contagious fever.

The year 1800! The crucial period of national trial is safely passed. By the ratification of the Federal Constitution the United States has become a nation. Washington was inaugurated in New York eleven years ago as President of eleven United States. During the year, North Carolina ratified the Constitution and entered the Union. Ten years ago, Rhode Island, the last of the original thirteen States, came in. Nine years ago, Kentucky followed; four years ago, Tennessee made the third. Sixteen States in 1800. The first census (1790) shows a population of something over 4,000,000. This decade will advance it a million. One hundred years ago! How must one shrink to fit the environment! Westward the national boundaries extend to the Mississippi river; southward to the mouth of the Yazoo river near Vicksburg, but nowhere touching the Gulf of Mexico. Spanish Florida, joining hands with Spanish Louisiana, blocks the way southward and westward. This very year Louisiana—a veritable empire of territory—will be retroceded to France, and three years hence Jefferson will buy it from Bonaparte, whose fear of Admiral Nelson surrenders colonial empire for the paltry sum of $15,000,000. The great Northwest territory, ceded by Virginia and conquered by George Rogers Clark, has been open to settlement for three years. Only four years ago, in tardy compliance with the treaty of 1783, the English garrisons were withdrawn from the forts which dominated it. Five years hence, a brother of the same Clark, with Merriwether Lewis, sent out by the same Jefferson, will add to the national domain by exploration the vast territory now covered by Oregon, Washington, and Idaho. The French Revolution, which painted red the skies of the world, has given place to the Directory, which is Napoleon

Bonaparte. An indiscreet envoy from that republic, impatient at Washington's wise forbearance to embarrass our new nation with entangling alliances, has recently appealed from the President to the people, and by private canvass and agitation stirs up a commotion whose rebuke led up to the threshold of war with France and unsealed the triumphant thunders of Truxton's guns.

One hundred years ago! It is just eight years since Eli Whitney, at Savannah, invented the cotton gin, which will revolutionize the industrial world. And, though there are some people, both North and South, projecting with the application of steam to navigation and commerce, it is yet seven years to Fulton's steamboat and thirty years to the first railroad and forty-four years to the first telegraphic message. The reaper, the power loom, and a thousand other mighty inventions are in the unknown future. Each community is isolated from every other by land travel. Philadelphia hears on New Year's Day how New York celebrated Christmas, and one adventurous man had travelled overland from Atlantic tidewater to Oregon in only eight months. Fenimore Cooper and Washington Irving are boys of seventeen, and William Cullen Bryant is a lad of seven.

But what about the Baptists of that day? In the United States, we have as data, contemporaneous with the first census in 1790, Asplund's Register, which shows in statistics, State by State, that there were in this country 564 Baptist preachers,

748 churches, 60,970 members. But that was ten years ago. A circular letter, to be read next year (1801) before the Philadelphia Baptist Association, will say: "We have entered upon a new century, and, while it is yet the morning of it, let us take a view of some of the works of God in the last. Ninety-four years have rolled on since the first meeting of this Association, the first in America, and then composed of only five churches; but, viewing the present state of our connection in this country, we perceive it to be as the thousands of Israel, embracing numerous associations, composed of at least 1,200 churches, including more than 100,000 members." You see, by the way, that these early Baptists knew when a century commences. The writer does not give the original sources of information from which he obtained his figures; but he seems to speak advisedly and with confidence.

Fortunately, we have the full text of the centennial sermon commemorative of the 100th anniversary of the organization of the Association, which was preached in 1807. The preacher is Samuel Jones, a noted man in his day. He preached from William Carey's text to show that the great things expected and attempted fourteen years ago have been marvellously fulfilled. Without accurate statistics before him from other associations, the preacher concludes that there are 122,500 Baptists in the United States in 1807. He reckons 194 churches in Massachusetts and 150 in New York. He observes with pleasure that religious persecution of his brethren had ceased in Virginia and had abated in Massachusetts. He calls special attention to the missionary spirit prevalent for years in many places, tending to carry the gospel to the heathen world, and expects the millennium to come by the opening of the twentieth century. We can testify that it has not yet arrived.

Unquestionably, the great and historic association in the Western world 100 years ago was the Philadelphia Association. It is the Mother Eve of American associations. From the beginning it has been sound in faith and missionary in spirit. We hear much in that olden time of Virginia and the Carolinas sending help in many ways to New England, but Philadelphia sent help southward, and her gospel came with healing in its wings. There was in 1800 no State or national organization of our people, but there were general committees and widespread co-operation for missions, education, and particularly for mutual protection against civil and religious persecution. There were no Sunday schools of the modern kind, but there was much private and catechetical instruction. All the principles underlying the wider forms of present co-operation were then in full force.

OLD VIRGINIA.

My heart always thrills at the name. The history of two States in this Union furnishes higher themes for epic poems than the less heroic affairs which inspired the songs of Homer and Virgil. One of the two is Virginia—modesty forbids that

I name the other. From the beginning of its entrancing history until this good hour, life in the Old Dominion was set to heroic measure. Higher criticism has utterly failed to destroy the historic verity of the romantic story of John Smith and Pocahontas. You know Virginia once extended on the Atlantic coast from Cape Cod to Florida and straight westward to the Pacific Ocean, supposed to lie somewhere back of the Blue Ridge. There is yet preserved the record of an old-time writer who states his case in a charming way. He calls attention to the intrusion of some Swedes upon Virginia soil, who were making their way up a river called Delaware, and of certain nosing Dutch who were also trespassing on a river called Hudson. He wonders at two things—first, how far it may be from the falls of the James river, afterwards the site of Richmond, to the Pacific Ocean, Virginia's other boundary, where Drake had been sailing; and, second, that the 20,000 Puritans of New England did not leave their cold and barren shores and come down to God's country, where wild turkeys weigh sixty pounds, where raccoons are as good as lambs, 'possums as good as hams, artichokes as sweet as yams, and where are such worlds of good tobacco, and where the rivers teem with bass and shad. You see there was some imagination there, even then. The religious denominations were famous in old Virginia. The Episcopal was the State church, which, for support, made awful inroads on Baptist tobacco. Their own Bishop

Meade tells us some marvellous stories of the gambling, swearing, horse-racing, cock-fighting, and drunken clergy, who assumed to monopolize gospel functions. One of them was a noted pugilist, who, getting into some trouble with his vestrymen, floored them all in a knock-down and drag-out fight. The following Sunday, he commemorated his victory in a sermon from this text of Nehemiah: "And I contended with them, and cursed them, and smote certain of them, and plucked off their hair."

After the Revolutionary war, there were wonderful revivals among the Virginia Baptists. In 1790-2, there were 200 churches and 20,000 members, to become as the new century opens nearly 400 churches, with 35,000 members, and that, too, after peopling Kentucky by migration. Oftentimes a whole church, pastor and people, would move together to a new field, without a break in organization or regular service. As in the beginning "the groves were God's first temples," so the camp-fires of these moving Virginians lighted up the primeval forest as they worshipped God. In the first church to which I ever preached was a colony of Virginia Baptists, all members of one of the churches ministered to by that venerable Andrew Broaddus, Jr., of Caroline, who recently passed away. Often have I read the manuscript copy of his farewell sermon to these pilgrims, one of whom, his kinsman, another Andrew Broaddus, became a distinguished Texas lawyer and for years was the president of our State Baptist Convention. A century ago, there were twice as many Baptists in Virginia as in New York, and more than in all New England. Only last year (1799) their General Committee gave way to their General Conference, which, in turn, will become their General Association. Their annual meetings were famous for spiritual power, and never failed to leave a lasting and favorable impress behind. A Methodist preacher once told me that the Baptists captured Virginia by the power of their annual meetings, particularly of the old Dover Association and their General Association. Perhaps the three greatest leaders in Virginia 100 years ago were John Leland, Andrew Broaddus, Sr., and Robert Semple. John Leland was a mighty man of affairs, and played no small part in the revolutionary movements of his day. And, while I am proud of the association of his name with that of James Madison, I delight most to think of him in one of his happy pulpit efforts. It was a time of strong doctrine, and many Baptists were hyper-Calvinists in their views. But Leland himself tells us how one day, while preaching, "his soul got into the gospel trade winds," which so filled his spiritual sails that he forgot about election and reprobation, and so preached Christ to sinners that many accepted him as their Saviour and Lord. And, oh, I would to God that his people now, like old John Leland of long ago, would get into the gospel trade winds and bear away with flaming canvas the everlasting gospel to earth's remotest bounds! Andrew Broaddus was every way a remarkable man. Think of it, ye aspiring young preachers, who long for fat city pastorates, how this man kept refusing calls to New York, Boston, Philadelphia, and other mighty centres, that he might abide with his dear old country churches. Semple became the historian of that historic time, and you would do good to yourself by adding to your library his valuable record, so recently and commendably reproduced by the Religious Herald men.

THE FOUNTAINS OF THE PAST FROM WHICH FLOW THE STREAMS OF TO-DAY.

Any careful retrospect over the field of modern Baptist history reveals at a glance certain mighty facts or movements, uplifting themselves into clear visibility far above the dead level of ordinary events, as mountain peaks tower above the plain. These are the mile-stones and sign-boards along the highway of human progress. Look back yonder, while I point them out, peak by peak, and discern the mountain springs from which flow the streams whose mingled currents make up the river of present denominational power:

1. First of all, the giving of the Bible to the common people of the English-speaking world. The Bible in the mother tongue, without note of expert or comment of scholar, without a priestly shadow to darken one luminous page—the naked Bible, the Father's message to men, naturally makes Baptists. One of the most thrilling and instructive classics in our language is Harwood Pattison's "History of the English Bible." A few days ago, while dining in Judson Memorial Hall with a son of Adoniram Judson, I found myself commending this book to a bright young man, who proved to be Pattison's own son. He promised to read the book.

2. Next comes, as the natural sequence of a free Bible, that mighty struggle between the Parliament and Charles I., which culminated in the Commonwealth. To ignore that period seals up history. Ignorance of it makes it impossible to understand the Baptists of to-day. It was a colossal strife for civil and religious liberty. Victories were won in that day whose laurels will never fade and whose influence will never die; and whenever and wherever that fight has raged in the last nineteen centuries you may count that Baptists were in it, as confidently as you look for an Irishman at a wake. Wherever Cromwell's armies marched, the Baptists, who constituted a large, heroic, and influential part of them, deposited the imperishable seeds of their principles. In his Irish garrisons

(1655) were twelve Baptist governors of cities, ten colonels, three lieutenant-colonels, ten majors, and forty-three company officers. Hence Richard Baxter's growl: "In Ireland, the Anabaptists are grown so high that many of the soldiers were rebaptized as a way to preferment." In Scotland they stood unabashed under the frowns of John Knox, resisting even Cromwell's later ambition, reminding him of their timely help at Dunbar, and still later petitioned the famous General Monk, the king restorer, for high civil and religious rights. The times ripened their literary genius until it kindled flames whose light illumined the skies of the world and whose aspiring sparks hailed the stars. "The blind old bard of Scio's rocky isle" was outsoared in epic fame by a blind Baptist bard, iron Cromwell's Latin secretary. A pilgrim crept through the bars of Bedford jail and went forth into more byways and highways, knocking at more doors, and speaking to more peoples in their mother tongues than ever before or since a literary pilgrim has done. The Tinker is dead; his statue stands where four roads meet—"a very grave person, the world behind him." The tinker is dead; the statue stands. The Pilgrim moves on, outlasting the wandering Jew. Indeed, the tall, widespreading Baptist tree of to-day is deep-rooted in Cromwell's time.

3. Next in order of time and natural sequence comes *"The Act of Toleration"* (1689), during the reign of William and Mary. This was life to England, as the revocation of the edict of Nantes was death to France. They will stand over against each other till the judgment, in everlasting contrast, as light and darkness. That evil stroke of the pen of Louis XIV. hurt France more than the defeats at Blenheim, Oudenarde, and Malplaquet. That signature of William III. uplifted England more than all Marlborough's victories; and both mightily built up the Baptist power in England and her colonies.

4. Later in date, but more far-reaching in power, is William Carey's foreign mission sermon. When he spoke, the sleeping world heard two far-off cries—one from heathen lands, "Come over and help *us*," and one from the mount of ascension, "Go ye into all the world, and preach the gospel to every creature." And, wherever and whenever since, oppression lifts its heavy hand from Baptist necks and God sends revivals, they hear those two voices made audible by Carey's sermon. The cobbler's body lies moldering in the ground, but the cobbler's soul goes marching on.

5. Passing over to the New World, the struggle for religious and civil liberty in America, culminating when the members of the old Philadelphia Association, then holding their seventy-fourth session, were roused at midnight by the watchman's cry: "Past 12 o'clock and all is well, and *Cornwallis has surrendered*." Hence their resolution: "And now, dear brethren, we feel ourselves constrained to acknowledge the great goodness of God towards us, and to call on you to join with us in thankfulness and praise, as well for the unanimity and brotherly love which prevailed throughout our meeting as for the recent signal success granted to the American arms in the surrender of the whole British army under the command of Lord Cornwallis, with the effusion of so little blood." Cornwallis surrendered October 19, 1781, at Yorktown, Va. This resolution was adopted in Philadelphia four days later. Happy people who are able to reckon unanimity and brotherly love as great a cause for praise as the surrender of an enemy's army. Lord, help *us* ever to keep the lesson in mind! I can never think back into this period of fiery trials without seeing pictures. They fill a gallery in my mind. I walk among them and look up at them with bared head, in awed silence, while my heart is burning. There they are. I can see

them now. I see Roger Williams, an outcast, wandering in winter snows. I see the bared back of Obadiah Holmes, scarred with bloody stripes. I see the disgraceful spoliation of my brethren at Ashfield—their orchards, yards, fields, and the very graves of their dead sacrificed under forced sale to supply funds for a needless meeting-house of another denomination and to pay this Pedobaptist preacher's salary—himself there bidding in their property for a song. And this only six years before the battle of Lexington, and not so very far from that historic field. I see the venerable Isaac Backus at the meeting of the first Continental Congress, laboring vainly with the Massachusetts delegates in behalf of religious liberty for his persecuted people, and hear the reply of John Adams, that "you might as well attempt to turn the heavenly luminaries from their course as to ask Massachusetts to give up the union of Church and State." In this year (1800) Backus has yet seven years to live, and it will be twenty-seven years more before this unnatural union is dissolved in Massachusetts. It will be 1820 before Connecticut has religious liberty.

But we are yet in the picture gallery. This time the scenes are from old Virginia. I see Lewis Craig, John Burrus, Edward Herndon, James Goolrick, Bartholomew Choning, Edwin Saunders, and John Waller in jail for the crime of preaching the gospel without Episcopal license. I see letters written to them while incarcerated and their replies from behind prison bars. I hear them preaching through prison windows to friends gathered outside. I read the Baptist addresses and memorials and petitions addressed to the House of Burgesses, to the President of the United States. They bear familiar signatures—Samuel Harriss, Reuben Ford, John Waller. I see the historic forms of Washington, Jefferson, Madison, and Patrick Henry, giving better counsel and help than John Adams gave to Father Backus. Brethren, in the war of the Commonwealth in England and in our Revolutionary war the Baptists were all patriots. In a long list of published Tories there is not a Baptist name. Dearer to a Baptist than life is soul liberty. They are like the grim Douglas, who said that "the smell of one faggot on the Tay" would bring him back from the English Marches. And let me tell you that soul liberty in these United States means soul liberty one day for the whole world.

THE LEADING MEN OF 1800.

Truly "there were giants in those days." Look at them! In Europe were Carey, Fuller, Robert Hall, Christmas Evans, and Carson. In the North stands the venerable Backus at the head of the list. With him are Manning, Stillman, Staughton, Gano, and a host of others. In the South are John Leland, Andrew Broaddus, Semple, Richard Furman, Jesse Mercer, Henry Holcombe, and many others. And what men they were in character and power! Who over-tops them now? And shall we not be called on to put forth all our strength to maintain the standards they established and transmit unimpaired the priceless legacies they bequeathed? Oh, that I had time to speak of the laymen and of that vast host of modest country preachers whose names are omitted from the historic page, but who snatched civil and religious liberty from tyranny's grasp, broke the bonds uniting Church and State, filled all the woods of the New World with campfires of revival, and made every river, lake, and pool bear testimony by baptism to the resurrection of the dead! Heaven is peopled by their converts, and myriad expectant cells of hell left forever vacant, because of the brands they plucked from the burning.

"Before showing wherein Baptists differ from other Christian denominations, it may be well for me to say that in many things there is substantial agreement . . . but there are points of difference. On these points *Baptists hold views which distinguish them* from Presbyterians, Episcopalians, Congregationalists, Lutherans, and Methodists. These views they deem so important as to justify their denominational existence; and because they hold these views they are a people 'everywhere spoken against.' If, however, the *distinctive principles of Baptists* have their foundation in the Word of God, they should be not only earnestly espoused, but maintained with unswerving fidelity. No truth taught in the Scriptures can be considered unimportant while the words of Jesus are remembered: 'Whosoever therefore shall break one of these least commandments, and shall teach men so, he shall be called the least in the Kingdom of Heaven; but whosoever shall do and teach them, the same shall be called great in the Kingdom of Heaven' (Matthew 5:19); 'Teaching them to observe all things whatsoever I have commanded you' (Matthew 28:20). . .

The foregoing pages show that there is something distinctive in the principles of Baptists. They differ from all other denominations; and the difference is so great as not only to justify, but to demand, their separate existence as a people . . . Should their testimony be suppressed, in what religious denomination could 'the whole truth' concerning the subjects of baptism be found? . . . Who but Baptists declare 'the whole truth' with regard to the exclusive baptismal act and the symbolic import of the act? If there are others, where are they? We know not. Nor do we know of any people, besides Baptists, who maintain 'the whole truth' on the subject of a regenerate church-membership, embracing, as it does, the vital point that we come to the church through Christ, and not to Christ through the church and its ordinances. Baptists proclaim in the audience of the whole world that persons have nothing to do with church relations and gospel ordinances until they are regenerated . . . Truly, Baptists are important witnesses, for they testify important things . . . Baptists should be ready not only to meet and to repel attacks made on their principles, but should earnestly engage in the propagation of those principles . . . This is one fault of some of the Baptists of this generation - that they do not zealously propagate their distinctive views. They should see to it that the truth as embodied in their distinctive principles is brought into direct, positive, constant, exterminating contact with the error opposed to those principles. What distinctive mission have the Baptists, if this is not their mission? - to present the truth in love on the matters wherein they differ from Pedobaptists. What is there but this that justifies their separate denominational existence and saves them from the reproach of being schismatics? *If they have a right to denominational life, it is their duty to propagate their distinctive principles, without which that life cannot be justified or maintained."*

J. M. PENDLETON
Distinctive Principles of Baptists
(Philadelphia: American Baptist Publication Society, 1882)

APPENDICES A - D

A - IMMERSION ESSENTIAL TO CHRISTIAN BAPTISM
by John A. Broadus

B - THE EVILS OF INFANT BAPTISM
by Alvah Hovey

C - PROTESTANT PAEDOBAPTISM AND THE DOCTRINE OF THE CHURCH *by Howard Osgood*

D - THE POSITION OF BAPTISM IN THE CHRISTIAN SYSTEM *by Henry H. Tucker*

JOHN ALBERT BROADUS, D. D., LL. D.
1827-1895.
President of Southern Baptist Theological Seminary.

IMMERSION

ESSENTIAL TO

CHRISTIAN BAPTISM.

BY JOHN A. BROADUS, D.D., LL.D.,
PROFESSOR IN THE SOUTHERN BAPTIST THEOLOGICAL SEMINARY,
GREENVILLE, SOUTH CAROLINA.

PHILADELPHIA:
AMERICAN BAPTIST PUBLICATION SOCIETY,
1420 CHESTNUT STREET.

IMMERSION ESSENTIAL TO CHRISTIAN BAPTISM.

THE object set before us is to maintain the proposition, that *Immersion in water is essential to Christian Baptism.*

The point here involved is not by any means the most important of those upon which Baptists differ from many of their fellow Christians. The questions: Who ought to be baptized? and, What does baptism signify and effect? appear to us, so far as it is proper to assign degrees in matters of divine ordinance, to be of far greater consequence.

To insist on the scriptural act of baptism is a necessary consequence of a great fundamental principle, which was once held by Baptists almost alone, but which many of our brethren of other connections are now coming to share—the exclusive authority of Scripture. We do not say simply the authority, nor the paramount authority, but the exclusive authority of Scripture. Baptism is performed at all, simply because the Scriptures direct us to perform it; therefore we feel bound to inquire what it is that they direct, and to do that. We cannot acknowledge any other authority. The opinions and practices of eminent Christians in past ages, yea of our own best friends, our pastors, our parents, must not be regarded, except so far as they may help us to determine what is taught on the subject in the Scriptures.

And it is not an inquiry as to the mere *manner* of performing a duty. The popular phrase, "*mode* of baptism," seems to us to beg the question. The real question is, What *is* baptism? Compare the case of the Lord's Supper. No Protestant insists strongly on any particular *mode* of observing the Lord's Supper. We may have our preference, and may recommend it—as sitting around a table, kneeling around a railing, sitting in the pews, etc.,—yet we do not insist. But when the Romanist gives only the bread to the laity, reserving the cup for the priests, all Protestants cry out. The Romanist might say, "Why, does not the bread really represent the great fact that Christ gave *himself* for us? Does not the body include the blood? May we not get all that is essential to the ordinance in taking the bread alone?" We—all who are commonly called Protestants—answer two things. First, to take the wine also, makes a more complete and expressive representation. Second, our Lord *told* us to eat bread and drink wine in remembrance of him; what right have we to alter that which he appointed, as if we knew better than he? Now just the same ground do Baptists take as to baptism. They do not insist strongly on the mere manner and circumstances of its administration. Thus, it is a mere question of taste and convenience whether it shall be performed in a stream or a baptistery. Dr. Judson preferred to baptize face foremost. Even the practice of trine immersion, which was once very common, and still exists in some quarters, while it is in our judgment unwarrantable and improper, may be considered a matter of no great importance. The question is, not what is the most appropriate manner of performing baptism, but what is the act to be performed. And when any think proper to alter this act, we object most earnestly, and for the same two reasons as in the other case. First, the act enjoined gives a more complete and expressive representation of those things which baptism denotes; in fact without it, the representation is grievously defective. Second, our Lord *told* us to baptize; what right have we to alter his appointment? He did not tell us to recline at a table as he was doing, and take bread and wine, but he told us to take bread and wine; and we do not insist on the reclining, we insist on the bread and wine. He did not tell us to be baptized in the Jordan, or in a river as he was, but he told us to be baptized; and we do not insist on the Jordan, or any river, or any other mere circumstance, but we insist on the baptizing.

What then do the Scriptures teach as to the action which constitutes baptism? Every one should try to decide this question for himself. It is the duty of Christian people to settle every religious question, if possible, by their own personal examination of Scripture. Luther contended for the *right* of private judgment; is there not a corresponding *duty* of private judgment?

A plain man of average intelligence has become a believer in Christ, and knows that he ought to be baptized. He knows, also, that there is a difference among Christians around him as to what is baptism; that three different actions are called baptism. He takes up his New Testament, to read in his own tongue, and to see if, as a matter of private judgment, he can determine what constitutes the baptism which his dear Saviour enjoined. What does he find? The word *baptize* is only borrowed into the English language, and for him does not determine anything, being used, he knows, by different persons in different senses. And he is not acquainted with Greek.

But he finds the record of our Lord's own baptism; that it was in the river Jordan; that after his baptism he came up out of the water. Does some one feel like interrupting me here to say that literally it is "came up *from* the water?" I answer, that is true in Matthew; but in Mark, according to the correct Greek text, it is "out of." And in Matthew, while the word "from" does not itself show that he had been in the water, it does not at all show that he had not; and the connection makes it so plain that he had, that the versions of Tyndale, Cranmer, Geneva, and King James all render "out of." The expression is like, "Let me cast out the mote *from* thine eye," and the statement in Tobit that "a fish leaped up *from* the river and wished to devour the lad." So our friend is not misled by his English Bible as to this expression. He finds also that when John, after long baptizing in the Jordan, left it for another place, he went to Ænon, "because there was much water there." In reading Acts, he finds that when Philip was about to baptize the eunuch, they went down into the water, and after the baptism they came up out of the water. In reading Romans, he finds the apostle likening baptism to a burial, and arguing that believers must not and cannot continue in sin that grace may abound, seeing that their very baptism, at the beginning of their Christian course, had reference to the death of Christ, and they were buried with Christ by baptism unto death, in order that as Christ was raised from the dead, even so they also might live a new life.

Now what can this man conclude, but one thing? Pardon a homely story. The summer after the battle of Gettysburg, I was preaching in a Virginia brigade at the camp below Orange Court House, during the great and blessed revival in Lee's army. Many soldiers were finding Christian hope. After preaching one day in an old church near the camp, a Presbyterian chaplain arose, called up several soldiers, and proceeded to "baptize" them, as he termed it, from a little bowl of water. When the services were about to close, a Baptist chaplain invited the congregation to go after dismission to a baptistery which had been prepared at the foot of the hill, where the ordinance of baptism would be administered. He handed me his Bible as we went down the hill, asking me to read some passages and pray. I read the account of the baptism of Jesus, the commission in which he enjoins baptism, the account of Philip and the eunuch, and the passage in Romans, and then many soldiers were baptized. As the crowd went away, a soldier was heard to say to his comrades, "I tell you what, fellows, this that they did down here was a great deal more like them Scripturs than what they did up yonder." Can anybody wonder that he thought so? Would not this be the general verdict of plain men, if they would just look on and consider? If anyone should say that this was but an ignorant man, I will add that a Virginia gentleman of high position and culture, and not a Baptist, once said to me, "Anybody can see that immersion is baptism, and I grant that it takes a good deal of argument and explanation to show that something else is baptism too."

Now remember that the Bible is a book for the *people*—given, in order that the people may read and learn and judge for themselves. We who are called Protestants all contend for this; *we* are not afraid the people will be misled, if they humbly and prayerfully search the Scriptures. It follows that the *obvious* teachings of Scripture—the ideas which lie plainly on its surface, so as to commend themselves to ordinary readers—are, to say the least, extremely apt to be what Scripture was meant to teach. We all insist much on this principle as regards the divinity of our Lord, and the fact that he died to save us. So here; the plain teaching of the English New Testament, to a plain man, who comes to it for information on this subject, will be that baptism is not a sprinkling, or pouring, but an immersion.

Does some one think our friend's *translation* has misled him on this subject? That would be strange, for the translation certainly was not made by Baptists. (The fact that some Baptists have recently made a revised version does not affect this argument.) The translation he reads, our cherished Bible, was made by Episcopalians, members of the Church of England. And what we Baptists ask of everybody is, Do read your own Bible with your own eyes, and earnestly and prayerfully try to find out this matter, and all such matters for yourself. But it is asserted that here the plain and obvious meaning of our English Bible is not the true meaning. That would seem matter of deep regret. Is it so, that an honest inquirer, who has sense but not erudition, will be led astray on such a point by the very best popular version of the Scriptures that can be found on earth? Still, it is insisted that our inquiring friend must not trust his own judgment of the meaning of his own Bible—he must ask *scholars* what the *original* means. For the sake of the argument we reluctantly consent that he shall do so. This word *baptize*—it is said to be borrowed from the Greek βαπτίζω, which is said to be the word invariably used where our version has baptize—what does that Greek word mean?

Well, whom shall we ask in our friend's behalf? It is a question of scholarship. Therefore we ought to ask those who are unquestionably able and leading scholars. And they ought to be as nearly as possible *disinterested* as to the matter in hand. Such are the conditions required when we refer any matter whatever to the decision of others.

Now as to the meaning of this Greek word, I will just consult in our friend's behalf the three most recent standard lexicons, one of classical and two of New Testament Greek, which are acknowledged by all scholars as scholarly, scientific, and eminently authoritative. They are first, Liddell and Scott's Lexicon of the Greek Language in general, the sixth edition, revised and greatly augmented, and published last year by two scholars of the Church of England; second, Grimm's edition of Wilke's Lexicon of New Testament Greek, published four years ago in Germany, and now in process of translation by a Congregationalist scholar in this country; third, Cremer's Biblico-Theological Lexicon of New Testament Greek, published six years ago in Germany, and recently translated in England.

Liddell and Scott say, *baptizo*, "to put in or under water." And they go on to explain various secondary and metaphorical uses as derived from this, *e. g.* to *sink* a ship, a man *soaked* in wine, *over head and ears* in debt, *drowned* with questions. They do not recognize or hint at any other meaning.

Grimm's Wilke translates it, (1) "immerse, submerge;"—then (2) "to wash or bathe by immersing or submerging"—which he says is the meaning in Mark vii. 4, and in the cases of Naaman and Judith;— (3) figuratively, "to overwhelm," as with debts, misfortunes, etc. So much he gives as to the *general* use of the word. In the New Testament rite, he says it denotes "an immersion in water, intended as a sign of sins washed away, and received by those who wished to be admitted to the benefits of the Messianic reign." No hint of its meaning anything else.

Cremer gives as the general meaning "immerse, submerge;" and says that in the peculiar New Testament and Christian use, the word "denotes immersion, submersion, for a religious purpose."

Such is the rendering of this word by the three most recent lexicons of acknowledged scientific value; the three which any competent scholar, if asked to recommend lexicons to a student of New Testament Greek, would be sure to name. I might add that the two German commentators on the New Testament, who are the foremost of the century as to full and accurate scholarship, Fritzsche and Meyer, furnish like testimony as to the meaning of this word.

But why, it may be asked, do some Greek lexicons, besides the renderings "immerse," "put in or under water," etc., give the meaning "pour," "drench," etc.? The classical lexicons which give this meaning base it on such expressions as I have mentioned, viz., baptized with wine, sleep, misfortunes, debts, etc. Now in these cases (all figurative, you will observe), some such other sense would be possible, perhaps appropriate— the idea then being that wine, debts, etc., are poured over one so that he is drenched with them—but certainly it is not *necessary*. This is shown by Liddell and Scott, who explain all such uses as derived from the primary sense of "put in or under water," comparing such English expressions as soaked in wine, over head and ears in debt, etc.; and we may add, immersed in business, in study, sleep, debt, troubles. Now an important general principle is here involved, a principle indispensable to all reliable interpretation of language, namely this: We are not at liberty to assign to a word a new meaning, quite different from its primary and established meaning, until we find some passage which absolutely *requires* it. Examples in which such a new and different meaning would be possible, or even appropriate, or even most natural, will not justify our assigning it, as long as the established meaning will suit even tolerably well. Only when the common meaning is impossible or utterly unsuitable, is it proper to give a new and very different meaning. Unless this principle be followed, interpretation of language, I repeat, becomes utterly uncertain and unreliable. Now it cannot be said that the notion of immersed in debts, etc., is an unnatural or unsuitable image.

To say that the other conception of having debts poured over one would also fit, is nothing to the point. We must, of course, hold on to the common and recognized sense as long as that will answer. It will thus appear that the classical lexicons in question have no right to give such a meaning as "pour," because it differs widely from the established and familiar use of the word, and the examples they cite do not *require*, and therefore do not *warrant* any such meaning. As to the lexicons of New Testament Greek, which claim that some passages in the Bible justify the meaning " pour," I shall speak afterwards.

Such, then, is the testimony of the leading lexicons. To this I need add but one fact, namely, the practice of the Greek Church. Their rule is, and always has been, to immerse. I myself saw a child thus baptized in a Greek church at Scanderoon, or Alexandretta, at the north-east corner of the Mediterranean. They laugh to scorn the idea that their Greek word *baptizo* can mean sprinkling or pouring. Now the Greek is not really a dead language; scholars, in Germany, England, and America, are every day seeing this fact more clearly, and recognizing more fully its importance. I remember when at Athens, a few years ago, a Scottish gentleman, who had spent most of his life in Greece, and had given very close attention to the language, told me of his own accord, that, although a Presbyterian, he thought the Baptists were quite right about the meaning of *baptizo;* and he hunted up a book in modern Greek, on Natural Philosophy, in which I found the word repeatedly employed. The Greeks usually leave this as the sacred word, and take other terms for common actions. But this writer, in describing the mode of determining specific gravity, explained that we first weigh a body in air, and then immerse it in water, and weigh it thus, being suspended by a cord; and this action of immersing he constantly and naturally describes by "baptize." There was recently published in this country a copious and valuable lexicon of Greek usage in the Roman and Byzantine periods, from B. C. 140 to A. D. 1000, by Professor Sophocles of Harvard College, who is himself a Greek, long resident in America. He defines *baptizo* as meaning to dip, to immerse, to sink—and then gives a great variety of uses, all explained as having this same force; *e. g.* soaked in liquor (intoxicated), sunk in ignorance, bathed in tears, he plunged the sword into his own neck—then, derivatively, to bathe. And as to the New Testament use he says expressly, "There is no evidence that Luke and Paul and the other writers of the New Testament put upon this verb meanings not recognized by the Greeks."

This, then, is the practice of the Greek Church, and this the testimony of the living Greeks who belong to it. The word involved is to them not foreign, but their own word. And one of their constant complaints against the Latin Church— the Church of Rome—is, that these have altered the ceremony of baptism. A modern Greek scholar has said, "The Church of the West commits an abuse of words and of ideas in practising baptism by aspersion, the mere statement of which is in itself a ridiculous contradiction." Soon after the taking of Constantinople, five centuries ago, as we learn from Dr. Döllinger and others, a council of Greek patriarchs agreed, not that they would practise pouring or sprinkling, but that they would recognize it in the Westerns as valid baptism. They were almost ruined, in danger of being utterly swallowed up by the conquering Turks, and wanted to make friends with the Latin Christians. But at a later period, the Greek patriarchs retracted this. It is still observed in Russia, but those to whom Greek was the native language could not stand it. They said that instead of a *baptismos* the Latin Church practised a mere *rantismos*—instead of an immersion a mere sprinkling.* To a man who spoke Greek every day this was " a ridiculous contradiction."

Such, then, is the evidence which may be given our unlearned friend from scholars, the lexicons, and the living Greeks, concerning their own word. Much more might be added in the way of confirmation; but he would probably say, "Well, it is plain that I *can* trust my English Bible. What these great scholars say—none of them Baptists—and what the living Greeks say and do, accord exactly with the impression I got from my own Bible; and so the evidence is enough; I care for no more."

He for his part might stop there, being con-

---

* Döllinger, " Kirche und Kirchen," s. 188.

cerned only to determine his own conduct. But I have another and a different task to perform.

In the face of such facts as have been stated, on what ground do any Christian people defend the practice of sprinkling for baptism? Well, some of them have really never known the facts, or never stopped to think about them. But others, with the facts before them, still defend sprinkling. Respect for my fellow Christians requires that this matter be as carefully considered as the time will allow. Yet I can but briefly mention, and rapidly discuss.

There are several distinct grounds which are relied on by the same or different classes of persons.

I. Grant that New Testament baptism was immersion, some hold that "the church has authorized a change."

Yes, *clinic* baptism, baptism of a sick person in bed, began as early as the third century to be allowed by some ecclesiastics, *e. g.* Novatian. They poured water copiously around the dying or very sick man as he lay in bed. This practice arose from exaggerated notions of the importance of baptism. We should say, if the man was too ill to be baptized, it was not his duty; but they were afraid to let a man die without baptism, and as real baptism was impracticable, they proposed a substitute, which by copious pouring would come as near it as possible. There were many disputes as to the lawfulness of this, but it came by degrees to be generally recognized as lawful. As the centuries went on, there was gradual progress. The more convenient substitute was preferred in other cases than illness, was further reduced to mere sprinkling, and became increasingly common. It was long withstood by Popes and Councils, but grew in popularity through the Dark Ages; until in the thirteenth century—one thousand years after clinic pouring began—the Pope finally yielded, and authorized sprinkling in all cases.

So the Reformers found it. And, unfortunately for our modern Christianity, they did not insist on a change. *Luther* repeatedly said a change *ought* to be made, *e. g.*, "Baptism is a Greek word, and may be translated immersion, as when we immerse something in water that it may be wholly covered. And, although it is almost wholly abolished (for they do not dip the whole children, but only pour a little water on them), they ought nevertheless to be wholly immersed, ... for that the etymology of the word seems to demand." Again, he says that baptism does not simply represent washing for sins, but "is rather a sign both of death and resurrection. Being moved by this reason, I would have those that are to be baptized to be altogether dipt into the water, as the word means, and the mystery signifies." So elsewhere.* In like manner *Calvin*. In commenting on the baptism of the eunuch by Philip, he says: "'They descended into the water.' Here we perceive what was the rite of baptizing among the ancients, for they immersed the whole body into the water; now the custom has become established that the minister only sprinkles the body or the head. But so slight a difference of ceremony ought not to be esteemed by us so important, that on account of it we should split the church or disturb it with quarrels. For the ceremony of baptism itself indeed, inasmuch as it was handed down to us by Christ, we should a hundred times rather fight even to

---

* See Ingham's "Handbook of Baptism," p. 89.

death, than suffer it to be taken away from us. But when in the symbol of the water we have a testimony as well of our ablution as of our new life; when in water, as in a mirror, Christ represents to us his blood, that from it we may seek our purification; when he teaches that we are fashioned anew by his Spirit, that being dead to sin, we may live to righteousness—it is certain that we lack nothing which pertains to the substance of baptism. Wherefore from the beginning the church has freely permitted herself, outside of this substance, to have rites a little dissimilar."* The ancients, in the time of Philip and the eunuch, practised immersion; a different custom has now become established, the church allowing herself liberty.

The leaders of the Reformation in England attempted a return, not, indeed, to the full New Testament plan, but that of the Fathers in the third century. The rubric of the Church of England has always been, from the Reformation till now, "shall dip the child in the water . . . . but if they certify that the child is weak, it shall

---

* "Calvin on Acts," viii. 38.

suffice to pour water upon it." This is essentially the principle of the old clinic baptism. And this the Greek Church also tolerates as an exceptional practice. But among the Reformers, on the continent and in England, the custom of several centuries, with convenience, etc., triumphed over these attempts, and pouring, nay, even sprinkling, became the common practice.

In this sense, then, "the church" has changed the act of baptism. On this ground the Roman Catholics stand—*the church* has changed it—so they always meet the complaints and censures of the Greek Church. And intelligent Romanists see exactly how the matter stands among us who are called Protestants. Thus the famous Dr. Döllinger says: "The fact that the Baptists are so numerous, or even the most numerous of all religious parties in North America, deserves all attention. They would, indeed, be yet more numerous, were not Baptism, as well as the Lord's Supper, as to their sacramental significance, regarded in the Calvinistic world as something so subordinate, that the inquiry after the original form appears to many as something indifferent, about which one need not much trouble himself. The Baptists are, however, in fact, from the Protestant standpoint, unassailable; since for their demand of baptism by submersion they have the clear Bible text; and the authority of the church, and of her testimony, is regarded by neither party."* I may remark here, that, on this subject, the Baptists belong to the majority. It is often objected to us that we are an insignificant minority of the Christian world, and it is a point about which we are not greatly solicitous. But if anybody cares greatly for majorities in such a matter, let him observe that, in contending for immersion as necessary to the baptism taught in the New Testament, we have on our side the whole Greek Church, and the whole Roman Catholic Church, and a very large proportion of the Protestant world, particularly of the Protestant scholars.

To return. This is an intelligible position. New Testament baptism was immersion, but the church has changed it. Accordingly, in the Church of England, few scholars ever, for a moment, question that *baptizo* means immerse,

---

* " Kirche und Kirchen," s. 337.

or that the New Testament baptism was immersion.

The church has changed it. Very satisfactory for a Romanist, but how can a Protestant rest on this? Chillingworth, the Church of England scholar, left a dictum which has grown famous: "The Bible, I say—the Bible only—is the religion of Protestants." Was this all a mistake?

II. Christian Liberty is the ground on which others proceed.

They say Christians may choose for themselves about mere outward forms; these make no difference if you have the *essence* of the thing. Yes, and so says the Quaker, more strongly still. What would you say to the Quaker? I asked this question of an esteemed friend, who is an Episcopal clergyman. The Quaker tells us the mere outward form of baptism is unnecessary; the essential thing is to have the baptism of the Spirit, and water baptism need not be observed at all. What would you say to him? "I would tell him the Scripture teaches us to baptize *in water*." Very well, I replied, and so it teaches us to *baptize* in water. If you have an *outward ceremony* at all, you have a form, and can you say that the *form* of a *ceremony* is of no importance? How will such an one answer the Quaker, except upon the Baptist principle? The state of mind represented, the baptism of the Spirit, is, of course, the essential thing; *without* it, the outward ceremony is an empty form. But our Lord has appointed a form, a ceremony. We ought to observe this because he has appointed it; and plainly, therefore, ought to observe it as he appointed it. Either the Baptist ground, or the Quaker ground.

"But suppose," one says, "that immersion is impracticable, or excessively inconvenient; there is no water, or it is too cold; why not substitute another use of water, and attach the same meaning to it?"

Well, suppose you want to observe the Lord's Supper, and there is no wine to be had—a thing much more likely to happen than no water, and which I once knew to happen in a country neighborhood—why not take some other beverage, and let that represent to us the same thing as wine? We should all unite in raising two objections. First, our Lord told us to eat bread and drink *wine*; if circumstances really prevent our doing that, let us do nothing, feeling that we are providentially hindered. Second, while any liquid, as water, might, in some sort, represent the blood of our dear Lord, yet it is obvious that wine much more clearly and strikingly represents it. Even if we did not perceive this, we ought to do just what he said; and much more when we *do* perceive it. And so, if immersion be really impracticable, we should make the *same two points*. First, we must do what he told us, or do nothing. What is really impracticable, is not our duty. Second, while sprinkling with water may represent purification, yet even this part of the meaning of baptism is much more strikingly represented by immersion; while the other part, the idea of burial and resurrection, which the apostle twice connects with baptism, sprinkling does not represent at all. Even if we did not perceive that what he appointed is more expressive, we ought to do just what he said; and much more when we *do* perceive it. Either, then, what he told us to do, or nothing.

But some one is dying—shall we deny him the satisfaction of being baptized? Why not?

How was it with the thief on the cross? Suppose the same dying man wants the Lord's Supper, and you have no wine?

Nay, my friends, such pleas look like *making too much* of baptism. In this, as I said, began clinic baptism; and pray notice how the argument we are discussing—a favorite argument with some—just comes back to the same thing, attaching an unwarranted importance to baptism. If Baptism or the Lord's Supper be providentially impracticable, surely there is nothing lost, and no guilt incurred, by failing to observe it.

III. Others, without going into an argument as to the teaching of Scripture, while neither admitting nor denying that it teaches what we claim, urge *general* reasons why they cannot believe that immersion is obligatory.

1. They will say, as before, that immersion is sometimes impracticable, and so it cannot be necessary to baptism. We answer, when baptism is impracticable it is not our duty; when it is practicable, let us practise it, and not substitute something else.

2. But immersion is often really dangerous. What! a cold bath dangerous, taken promptly,

when a person is sustained, too, by strong excitement, and its effects quickly removed? In a few cases of illness, or extreme feebleness, it might be dangerous, but then it is not our duty. There is, perhaps, nothing in this world which may not sometimes be dangerous.

3. Immersion is indecent. Will you allow a bit of personal experience? My boyhood was spent in one of the counties of Virginia, where Baptists were numerous. The country church to which the family belonged commonly repaired, for baptizing, to my father's mill-pond, which was a very convenient and a very pretty place. I always went to witness it, with eager interest. I was, of course, like other boys, not too good to have noticed and laughed at anything indelicate. But when I grew up and went to the university, and a Presbyterian student one day said that he thought immersion was indecent, the idea was to me utterly novel; it had never, in all my life, entered my head. Such a notion is a mere prejudice of education. If you think baptism indecent, I should beg pardon for saying you have not been "well-raised" in this respect. In many circumstances of life there may be per-

sonal exposure, through bad arrangements, or awkwardness, or accident; as in alighting from a horse or a carriage, in passing a muddy street-crossing, in descending the steps of a church. What does that prove, except that, wherever there is danger of exposure, we must take care to avoid it? If, in any of these cases, or in baptizing, there is great awkwardness or bad management, we condemn the managers. If there is merely accidental exposure when a lady alights from her carriage, or when a lady is baptized, well-bred people will only feel regret and sympathy. Besides, what about sea-bathing? The very persons who oftenest complain of immersion as indecent, are those who most delight in sea-bathing.

4. So many good people have believed in sprinkling, and felt that they were blessed in receiving, administering, or witnessing it. This is, with some, a favorite argument. But consider. Transubstantiation has, from early centuries, been believed in by multitudes of deeply devout people, including such men as Thomas à Kempis and Pascal. They have felt that they were blessed in worshipping the host as the very body

of Christ. So, also, as to the worship of the Virgin Mary; many who were deeply devout have found in it great delight. Good people are not infallible. And God may, and doubtless does, bless people in holding opinions and observing practices that are not in themselves according to his will. This must be so to some extent—else who would be blessed? David was greatly blessed of God, and David was a polygamist. Now, if it is true, to some extent, that he blesses those who have principles and practices which he does not approve, we cannot tell how far it may be carried, and must leave that to God. But one thing follows inevitably, that we must not take the fact of God's blessing a man, or an association of men, as proving that he approves all their doctrines and all their practices.

5. But sprinkling has not only been widely believed in and practised by good people, it has been *defended* by many able and devout men, after careful investigation. Very well, we may answer. You are a Methodist, or an Episcopalian; what do you think of the doctrine of Election, Reprobation, Limited Atonement? Yet you know that for ages these doctrines have been

held and rejoiced in by many good Christians; and defended, after careful investigation, by some of the greatest intellects of the human race. Or you are a Calvinist; what do you think of the doctrine popularly called "falling from grace?" Yet you know that it is held and defended by not a few of the most zealous, fervent, and useful Christians on earth.

But it may be said, this is not a parallel case; these are *doctrines*. That makes no difference as to our argument. If grave errors as to *doctrine* exist, and have long existed, among persons very devout and often richly blessed of God, the same must certainly be true as to the less important matter of *ceremonies*—something may be quite erroneous though held and earnestly defended by some good and wise men. But take the case of Church Government. You are a Presbyterian, and do not believe that Episcopacy is scriptural or expedient; yet how many pious people believe in it and live under it with joy and with religious growth and usefulness; and how many great men defend it after careful investigation, for example, in the Church of England? Or you are an Episcopalian; how many Congregationalists, Presbyterians, Lutherans, there are in America, Scotland, England, France, Switzerland, Germany, who are neglecters and opposers of Episcopacy, yet are devout, learned, honest?

What is the conclusion from all this? Why, that we are *compelled* to think for ourselves. We may err, as so many have done; but we must not be content without the most earnest efforts to escape error that our circumstances will allow. I repeat, there is not only a *right* of private judgment, there is a *duty* of private judgment. Every man shall give account of *himself* unto God. And how can we square it with our consciences if we do not personally strive, in all possible ways, to find the truth in all things? There is here but one alternative. Either we have no right to be sure that anything is true, or we are bound to assure ourselves by personal inquiry. Either universal skepticism, or private judgment.

IV. But another class of persons endeavor to go deeper, not relying upon the opinions of others. They say, grant that the classic use of *baptizo* is as the lexicons mentioned, wash, that it always means immerse, and kindred ideas; yet the *Biblical* use is very different, for in the Bible it certainly sometimes means sprinkle or pour. The attempt is made to show this from various passages; really it seems that so many are tried because it is felt that none of them are exactly conclusive. I should be glad to go over all that have been thus appealed to, but time does not allow that, and I can only mention those which are most frequently relied on, or which seem most plausible.

1. It is said that in the case of certain other words, such as pastor, bishop, elder, church, supper, the sacred use is frequently quite different from the classical use; and this is thought to afford a presumption that there is also a difference as to the word *baptize*. But most of these words have not changed their meaning to something quite different; there is only a figurative or novel application, while the ground idea remains the same. Thus the pastor *is* a shepherd (figuratively), the bishop *is* an overseer (spiritually), the church is an assembly (actual or ideal). So *baptize* is still an immersion, having only a special reference and mean-

ing. The word "supper" has been much insisted on, as having a wholly different sense in the New Testament from its classical use. But when the Apostle Paul speaks of the Christians as coming together to eat "the Lord's Supper," it *was* a supper. *We* continue to apply the term "supper" when it is eaten at other times of the day, but *Scripture* does *not* so apply it. Besides, our Lord did not tell us to eat a supper, but to eat bread and drink wine. This is what we must do; and we make here no substitute, either for the elements (bread and wine), or for the action (eating and drinking). So the appeal to "supper" is quite inappropriate. The use of "elder," however, seems to be a case in point, for this word has changed its meaning. But the change is not in *sacred*, as distinguished from secular use. The application of the term "elder" to a person who is not old, is found in classical Greek, as also in Latin and English. The Greek word *presbus*, an old man, is used in classical Greek to denote an honorable man, an ambassador, a senator. So with the Latin *senator*, senator, and the English *alder*man. This, then, is not a case in which the word acquires an entirely different sense in sacred from what it had in classical use. And so all the examples cited break down, and this supposed analogy and consequent presumption, much relied on by some, amounts to just nothing.

2. There is the purification theory, put forward by Dr. Edward Beecher and others. In John iii. 22-5, we are told that Jesus was baptizing (through his disciples); next, that John also was baptizing, for he was not yet cast into prison; and then it is added: "Then there arose a question between some of John's disciples and the Jews" ("a Jew" is the correct reading), "about purifying." From this it is argued that the word baptize is synonymous with purify. Now baptizing was certainly a very striking form of purification. The fact that baptism was going on might very naturally lead to a discussion between some of John's disciples and a Jew about the general subject of purification, and the relation of this to other purifications. Being a peculiar, remarkable, and novel purification, it was perfectly natural that baptism should lead to discussion of the general subject. But why in the world are we to say that the

terms baptism and purification are synonymous, that baptism means nothing more definite than purification, and that any form of purification might be called a baptism? Suppose a *murder* has occurred, and leads some persons into a discussion concerning *death;* are we to conclude that the terms murder and death are synonymous, and that any form of death may be called a murder? Yet because the occurrence of baptism led to a discussion concerning purification, we are told that these terms are synonymous, and that any form of purification is a baptism. Now upon this assumption rests Dr. Beecher's theory—a huge inverted pyramid resting upon a single point, and that point a mere assumption, and one in itself unwarrantable and unreasonable.

3. But besides these more general considerations, various particular passages are urged as showing that the word *baptizo* in the New Testament is not always taken in the classical sense of immerse and kindred ideas.

(1) The river Jordan is mentioned. I learn that *recently* a clergyman in South Carolina stated that the Jordan is quite too small a

stream to admit of immersion. It is more than two hundred miles long, and in all the region where the baptizing is described as performed, is very hard to ford even at the lowest water of summer. On the other hand, an estimable minister who died not long ago in South Carolina, stated in a sermon that he had been to the traditional place of our Lord's baptism, and that the bank is so steep and the current so swift and deep and strong as to make immersion there impracticable. Now this gentleman perfectly knew that every Spring, when the river is high as he saw it, in the week preceding Easter, there come four or five or seven or eight thousand pilgrims from all parts of the East to this very place, the traditional place of our Lord's baptism, and there these thousands, men, women, and children, do actually immerse themselves and one another in the river—not as baptism (for they have received that in infancy), but as a sacred bath at that holy spot. He knew as well as I do that this happens every Spring at that very place, and yet it never occurred to him to connect that fact in his mind with his own timid notion that immersion would there be impracticable. I am satisfied he was a good man, and have no idea he meant to deceive, but how strangely good men can sometimes manipulate their own minds. The traditional place is not particularly well suited to baptism when the river is high. As to the bank, it could be cut down and made perfectly convenient in an hour. But there are better places higher up the Jordan (towards the Sea of Galilee I saw some which struck a practised eye as admirably convenient and beautiful), and that may possibly have been one reason why John moved up the river, as he appears to have done.

(2) Much is said about the scarcity of water in Jerusalem, rendering it unlikely that the three thousand on the day of Pentecost were immersed. This seems to some unreflecting people a very strong argument, when they are told that around Jerusalem there is, in ordinary dry weather, no running stream whatever, except the little rivulet from the fountain of Siloam; that even the brook Kidron does not contain a drop of water except when it rains, and the city was supplied by aqueducts, pools, and cisterns. Accustomed to think, with the

school boy, that it is a remarkable providence that great rivers so often flow by great cities, and having never studied the water arrangements of ancient Jerusalem, these persons very naturally say, "Why certainly, in a city without a river, a city so scarce of water they would not have spared enough for immersing three thousand men." But only think a moment. Even if we knew nothing of the methods by which Jerusalem was actually supplied, here was a city of say two hundred thousand as its ordinary population, besides several hundred thousand visitors for a week at a time during the great feasts—a great population with all their wants, including the washing of their clothes, and a people who attached extraordinary importance to ceremonial purifications and to personal cleanliness—and you say that in this great city they could not spare water enough for baptizing three thousand persons? Besides, Jerusalem was repeatedly besieged. During the great siege by Titus, a vast multitude from the country crowded the space within the walls, an were kept inclosed there from April to Septe ber. There was scarcity of food, but in none of the great sieges, not even in this last, of which we have so minute an account in Josephus, is there a word said about scarcity of water. It is plain that Jerusalem must have possessed remarkable arrangements of some kind, giving an immense supply of water. And examination has sufficiently disclosed the character of these arrangements, as various writers have shown.* I will add, not as caring to lay any stress on it, that in observing the remains of the immense pool, just outside of Jerusalem on the West, which Robinson identifies with the Lower Pool of Gihon, I was struck with its adaptation to baptism. The pool, six hundred feet long, was made by building two walls across the deep ravine, so as to retain the water brought down in the rainy season. The steep banks on either side present a succession of flat limestone ledges at various depths, and often many feet wide; so that at whatever depth the water might be standing in the pool, there would be excellent standing room for a great number of persons,

---

* See especially a tract by Dr. G. W. Samsor, "On the Water Supply of Jerusalem," published by The Bible and Publication Society.

with the proper depth for baptizing. As there was an abundance of drinking water in the city from the cisterns and aqueducts, this pool was probably used for watering cattle, and perhaps for washing clothes, while the limestone sides and bottom would keep it always clear. Persons who have educated themselves to dislike immersion might fear to stand on these ledges and practise it, but the Jews of that day were accustomed to purificatory immersions, and would have no fear nor difficulty.

(3) The gospel according to Mark (vii. 1-5) tells us that it was the custom of the Jews to baptize (immerse) themselves when they came from the market, and to baptize (immerse) cups, couches, etc. It is said with great confidence, that *of course* this cannot have been immersion. But did you ever notice that if you understand it as merely washing (as in our version), you make the latter part of the evangelist's statement feeble and almost meaningless? Some Pharisees and scribes were watching Jesus and his followers to find fault with them. And seeing some of his disciples eating bread without having washed their hands, they asked Jesus why his

disciples did not walk in this matter according to the tradition of the elders. In narrating this, the Evangelist Mark, who writes especially for Gentiles, pauses in the midst of the narrative to explain to his Greek and Roman readers that the Jews were very particular about this matter of washing the hands before eating, and washing them "with the fist," scrubbing one hand with the other, that is, washing very carefully—observing the tradition of the elders. In fact, he says, they do something more remarkable than this; when they come from the market (where some unclean person or thing may have touched some portion of their body), they do not eat till they have immersed themselves. And he adds that many other things they have received by tradition to hold, immersions of cups and pots and brazen vessels and tables (or it should be "couches"). These practices were so wonderful, and gave such proof of the extreme scrupulosity of the Jews, that it is not strange the writer of the gospel should have gone on to mention them, though nothing was necessary to explain his narrative but the first statement, that they did not eat without having washed their hands. But if you say that the word *baptizo* in the fourth verse only means "wash," as the word *nipto* does in verse second and verse third, then what was the use of adding verse fourth at all? If according to verse third they do not eat without having carefully washed their hands, what is the use of adding that when they come from the market they do not eat unless they have washed? This certainly must mean something different from washing their hands, and something much more remarkable, or it would have been a waste of words, a very empty tautology, first to tell us that they do not eat at all, under any circumstances, without having carefully washed their hands, and then to add that when they come from market they do not eat without having washed. One would suppose not, if they wash before eating even when they have *not* been to market. Perhaps, some one says, the washing in verse fourth means purifying, they purify themselves when they come from market. Of course it means a purification, but the washing of verse third is a purification too. That of verse fourth must be a different and more thorough purification, something more than the careful washing of hands, or else you make the inspired evangelist talk nonsense.

And notice the further addition. He goes on to tell his Gentile readers that these singular and scrupulous Jews have many other traditional observances, as immersions of cups and pots and brazen vessels and couches. Now if you say this cannot have been immersion, but only washing in some other way, then why should the sacred writer have gone so far away from the immediate subject of his narrative merely to say that the Jews washed cups and pots? Most people do. And if it be said the point is that this was a ceremonial washing, a religious purification of the articles mentioned, we may answer that that would not seem remarkable to the Romans. They practised numerous lustrations. A Roman shepherd would sprinkle his sheep with water once a year, accompanied by sacrifices, to preserve them from disease and other evils. Why should Mark go out of his way to inform Romans that the strange Jews made lustration of cups and couches? But understand *baptizo* in its own proper sense, and all becomes plain and forcible. The Jews not only wash their hands carefully before eating, but when they come from market, where they know not what may have touched some part of their persons, they immerse themselves; and this suggests, and leads the evangelist to mention, that they have many other like thorough and painstaking purifications enjoined upon them by their traditions, as immersions of cups and pots and brazen vessels and couches. Thus the several facts of verse third and verse fourth rise as a climax, and we see the propriety of pausing to mention these various proofs of painstaking scrupulosity.*

But one says, "I cannot believe that they immersed beds; that is absurd." Well, the beds might mean pallets, consisting of several thicknesses of cloth quilted together—as when the paralytic was told to take up his bed and walk, or like the beds they give you now in some houses of Palestine. More probably, however, they mean the couches beside the table, on which the guests reclined to eat, as the subject of the whole connection is their observances about eating.

---

* Compare Meyer on Mark.

Now suppose there has been contagious disease in one of our homes, that a person has died of small pox, or even of typhoid fever, will any careful housewife think it too much to take the bed on which he died all to pieces—if in fact she does not burn it—and carefully cleanse every part of it? Well, if she would be thus anxious to avoid contagion in her household, the Jews were equally anxious to avoid ceremonial impurity, when, for example, some "unclean" person was found to have reclined on one of their couches. And if she would not shrink from such pains in order to effect a thorough cleansing, why should we pronounce it incredible that the scrupulous Jews would take equal pains to effect a thorough religious purification?

Grant that in such cases the law of Moses did not always require immersion of the unclean object or of the person. The evangelist is expressly speaking of the *traditional* observances, and the Jews had become so very scrupulous that the tradition often required more than the law did. So we find them still doing in the time of Maimonides (twelfth century), and he asserts that such was the real requirement of the law. "Whenever in the law," he says, "washing of the flesh or of the clothes is mentioned, it means nothing else than the dipping of the whole body in a laver; for if any man dip himself all over, except the tip of his little finger, he is still in his uncleanness."

"A bed that is wholly defiled, if a man dips it part by part, it is pure."* This last statement of his may relieve the extreme solicitude sometimes expressed as to how a bed could be immersed; and both statements show how scrupulous the Jews had become in employing the most thorough form of purification even where it was not required. This also explains the conduct of Judith in the Jewish romance, who, living in a heathen tent and eating the food of the heathen, goes at midnight with her maid into a ravine and immerses herself, and returns "clean."†

---

* Quoted in Ingham's "Manual of Baptism," p. 373.

† The church-Father, Epiphanius, born in Palestine of Jewish parents in the fourth century, describes, in his great work on Heresies, a party of Jews whom he calls *Hemerobaptistæ*, "Daily baptizers," whose doctrines he says are the same as those of the scribes and Pharisees. Their peculiarity is that "both spring and autumn, both

(4) Another passage relied on by some *is* 1 Corinthians x. 1, "That our fathers were all under the cloud, and all went through the sea, and were all baptized unto Moses in the cloud and in the sea." This, we are told, cannot be understood as an immersion. Certainly, not a literal immersion. What happened to them was only *something like* baptism; and it was certainly quite as much like immersion as it was like sprinkling or pouring, and most people would think a good deal more so. They left the shore, and going down into the bed of the sea, with the

---

winter and summer they baptize themselves every day, maintaining that a man cannot live unless he baptizes himself in water every single day, washing himself off and purifying himself from every fault." Epiphanius says, this shows lack of faith; for if they had faith in yesterday's baptism, they would not think it necessary to repeat it to-day. And he declares that if they keep sinning every day, thinking that the water will cleanse them, it is a vain hope; "for neither ocean, nor all the rivers and seas, perennial streams and fountains, and the whole rain-producing apparatus of nature combined, can remove sins when, namely, it is done not according to reason nor by the command of God. For repentance cleanses, and the one baptism through the naming of the mysteries." The same "Daily baptizers" are mentioned in the so-called Apostolical Constitutions, supposed to have been written in the third century.

sea on either side and the cloud above, they were in a position somewhat resembling baptism. And as Christians publicly begin to follow Christ by being baptized unto him, so it may be said that the Israelites began following Moses by being baptized unto him in the cloud and in the sea. Some persons actually tell us there was a sprinkling or pouring, because of the poetical expression in Psalm lxxvii. 17, "The clouds poured out water." Do they really believe the Israelites were made to cross the Red Sea during a pouring rain and a terrific storm of thunder and lightning? The Psalmist alludes in verse sixteenth to the division of the Red Sea, but then passes to speak of the general phenomena of storms. At least so it is explained in the commentary of Addison Alexander, the learned Presbyterian Professor.

(5) One more passage may be mentioned, which some think quite conclusive against immersion, viz.: "baptized with the Holy Ghost." John the Baptist predicted that the mightier One who was coming would baptize with the Holy Spirit. (Literally it is "in the Holy Spirit," and this primary and common signification of the prepo-

sition ought certainly to be retained unless it can be shown to be inappropriate.) And just before his ascension our Lord said, "Ye shall be baptized with (in) the Holy Spirit not many days hence." On the day of Pentecost this was fulfilled. "There came a sound from heaven, as of a rushing mighty wind, and it filled all the house where they were sitting. And there appeared to them distributed tongues as of fire, and it sat on every one of them, and they were all filled with the Holy Spirit." And Peter, in defence and explanation of the speaking with tongues, says that this is that which was spoken through the prophet Joel, "I will pour out of my Spirit upon all flesh . . . ." Here a baptism with (in) the Spirit is promised, and the fulfilment is represented by a tongue-shaped flame of fire, resting over the head of each person, and is afterwards described as a pouring out; therefore, we are told, there may be baptism without immersion. But if you contend that the symbol must be the same in the fulfilment as in the promise, pray notice that the Spirit is as truly represented by the sound which filled all the house, so that they were enveloped in it, as by the tongue-shaped flame over the head. But what is the sense of maintaining that when two symbols or images represent the same thing, they must therefore be the same image or symbol? What was predicted as a baptism is afterwards described as a pouring. Well, if I say a man is bathed in pleasure, and presently speak of him as drinking from the cup of pleasure, would any one argue that the action of bathing is the same as drinking from a cup? Peter quotes the prophet as using the image of pouring, while our Lord had used the image of baptism; therefore pouring and baptism are the same thing. Christ is called a lamb, and is also called a shepherd; therefore a shepherd and a lamb are the same thing.

But some say it is absurd in itself to speak of immersion in the Holy Spirit. Why? You cannot conceive of this, and you can conceive of the Spirit as poured out. But both are of necessity figures. The Spirit was not literally poured out, any more than men were literally immersed in the Spirit; and why is the one *figure* any harder to conceive than the other? Cannot you conceive of breath, wind (that is what the word

Spirit means) as filling a space, and men immersed in it? Surely that is a perfectly conceivable figure. And does it not most strikingly represent the persons as completely brought under the influence of the Spirit, as encompassed, surrounded, pervaded by it? We are at present more familiar with the image of the Spirit as poured upon men, but how can one deny that the image of men as immersed in the Breath of God is both conceivable and impressive?

Some other passages are occasionally brought forward, as being supposed to yield an argument against immersion. I have mentioned those which are most relied on, and which look most plausible. And what do they amount to, when even cursorily examined? Remember, that it is necessary to find some case, in which the word not only *might*, but *must* have a different meaning. It is not enough to find passages in which some other idea would seem to you more appropriate, but to find one in which the established meaning of the word is quite impossible. If we abandon this great principle, all strict and sure interpretation of language comes to an end. And can it be said that the established meaning of *baptizo*, viz.: immerse, and kindred expressions, is impossible because of the condition of the river Jordan, or the imagined scarcity of water at Jerusalem, or the immersion of cups and couches, or the baptism in the cloud and the sea, or the baptism in the Holy Spirit? You might prefer some other conception, but is the idea of immersion impossible in any of these cases? If not, it must stand.

Men who are determined to get rid of an unacceptable teaching can always raise some doubts as to the meaning of the plainest words. The Universalist works away at the word "everlasting," until some minds grow confused, and those who wish to agree with him are misled. The Unitarian insists that instead of "and the Word was God," it *might* be translated, "and God was the Word." The orthodox answer is that language is necessarily imperfect. If God has mercifully given a revelation in human language, we should accept and follow its plain teachings, and not try to gather doubt around them, in order to escape what we do not fancy. And just this is what we say about the word *baptize*.

V. Before closing this long discussion, it is

probably desirable to refer briefly to a new theory as to the act of baptism, put forward by Rev. Dr. Dale, a Presbyterian minister of Pennsylvania. In three volumes, and with great fulness of detail and elaborate ingenuity, he explains and defends his view, but the substance of his argument may be stated in comparatively few words.

As to the primary meaning of the word *baptizo*, Dr. Dale does not differ materially from Liddell and Scott. They say it means "to put in or under;" he says it is to put within, which he expresses by a manufactured word, "intuspose," compounded from the Latin, and signifying "put within." This definition of Dale, and of Liddell and Scott,* is doubtless more correct than that which has often been given, that the word primarily means "to dip frequently." But Dr. Dale goes on to insist that *baptizo* is always broadly different in its meaning from the

---

* Dr. Conant, in his treatise on BAPTIZEIN, has also given nearly the same definition: "In its literal use, it meant to put entirely into or under a liquid, or other penetrable substance, generally water, so that the object was wholly covered by the inclosing element."

simple word *bapto*, the basis on which it is formed; that *bapto* alone means to dip, and *baptizo never* signifies to dip, but only to put within, giving no intimation that the object is to be taken out again. *Bapto*, according to him, would put an object in water and quickly take it out; but *baptizo* would put it in, and so far as the meaning of the term is concerned, would leave it there.* Suppose it were granted that this was true; then we should have Christ commanding us to put men within or under the water, as a religious ceremony, and, because he does not expressly add that we are to take them out again, we should be bound, forsooth, to let them remain there. If any of my esteemed brethren of other denominations should take this view of the matter, and request me to "intuspose" them, to put them within the water, in the name of our Redeemer, it may be assumed that my common sense and humanity will cause me to take them

---

* Does the word "dip" in itself denote that the object is to be taken out? It is connected with *deep*, as the German *taufen* (the word for baptize) is with *tief*, and the Greek βαφ, the root of βάπτω, is with βαθ in βαθύς (which means deep). See Curtius, Griechische Etymologie, s. 416.

out again, as their own common sense and prudence will then lead them to go off and change their garments, without needing an express command in either respect. If, then, Dr. Dale were right in maintaining such a broad and invariable difference between *bapto* and *baptizo*, and right in advancing to maintain, laboriously and amusingly, a similar invariable difference between the English "dip" and "immerse," and between the Latin *tingo* and *mergo*, all this would leave the practical duty the same. Let it be granted that dip and immerse are not only sometimes different, but always broadly different in the way maintained, still a command to immerse men in water would be practically plain enough for all who are trying to learn their duty. So it would all amount to nothing.

But such a broad and invariable difference between *bapto* and *baptizo* does not exist, any more than between the English words or the Latin words mentioned. Without discussing the numerous passages involved in this question, I merely mention a single one. Plutarch uses *baptizo* where he describes the soldiers of Alexander, on a riotous march, as by the roadside dipping (literally *baptizing*) with cups from huge wine-jars and mixing-bowls, and drinking to one another. Liddell and Scott say it here means *to draw* wine from bowls in cups, and add, " of course by dipping them." This is the obvious meaning, which no one can well mistake; and Dr. Dale's attempt to explain it away is simply amusing. Here, then, we have *baptizo* used precisely where Dr. Dale's theory would call for *bapto*. And there are numerous other cases, not always so obvious, but equally real.

It is a common tendency in language that a strengthened form of a word shall gradually take the place of the weaker. From *bapto*, to dip, came the verbal adjective *baptos*, dipt; and from this verbal adjective, by means of the termination *-izo*, was formed *bapt-izo*, which we may clumsily describe as primarily meaning to cause to be dipt, or to bring into a dipt condition, and may well enough render by put in, or under, or within. Being thus a stronger word, it is frequently used where the simple *bapto* would be less appropriate or less forcible. But by the tendency I have mentioned, the stronger word gradually came to be preferred to the weaker, with no substantial difference of meaning. The same thing has happened, still more completely, with the words signifying to sprinkle. From *raino*, to sprinkle, came *rantos*, sprinkled; and upon this verbal adjective was formed *rant-izo*, which would thus mean to cause to be sprinkled, or to bring into a sprinkled condition. But, here there is never any practical difference in meaning between the simple and the derived form. In the classics we find only the simple *raino*; in later Greek writers and the Septuagint, both this and the stronger *rantizo*; in the New Testament, only *rantizo*; in modern Greek, both; and nowhere is any practical difference discernible. There are other examples of the same sort.* While *bapto* and *baptizo* did not (like

---

* *E. g.*, φαντάζομαι, αἱρετίζω. The frequentative sense in which some verbs, as ῥιπτάζω, κυπτάζω, is probably derivative from the causative or active sense described above. Another derivation would be the intensive sense, where the termination is frequently appended, not to the stem of the verbal adjective, but to the simple verb root, as in αἰτέω, "ask," αἰτίζω, "beg;" ἕρπω, "crawl," ἑρπύζω, "creep." Curtius gives some indirect support to this view (Griech. Etym., s. 553-5), but the terminations in ζω have never been thoroughly studied.

raino and *rantizo*) become identical in meaning, but each has uses of its own, yet the stronger word came to be frequently employed in substantially the same sense as the weaker, seeing that the natural and common way of bringing a thing into a dipt condition is to dip it.

Thus far, then, Dr. Dale has made no important addition to our knowledge of the primary meaning of *baptizo*. He deserves the credit of having brought out that meaning more clearly than others, though he has not perceived its connection with the etymology. His attempt to establish a broad and invariable difference in meaning between it and the simple form *bapto* is a mistake, and even if he were right, it would make no practical difference as to the duty enjoined by *baptizo*. His elaborate efforts to show that Baptist writers, of different generations and countries, have differed in their views as to the mere *theory* of the word, prove nothing as to the real question at issue.

But Dr. Dale now takes an additional step which is novel and surprising. In the first place he confounds the literal and figurative uses of the term in question, and substantially claims that in the literal use it can have no more definite sense than it has in the figurative—a process destructive of all exact interpretation. He then attempts to show that the word is used in three different senses: first, intusposition without influence, as when a stone is intusposed in water; second, intusposition with influence, as when a man is intusposed in water, and—not being taken out—is drowned; third, influence without intusposition, so that whatever controllingly influences a thing, may be said to baptize it. This last can only be called a figment of Dr. Dale's fancy. By the same sort of process I could reduce to a nebulous condition the meaning of any word whatever. Anything which controllingly influences an object so as to change its condition, may be described as baptizing that object. Thus, if I should set fire to this piece of paper and change it to ashes, I should be baptizing it. If I hang a man, or stab him, or poison him, or corrupt his morals, I baptize him. This fanciful notion he attempts to support by a mass of painstaking, but utterly wild interpretation, such as can only excite one's astonishment.

And the grand result of his whole discussion

is, if possible, still more wonderful. Beginning with the position that baptize means immerse, he ends by maintaining that *immersion is not baptism*. This surpasses the jugglers. Here is the word baptize meaning immerse, or if you prefer it, intuspose; now a few passes of logical and philological slight of hand, and behold immersion, or intusposition, is not baptism at all. If you feel inclined to say the force of absurdity could no further go, be not too fast, for Dr. Dale, apparently fascinated by his fancies, has in his most recent production practised an utter *reductio ad absurdum* upon his own theory. Our blessed Lord speaks of his dreadful sufferings as a baptism, and also speaks of them as drinking a cup; and Dr. Dale deliberately infers that *drinking a cup is baptism*. I cannot hold this up to the sheer ridicule it deserves, because the subject is too sacred.

I have thus endeavored to show that the plain teaching of our English Bible, supported by the highest authorities as to Greek scholarship, and by the testimony and practice of the living Greeks, cannot be set aside either by the authority of "the church," the opinions of eminent individuals, or our own notions of convenience, nor yet by the attempts to establish a sacred, as quite different from the classical, sense of the term involved, nor by the strange and wild notions of a recent writer.

And now, this protracted discussion shall close with a single remark. I have spoken long and earnestly of a controverted question, one of those which divide Christians. But I am a rejoicing believer in Christian Union. It is too common to speak of this as having no actual existence; to speak dolefully of our Lord's prayer, "That they all may be one," as not at all fulfilled. Certainly it is not completely fulfilled in the present state of things; but it is fulfilled as really, and in as high a degree, as the prayer which precedes it, "Sanctify them through thy truth." Christ's people are by no means completely sanctified, yet they are sanctified; and though not completely one, yet they are one All who are truly his are one in him. Not only those belonging to what we call evangelical denominations, but many Romanists, for there are doubtless lovers of Christ among them, as there have been in past ages; and many of the Greek Church; and perhaps some Universalists, and Unitarians, possibly even Mormons; and Quakers, who reject all water baptism; and some who from mistaken views neglect to make any profession of faith, or as the phrase is, do not join any church;—whoever and wherever they may be, though many of their opinions be erroneous and their practices wrong, yet if they are truly Christ's people they are truly one in him. Let nothing prevent us from clinging to this great fact, and rejoicing in the thought of Christian unity. But assuredly it is desirable—eminently, unspeakably desirable—to have *more* of union, both in spirit and in organization. We who believe in the Bible ought to be standing together against the bold and arrogant infidelity which is coming in like a flood; we who are called Protestants ought to be laboring together against the aggressions of Romanism, which seeks to gain compensation in America for what it has lost in Europe. Now such completer union, of spirit and of organization, is possible only on Scriptural grounds; only by taking the Bible as our sole authority, and the Bible, as being a book for the people, in its plain meaning. All Christians, except the Quakers, make baptism a condition of church membership. And for the sake of a more complete and efficient Christian union, we urge upon our fellow Christians, as the plain teaching of God's word, that there is no baptism where there is not an immersion.

I close with the Apostle's words, "Grace be with all them that love our Lord Jesus Christ in sincerity."

ALVAH HOVEY, D. D., LL. D.,
1820-1903.

President of Newton Theological Institution.

EVILS

OF

INFANT BAPTISM.

BY REV. ALVAH HOVEY, D.D.

PHILADELPHIA:
THE BIBLE AND PUBLICATION SOCIETY,
1420 CHESTNUT STREET.

EVILS OF INFANT BAPTISM.

"A little leaven leaveneth the whole lump."—*Gal.* v. 9.

IT cannot for a moment be doubted that the servants of Christ should honor and defend his truth. And I mean by "his truth," comprehensively, "the gospel of the kingdom." For the Saviour of men, in his ever memorable response to Pilate, spoke distinctly of his kingdom as being not of this world, not dependent on the sword for existence, or growth, or defence, and then added this significant statement: "To this end have I been born, and to this end have I come into the world, that I may bear witness to the truth." From which language, interpreted by the context, I infer that the kingdom of Christ rests upon truth, and is to be enlarged and defended by faithfully manifesting the truth, that is to say, by declaring the facts, the principles, the laws, the duties, and the ends of that kingdom, or, to gather all into a single phrase, by preaching the gospel of the kingdom. Whatever Jesus taught, either by his own lips, or by the mouth of his apostles, is therefore embraced in the truth.

But is it necessary to oppose error in order to honor and defend truth? Must we protest in so many words against false doctrine, in order to "contend earnestly for the faith once delivered to the saints?" These questions may be answered, no, and yes, according to circumstances and the points in debate. For consistent thinkers the establishment of a given truth is doubtless the overthrow of the opposite error. And this method of action has sometimes great advantages. It is often more effectual than any other, and always more agreeable. It may be safely chosen when the views in question are plainly and directly opposed to each other. Thus the doctrine of universal salvation may be completely demolished by proving that some of our race reject the only means of salvation, and are lost forever; for that doctrine is a formulated denial of the final ruin of a single soul, and the simplest mind will see that it cannot be true, if any perish. But there are errors as to doctrine and duty which do not stand out in the light of day, each over against an opposite truth, and so sharply defined, so equally matched with that contrasted truth, that the reception of the one carries with it perforce a rejection of the other. Far oftener is error associated with truth, or clad in the garments of truth, and so able to deceive the unwary. Far oftener is it a tincture of evil permeating the mass of truth, like the leaven of which the apostle speaks in my text.

For it is agreed by the best interpreters that in this place leaven is an emblem of evil, that it symbolizes either teachers of error, or the error which they teach. I adopt the latter sense, as being more natural and obvious than the former; but if the former was intended by the apostle, the text is still pertinent to my theme—the "Evils of Infant Baptism,"—for false teachers do evil by means of the error which they diffuse. It is not their personal influence, their eloquence, or their persuasiveness which, in and of itself, poisons and corrupts, but it is the false doctrine commended thereby. Silently, secretly, steadily, does this work its way through every particle of the lump, and though small in amount, effects a startling change in the quality and state of the whole. Judaism, sometimes represented in this epistle by circumcision, its initial rite, is here in the mind of Paul, and is denounced by him as leaven pervading the whole lump with evil. A small error it might have seemed to those who thought it an error; not a formal rejection of Christ, the Lord, but only a perpetuation of the type with the reality which it typified; only a clinging to the shadow as well as the substance which it outlined; only a retention of the carnal ordinance along with the law of life; only a commingling of the natural with the spiritual, of that which constituted one a Jew outwardly with that which constituted one a Jew inwardly, tending to obscure the truth and darken the mind—this it was, and only this, which the apostle looked upon as an error endangering the very life of a pure Christianity and church. Good as Judaism certainly had been in its own day and for its appointed service, it was no more fit to be connected with a Christian church, than is the body of a worm to be united with the butterfly that has escaped from it, or the natural body of man to be joined with his glorified body; and every attempt to combine the two must result in harm to Christian doctrine and life.

A similar view must be taken of infant baptism. It has no natural place in the kingdom of Christ. Hence those who hold, in other respects, the apostolic doctrine as to that kingdom, find it the hardest task to justify this practice, and make it coalesce with the remaining elements of their creed. The farther one moves from the Papal Church towards the Apostolic, the more difficult does the comprehension of infant baptism become, and the more liable is it to be neglected as a practice of uncertain origin. The rite seems to be at home in the Papal Church, and everything else agrees so perfectly with it, that one is justified in surmising that infant baptism is, in fact, the "little leaven that has leavened the whole lump," the tincture of error which has corrupted every part of the system. But I must pass from this general statement, and endeavor to point out with all fidelity, and at the same time with sincere good will to Christians of every name, some of the evils of infant baptism.

I. *Infant baptism takes away from the Christian ordinance a large part of its meaning.*

If the Papal theory of a mysterious, sacramental virtue in baptism is unworthy of confidence, and the efficacy of the rite, as a means of grace, depends largely upon the truth which it brings into the mind and heart, anything which weakens its significance must be an evil; and the greatness of the evil must correspond with the amount of truth thus ignored and lost.* Now, the Sacred Record shows that in the apostolic age, Christian baptism was a solemn profession of faith in Christ on the part of him who received it. For, in his letter to the Galatians, Paul says to the Christians of that province:

---

* The translator, reformer, and martyr, Tyndale, says of the sacraments: "There is none other virtue in them than to testify and exhibit to the senses and understanding the covenants and promises made in Christ's blood;" and, "where the sacraments or ceremonies are not rightly understood, there they be clearly unprofitable."—*Tulloch's Rational Theology in England.* etc., p. 41.

"Ye are all sons of God through the (your) faith in Christ Jesus. For all ye who were baptized into Christ did put on Christ." Here the apostle alleges the fact of their having put on Christ, by their own act, in baptism as an evidence of their faith in Christ, and so of their sonship to God. "Ye are all sons of God, for ye have all believed in Christ, and ye have all believed in Christ, for ye have all taken him solemnly to be your Lord and your life, by submitting to baptism. If your profession in this act was sincere, ye are truly identified with Christ by faith, and therefore are sons of God." The only alternative to this view of Paul's language, is one that makes it teach the doctrine of baptismal regeneration; for he could not have appealed to the fact of their baptism as an evidence of their faith, unless it was either the root or the fruit of faith, unless it either originated or attested faith; and I need not state to this assembly the reasons which require us to look upon the act of putting on Christ in baptism as an avowal of faith, rather than a production of it, for the first time, in the heart.

With this passage may be compared another, addressed by the apostle to Christians of his own day: "Know ye not, that all we who were baptized into Jesus Christ were baptized into his death? We were buried therefore with him through our baptism into his death; that, like as Christ was raised from the dead through the glory of the Father, so we also might walk in newness of life."

The translation which I have read is that of Dean Alford. A little further on they are exhorted to reckon themselves "to be dead unto sin, but alive unto God in Christ Jesus." In the baptismal symbol and profession they had died to sin, separating themselves formally from the love and service of it, even as Christ, their Lord, in another way and respect, had also died to sin, separating himself from its burden and curse forevermore. Their baptism was an act by which they renounced openly the service of Satan and accepted that of Christ. This was true of all the faithful in Rome; but it is not true of persons christened in infancy. Their own death to sin, their own entrance upon a new life, their own union with Christ cannot be expressed by an ordinance administered without their knowledge or consent.

In harmony with my interpretation of these two passages are the several notices of baptism in the Acts of the Apostles. When the hearers of Peter on the day of Pentecost gladly received his word, they were baptized, but not before. When the people of Samaria believed Philip preaching the things concerning the kingdom of God, and the name of Jesus, they were baptized, both men and women. When the Ethiopian eunuch listened to the same Evangelist proclaiming Jesus, and asked the privilege of putting on Christ by baptism, the rite was promptly administered. Saul of Tarsus was not baptized until he gave evidence of faith in the Lord Jesus; nor Cornelius until he received the gift of the Holy Spirit; nor Lydia until her heart was opened by the Lord to attend to the words of Paul; nor the jailer until he believed, and all his house. In every instance cited, baptism appears to have followed and attested faith in Christ; and I find no case recorded in the New Testament where this ordinance was not understood to be a declaration of such faith. Even

John's Baptism signified a change of mind,* an entrance upon a new and spiritual life, which had already brought forth its appropriate fruits. When, therefore, the rite of baptism is applied to infants, a large part, and it may be the most important part, of its meaning is lost; and if, as we all believe, it was divinely instituted to symbolize and emphasize certain great truths in "the gospel of the kingdom," it must be an evil and a sin to disavow, or even ignore, one half its original significance. If any man deems this language severe, let him weigh the following words from the last chapter of Revelation: "I testify to every one that heareth the words of the prophecy of this book, that if any one shall add to them, God will add to him the plagues that are written in this book; and if any one shall take away from the words of the book of this prophecy, God will take away his part from the tree of life and out of the holy city." It must not be forgotten by us that the truth of God is sacred, whether expressed in words or in

---

* Μετάνοια, a strong and far-reaching word, applied only in the New Testament to a radical and spiritual change.

ordinances; and it is not in our power to say confidently that more evil is done by adding to that truth than by taking from it; by introducing rites not prescribed by the Founder of our religion, than by mutilating or misapplying those prescribed.

It is also proper for me to suggest that the application of baptism to infants not only takes away from the Christian rite a large part of its meaning, but that it tends to a change of the rite itself, by substituting affusion or sprinkling for immersion, and thus diminishing still further its original significance. While saying this, I do not forget the practice of the Greek Church, numbering so many millions, but I am satisfied, nevertheless, that the feebleness of infancy has had much to do in reconciling parents and pastors to what Cyprian calls "a compend, or abridgment," of this holy ordinance.* To this conviction I am brought by the nature of

---

* See *Cypriani Opera*, i. p. 197 (Gersdorf's ed.). "In sacramentis salutaribus necessitate cogente et Deo indulgentiam suam largiente totum credentibus conferunt divina compendia." Cyprian is here speaking of cases where "adspergi vel perfundi videntur *ægri*, cum gratiam dominicam consequuntur."

the case and the records of history, without appealing to the valid principle that deviation from apostolic example in one respect renders further deviation comparatively easy.

But does the substitution of affusion or sprinkling for baptism lessen its significance? Beyond a doubt this is to be answered in the affirmative; for, according to the obvious meaning of Paul's language in the sixth chapter of Romans, baptism represents vividly the death, burial, and resurrection of the candidate, his dying, through faith in the death of Christ, to sin and the law, and his rising through faith to a new life unto God, and free obedience. But, quite apart from this inspired exposition of the symbolism of the rite, immersion suggests to the mind all that sprinkling does, and far more.

Not many years ago a thoughtful woman made known to me her desire to be immersed, although she had been sprinkled in early life. When asked why she felt so strong a desire for immersion, her reply included and emphasized this declaration: "I feel that I ought to express in baptism the devotion of my whole being to the Lord." And in a recent sermon by Mr. Spurgeon, the following words are addressed to the members of his church:

"We who have been baptized upon profession of our faith, were taught in that solemn ordinance to bless the Lord with our entire being, for we were not sprinkled here or there; but we were, in the outward sign, buried with the Lord Jesus in baptism unto death, and we were immersed into the name of the Triune God. If our baptism meant anything, it declared that we were henceforth dead to the world, and owned no life but that which came to us by the way of the resurrection of Jesus. Over our heads the liquid water flowed, for we resigned the brain, with all its powers of thought, to Jesus; over the heart, the veins, the hands, the feet, the eyes, the ears, the mouth, the significant element poured itself, symbol of that universal consecration which deluges all the inward nature of every sanctified believer. My baptized brethren, I charge you, belie not your profession."

Now if this appeal rests upon the symbolism of the rite, as I believe it does, and if the application of it to infants has tended to the substitution of sprinkling for immersion, the evil has been great. For truth has been hidden, truth which the Saviour came into the world to reveal, truth which he was pleased to signalize and enforce by a holy ordinance, truth which a disciple in the freshness of his first love wishes to confess in the clearest manner possible. Who can measure the evil resulting from the practice of withdrawing such truth from the eyes of men?

I must now add, that young converts do often, if not always, esteem it a privilege to put on Christ by baptism, and sometimes express regret at their being prevented from so doing by a rite imposed upon them in infancy. But what is even more to be deplored, some who believe it their duty to avow their new-born faith and love by following the Lord in baptism, are led by their regard for the feelings of others to stifle their own convictions and wrong their own souls. This surely is a sore evil under the sun; and, so far as I can see, it is due to the practice of infant baptism.

II. *Infant baptism ascribes to the ordinance an imaginary virtue.*

I do not for a moment claim that it originated a belief in baptismal regeneration; for an impartial study of the Christian literature of the first three centuries after Christ will reveal the fact, that a certain regenerating efficacy was attributed to baptism long before the latter was applied to infants. Decisive proof of this may be found in the First Apology of Justin Martyr,* and in the Shepherd of Hermas. The Shepherd was written about the middle of the second century, and it plainly asserts that not even the saints of a former dispensation could be saved through Christ, without going down into the baptismal waters and experiencing their life-giving virtue. Hence the apostles, after finishing their earthly course, are said to have preached Christ and administered baptism to the patriarchs in Hades. If, then, the question of priority between the doctrine of baptismal regeneration and the practice of infant baptism is answered from history, the doctrine must be said to have preceded the practice by more than fifty years. And, if it went before the practice, it must have led to it. For let any man believe two things, namely, that infants need the new

---

* See the account of Baptism, ₴ 61.

birth in order to be saved, and that this birth is only realized in baptism, and an argument of tremendous cogency will urge him to apply the rite to babes, even before they are eight days old.* But the writings of the early Christians reveal their belief of these two things more than half a century before the faintest traces of infant baptism appear. The nature of the evidence and the nature of the case compel us therefore to say, that the practice of infant baptism owed its first existence to the theory of baptismal regeneration.†

---

* Note the words of Cyprian (i. p. 168, Gersdorf's ed.). "Quantum vero ad causam infantium pertinet, quos dixisti intra secundum vel tertium diem, quo nati sint, constitutos baptizari non oportere, et considerandam esse legem circumcisionis antiquæ, ut intra octavum diem eum, qui natus est, baptizandum non putares, longe aliud in concilio nostro omnibus visum est. In hoc enim quod tu putabas esse faciendum, nemo consensit, sed universi potius judicamus nulli homini nato misericordiam Dei et gratiam denegandam." The whole letter and argument are a curiosity, but they show that baptism was deemed necessary to the salvation of infants.

† And this circumstance accounts for the slight resistance which it encountered at the outset. The tendency of the period was towards ritualism. Tertullian, who first refers to infant baptism, though only to oppose it, refers

EVILS OF INFANT BAPTISM.

But, if the theory originated the practice, the practice has reacted in favor of the theory. For the two are natural allies, and neither is strong apart from the other. As it is well-nigh impossible to maintain infant baptism without the aid of that theory, so I believe it would be found impossible to support that theory for a long time without the complement and strength afforded by the practice.

It is indeed true that some justify the practice on the single ground that infants are brought into covenant relations with Christ by baptism,

---

also to the sign of the cross as commonly employed; and to various established customs which followed baptism— the anointing of the candidate, the imposition of hands, the eating of milk and honey, and the refraining from the bath for a whole week. Now it is impossible for any one to show when these and other ceremonies were first introduced. Ritualism was in the air, and the introduction of new rites, or the wider application of existing rites, was natural and easy. Hence, the exact date of the rise of infant baptism can no more be given than the exact date of the rise of the other additions to apostolic baptism, or the time when other ceremonies were first introduced. The spirit of the age and the culture of the people made these ritual innovations welcome, and not until their evil effects began to be in some degree obvious, could we expect to meet with remonstrances against them.

while all who are not baptized are left to the uncovenanted mercy of God. The effect of the ordinance is not therefore supposed to be moral, in the heart or character, but rather civil or perhaps legal, in the standing of infants before God. They are more likely to be converted in after life, because the seal of the covenant is applied to them in infancy, securing to them a larger measure of privilege or grace. Thus, many years ago, an orthodox clergyman lost a disobedient son by drowning. There was very little, I suppose, in the lad's character to relieve the father's anguish, yet the latter expressed a hope, founded on the single fact of his early baptism, that his boy had fallen asleep in Jesus.* And this instance is but one of many. For all who believe in infant baptism have an

---

* That pious father, who had doubtless offered prayer a thousand times in the name of Jesus for his wayward son, and who knew and taught that the prayer of God's dear children will be heard by their heavenly Father, yea, heard it may be sometimes in the very hour of death, forgot all the promises of God in this respect, and found his only comfort in thinking of an outward rite administered to his child in infancy. I sympathize profoundly with his sorrow, but, with the New Testament in my hands, I wonder at the direction in which he turned for relief.

EVILS OF INFANT BAPTISM.

impression that, in some way and to some extent, the saving grace of God depends on the reception of this rite. Ignoring the proper use and blessing of baptism, as a sacred and symbolical confession of Christ, which contributes to growth in character and life, they fix their attention upon its supposed virtue in procuring or producing the new birth. Ten years ago I had a long interview with a distinguished theologian of Berlin, in which the progress of our views in Prussia was freely discussed. He conceded at once that neither sprinkling nor pouring was sanctioned by the apostles; their baptism included an immersion of the subject in water; but he strenuously asserted that the ordinance must be useless, if it be not either a cause or a condition of the new birth. He seemed unable to comprehend its value as a testimony to the truth and as a means of grace to believers. Moreover, he deplored the labors of our brethren in Germany for two reasons especially; first, because the most earnest Christians were drawn from the Lutheran Church into the Baptist ranks; and, secondly, because the religious welfare of the people was amply secured by the established faith. When reminded by me that great multitudes appeared to contemn the law of God, the gospel of Christ, and the holy Sabbath, he appealed to their having received baptism and the eucharist, as the ground of his belief in their ultimate salvation. His reliance was placed on sacramental grace. And this professor of theology is a representative man, a teacher of the faith that rules in the fatherland. His views are honored by the Lutheran Church of to-day.

Nor are they confined to the members of that Church, but are accepted by a large part of the Church of England and of the Church of Scotland, together with all who belong to either the Papal or the Greek Church. Baptismal regeneration is therefore taught by an overwhelming majority of those that apply the rite to infants. And is not this doctrine the logical result of their practice? If the church is the kingdom of Christ; if babes must be renewed in order to share the life of that kingdom; and if they are to receive baptism, which, in the case of adults, conditions or attests their entrance upon that life, must not this ordinance in some way rescue the infant soul from ruin by imparting grace? It can convey no truth to the mind of the babe; it can testify of no conscious change, experience, or purpose in the heart of the babe; but may it not, as a sacrament, work in the unconscious spirit, infusing the principle of a holy life? The application of the rite being conceded, what more comforting theory of its virtue can be imagined? This theory is a key which opens the lock and explains the usage; therefore it must be and is correct.

But if the practice were to be laid aside as unscriptural, or were to be everywhere neglected as of doubtful origin and utility; if baptism were for any good reason to be again restricted to persons who seek it of their own accord, how long would it be, think you, before nearly all that know the Lord would accept the obvious meaning of the New Testament, and see in this ordinance an acknowledgment of grace already received, a profession of faith already implanted in the heart, a symbol of the new birth from God, manifesting itself to the world in cheerful obedience? Let infant baptism pass away, and the seductive error of baptismal regeneration will not long survive. Let infant baptism pass away, and believers' baptism, ordained by Christ and honored by the apostles, will soon take its place—a change that cannot, I verily believe, be sought too kindly, too conscientiously, and too persistently by the friends of Jesus. Says Dr. Hodge: "The reception of baptism, so far as adults are concerned, is an intelligent, voluntary act, which from its nature involves, 1st, a profession of faith in Christ, and 2d, a promise of allegiance to him. This is clear from the command of Christ to make disciples of all nations, baptizing them in the name of the Father, of the Son, and of the Holy Ghost. A disciple, however, is both a recipient of doctrines taught and a follower. Everyone, therefore, who is made a disciple by baptism, enrolls himself among the number of those who receive Christ as their teacher and Lord, and who profess obedience and devotion to his service. This is further clear from the uniform practice of the apostles. In every case on record of their administering the rite, it was on the condition of a profession of faith on the part of the recipient. This has also in all ages been the practice of the church. No-man was admitted to baptism without an intelligent profession of faith in Christ, and a solemn engagement of obedience to him. The practice of Romanist missionaries, in baptizing the heathen in crowds, can hardly be considered as invalidating this statement." These sentences from the pen of a distinguished Pedobaptist divine, though perhaps a little too unqualified, confirm my position. For according to their testimony, the application of baptism to adults has in every age and in all branches of the church been restricted to those who avow their faith in Christ. But Paul distinctly affirms that "No one can call Jesus Lord, but in the Holy Ghost;" and John reiterates the same truth by saying, that "Every one who believeth that Jesus is the Christ, hath been begotten of God." Admit the statement of Dr. Hodge, that, by the common, if not universal consent of Christians, faith should precede baptism in the case of adults, and the testimony of the apostles, that the work of the Spirit in regeneration is presupposed by faith, and it follows, that the doctrine of baptismal regeneration would pass away with the practice of infant baptism, or at least would soon follow after it. The latter may therefore be justly charged with aiding and abetting the evil involved in the former.

III. *Infant baptism mars the constitution of the Christian churches.*

To prove this I am called to show that Christian churches ought to be composed of such persons only as give credible evidence of faith in the Lord Jesus; for infant baptism brings into them persons who do not give this evidence. Your attention is therefore invited to but a single feature of an apostolic church. It was a company of believers in Christ. I do not mean to say that there were no hypocrites in it, for Judas and Ananias and Simon Magus bore the name of disciples for a time; and so fair a show of sincerity did they make, that only an eye which pierces through every disguise could detect their falseness at the outset. But I mean that these few deceivers, as well as all the worthy disciples of Jesus, were baptized and banded together in churches upon a profession of their personal faith, a profession that was apparently honest and heartfelt, the utterance of a new life in the soul.

In support of this position, I refer you again to a passage in the Epistle to the Galatians: "Ye are all sons of God through your faith in Christ Jesus. For all ye who were baptized into Christ did put on Christ." This letter was addressed to the churches of Galatia, and the passage which I have read, to all the members of those churches. "Ye are no longer," is the meaning of the apostle, "kept as wards under the law, as minor children under a schoolmaster, but ye are all sons of God, by adoption, through your faith in Christ, which was solemnly professed by you in your baptism." Now, if children in their minority had been baptized in Galatia along with their believing parents, and on account of their parents' faith, and if this process had been going on for a period of ten years, since the first visit of Paul to this province, there must have been many in the churches, say, one-third or one-half the members, who did not by their own act put on Christ in baptism. How then could the apostle say: "Ye are all in Christ by faith, and, therefore, are sons of God, for ye did all put on Christ in baptism?" His language appears to be strained and unnatural, if addressed to companies of men, only a part of whom had avowed their personal faith in baptism, or indeed in any other way. And the same may be remarked of a passage in his First Epistle to th Corinthians: "For in one spirit also we were all baptized into one body, whether Jews or Greeks, whether bond or free; and were all made to drink of one Spirit,"—language which is best explained by supposing that baptism was administered to those, and those only, who were believed to have the Spirit of God, so that spiritual incorporation into the body of Christ went before professional and sacramental. For this epistle was sent, not to a part of the church of God in Corinth, but to the whole of it, "together with all that call upon the name of our Lord Jesus Christ in every place." It is true that the church is also described as those who are "sanctified in Christ Jesus," "called saints," not, however, to suggest the idea of a church within the church, but to remind the members, one and all, of the grace which they had received from God and had thankfully acknowledged before the world.

With equal certainty may it be affirmed that Paul addressed all the members of the church at Philippi as "saints in Christ Jesus," and as notable for their fellowship in respect to the gospel; for in his greeting he invokes "the grace of God upon all the saints in Christ Jesus which are in Philippi, with the bishops and deacons," naturally meaning the entire church of that city; and in the last part of his letter he remarks: "When I departed from Macedonia, no church communicated with me in account of giving and receiving, but ye only," which implies that the persons to whom he wrote composed a church. It would be easy to multiply citations from the letters of Paul, showing that membership in a Christian church was deemed by him presumptive evidence of genuine faith, and certain evidence of avowed faith; hence, until weighty reasons constrain us to believe that some were brought into the apostolic churches, who either would not or could not make any profession of their own faith, I must hold and teach that those churches were companies of believers, that such persons only were admitted to them as gave credible evidence of love to God and faith in Christ.*

But against this view of Christian churches in the first age, two objections have been

---

* The Augsburg Confession says: "Est ecclesia congregatio sanctorum, in qua evangelium recte docetur et recte administrantur sacramenta. . . . Lyra testatur: Ecclesia consistit in illis personis, in quibus notitia vera et confessio fidei et veritatis. . . . Ecclesia est . . . congregatio sanctorum, qui vere credunt evangelio Christi, et habent Spiritum Sanctum. Catechismus Major: Credo, in terris esse quendam sanctorum congregatiunculam et communionem ex mere sanctis hominibus coactam sub uno capite Christo, per Spiritum Sanctum convocatam, in una fide, eodem sensu et sententia, multiplicibus dotibus exornatam, in amore tamen unanimem, et per omnia concordem, sine sectis et schismatibus. Ch. of Eng.: Ecclesia Christi visibilis est coetus fidelium, in quo verbum Dei purum praedicatur et sacramenta, quoad ea quae necessario exiguntur, juxta Christi institutum recte administrantur. Scotch ch.: Unam ecclesiam constanter credimus, id est, societatem et multitudinem hominum a Deo electorum, qui illum recte per veram fidem in Jesum Christum colunt et amplectuntur, qui ejusdem ecclesiae solus est caput, quae etiam est corpus et sponsa Christi Jesu. Helvetic ch.: Oportet semper fuisse, esse et futuram esse ecclesiam, id est e mundo evocatum et collectum coetum fidelium, sanctorum inquam omnium communionem, eorum videlicet, qui Deum verum in Christo servatore per verbum et Spiritum S. vere cognoscunt et rite colunt, denique omnibus bonis per Christum gratuito oblatis fide participant."

pressed, one of them drawn from the parable of the tares, and the other, from the so-called Jewish Church. The parable of the tares, according to Dr. Hodge, proves "it is not the purpose of God that the visible church on earth should consist exclusively of true believers." "Our Lord," he remarks, "expressly forbids the attempt being made. He compares his external kingdom, or visible church, to a field in which tares and wheat grow together. He charged his disciples not to undertake to separate them, because they could not, in all cases, distinguish the one from the other. Both were to be allowed to grow together until the harvest." On this interpretation of the parable, and the corresponding use of it in the justification of infant church membership, I submit the following reflections: 1. Christ explains his own parable, and declares "the field" in question to be "the world," not "the visible church;" and his definite interpretation is to me an end of doubt. 2. He declares "the reapers," and so, by parity of reason, "the servants of the householder," to be "angels," not "the children of the kingdom." The children of the kingdom are represented in this parable, according to the Master's own word, by "the good seed." 3. He charges the introduction of the evil seed to "the devil," not to "the servants of the householder," much less, to the "good seed," "the children of the kingdom." 4. He says that the tares, or darnel, was sown by night, that is, secretly, and not by day, or openly. Would the defenders of infant baptism have the friends of Christ do that openly, in the face of the sun, which the Saviour himself ascribed to Satan, working stealthily under cover of night? I cannot withhold an expression of amazement at the use which they have made of this parable. The true meaning of it may be given in the words of William Arnot: "It appears to me, then, that the Lord's direct and immediate design in this parable is, not to prescribe the conduct of his disciples in regard to the conflict between good and evil in the world, but to explain his own. Knowing that their Master possessed all power in heaven and in earth, it was natural that Christians of the first age should expect an immediate paradise. Nothing was more necessary for the support of their faith in subsequent trials, than distinct warnings from the Lord, that even to his own people the world would remain a wilderness." In a word, the early Christians must be taught that their King, with all the powers of nature and of the heavenly world at his command, would not root out evil from the earth in which his children were, until the end should come; and what he would not allow his ministers, his servants, his angels, to do, until the end of the world, lest some of the children of the kingdom should be destroyed with the children of the wicked one, it may certainly be inferred that he would not have the children of the kingdom do themselves. Persecution is, therefore, implicitly condemned. The wicked are not to be exterminated by the righteous. But the passage has no reference to the discipline of offenders by the church; nor does it, in the slightest degree, sanction the introduction of ungodly persons into the church. It says not a word in respect to the constitution of the church, favorable to infant membership. The "good seed" are "the children of the kingdom;" "the tares" are *not* "the children of the kingdom," but *are* "the children of the wicked one." There is nothing, then, in the parable of the tares to show that the house of God should not be built exclusively of what are supposed to be "living stones," and much to show that it should be built, so far as intention goes, of such stones only.

The second great argument for recognizing certain persons who are not supposed to be converted as members of Christian churches, is the constitution of the Jewish nation. The terms of admission to a Christian church may be learned, it is said, from the terms of admission to the congregation of Israel. As in the latter, the condition of the children was determined by the condition of the parents, so must it be in the kingdom of Christ.* Says Dr. Hodge:

---

* In setting forth the nature of the visible church, Dr. Hodge lays down the following propositions: 1. "The visible church is a divine institution." 2. "The visible church does not consist exclusively of the regenerate." 3. "The commonwealth of Israel was the church." 4. "The church under the New Dispensation is identical with that under the Old." 5. "The terms of admission into the church before the advent were the same that are required for admission into the Christian church." 6. "Infants were members of the church under the Old Testament economy." 7. "There is nothing in the New

In the sight of God, parents and children are one. The former are the authorized representatives of the latter; they act for them; they contract obligations in their name. In all cases, therefore, where parents enter into covenant with God, they bring their children with them." Again he says: "If a man joined the commonwealth of Israel, he secured for his children the benefits of the theocracy, unless they willingly renounced them. And so when a believer adopts the covenant of grace, he brings his children within that covenant, in the sense that God promises to give them, in his own good time, all the benefits of redemption, provided they do not willingly renounce their baptismal engagements."

It will be observed that Dr. Hodge first asserts that *parents* and children are one in covenant relations, and then that *a man* and his children are one in these relations. There is a difference between the statements which must not

---

Testament which justifies the exclusion of the children of believers from membership in the church." 8. "Children need and are capable of receiving the benefits of redemption."—(pp. 547–558).

be overlooked. For in the earlier economy it was the father, not the parents, who represented the family; hence none but male children, who might become heads of families, were circumcised. The husband was as truly the representative of his wife as he was of his children, of his daughters as he was of his sons, and of his servants, with their children, as he was of his own wife and children. Will asserters of infant baptism apply this to the Christian economy, and, when a man is baptized on profession of his faith in Jesus, proceed to baptize his wife and children also, even though the latter are old enough to believe for themselves, but do not? Unless they are willing to go to this length, they cannot justly claim to make the Jewish congregation a model for Christian churches. But they do not commonly go to this length; for they see that it would ill accord with the genius of Christianity, in which the spiritual is all-controlling, while the formal and natural is wholly subordinate. When the Saviour, on a certain occasion, "stretched forth his hand toward his disciples and said, Behold, my mother and my brothers! For whosoever shall do the will of my Father which is in heaven, the same is my brother, and sister, and mother," he made manifest the ties which are recognized as alone valid in his reign. But this was not the only occasion when he uttered words relevant to my subject: he said at another time: "Whosoever shall confess me before men, him will I confess also before my Father which is in heaven. . . . Think not that I am come to send peace on earth; I came not to send peace, but a sword. For I am come to set a man at variance against his father, and the daughter against her mother, and the daughter-in-law against her mother-in-law. And a man's foes shall be they of his own household." Also, "He that taketh not his cross and followeth after me, is not worthy of me;" and by this language he pointed very distinctly to a new order of things, to a kingdom into which no one could enter without personal faith and confession, into which men would come as individuals, not as families, the father for himself and the son for himself, and in which all natural affinities and distinctions would be merged in the one sacred kinship of soul to Christ, and the one infinite distinction between faith and unbelief, life and death. I grant that the natural Israel was typical of the spiritual Israel; but the type moves on a lower plane than the thing typified; into the typical nation men entered by natural birth, into the nation typified men enter by spiritual birth; those born of Abraham according to the flesh were circumcised, those born of God by the Spirit are baptized.*

Besides, if the Christian church is but a continuation of the Jewish, how is the preaching of Christ to be explained: "Except ye repent, ye shall all likewise perish?" Had the Jews willingly renounced their circumcision and their covenant standing? If they had, by their self-righteousness, though not intentionally, have not all children baptized in infancy, and still impenitent at the age of ten or twelve, renounced their

---

*When it suits their purpose Pedobaptists are ready enough to recognize the disparity between the Mosaic economy and the Christian. Thus Cyprian, in reply to the argument that baptism should be deferred to the eighth day after birth, because circumcision was performed on that day, says in his letter to Fidus, containing the decision of a council: "Nam quod in Judaica circumcisione carnali octavus dies observabatur, sacramentum est in umbra atque in imagine antepraemissum, sed veniente Christo veritate completum," etc. (Gersdorf's ed. i. p. 170.)

baptismal vows in the same way? And if this be so, what advantage is there in the rite? Are vows renounced better than no vows at all? Is there aught in the New Testament to justify such a view? Was not rather the gospel offered freely to all? Did not God bestow his grace on the uncircumcised Gentile as largely as on the circumcised Jew? But if mere unbelief on the part of a baptized child does not, as I understand Dr. Hodge to say, destroy his standing in the church, nor deprive him of the blessing of the covenant, then I submit that the progress from the shadow to the substance, from a kingdom that made large use of carnal weapons to one that employs only spiritual weapons, has been small indeed. Until, then, it can be shown that the type is on a level with the thing typified, and that Pedobaptists christen wives and grown-up children, as well as infants, on the faith of their husbands and fathers, they cannot rightly go back to the Jewish theocracy to learn the constitution of a Christian church.

I therefore return with full confidence to my position that a Christian church, as defined by the New Testament, is a company of persons giving credible evidence of their own faith. It will of course be recollected that I am giving but a single feature or characteristic of a church. And it is needless for me to insist that infant baptism, according to the doctrine of its ablest advocates, either introduces unbelieving children into the church, or assumes them to be already in the church at birth, or implants in their hearts sacramental and regenerating grace. Those who reject the last theory—that of baptismal regeneration—do therefore deliberately sow tares, to use their own figure, in the field which is the visible church. To employ a second figure, they put stones that are not "living" into the building of God. They wittingly and willingly mingle the carnal with the spiritual, and, I may say without offence to truth, apply the name "saint" to many a one whom they believe to be utterly unsanctified in heart. To do this seems to me equally against the word of God and against sound reason. It puts us back into the ritual and typical dispensation, into the state of pupilage, and offers the shadow of a spiritual kingdom in lieu of the reality. And so it mars the testimony given by the very constitution of an apostolic church to the nature of Christ's kingdom, as one which is not meat and drink, but righteousness and peace and joy in the Holy Ghost.

It may, however, be said by some who practise infant baptism, that a covenant relation with God is not a church relation, that children are consecrated in baptism and brought into covenant relations with God, but are in no sense members of the Christian church. But the position given to christened yet unconverted children by this theory is too uncertain to satisfy the mind. They seem to be neither in nor out of the kingdom; as a Catholic might say, they are in a sort of "limbus infantum," akin to the everlasting home of children who die in infancy, unchristened. For one I am unable to comprehend the relation which they hold to the covenant, or the principle on which they have been baptized; nor do I see that those who take this view of their position have any more light than I.

IV. *Infant baptism facilitates the union of church and state.*

This, if I mistake not, has been denied, though

it stands before my mind as an almost self-evident truth. The testimony of history is not, perhaps, decisive on the point, but whatever force it has favors my position. The friends of infant baptism claim that this rite has the same place and office in the Christian church, as a visible body, which circumcision had in the Jewish theocracy; but that theocracy was a union of church and state, and circumcision was confessedly adapted to it. The story of the Jewish people shows how naturally a person could be claimed as a subject of both church and state by a rite applied in infancy. But this is not the only instance. Since the reign of Constantine many examples of the union of civil and religious authority in the same government are on record. In some instances that union has been formal and complete, in others it has been tacit and partial. The Pope wielded the two swords for ages over a part of Italy; and would not perhaps refuse, if invited, to wield them over the whole world. The Emperor of Russia has pontifical as well as imperial power. In Spain and Austria, in France and Bavaria, there has been no exact line of demarcation between the functions of the church and those of the state. The power of the state has, however, been nearly always at the service of the hierarchy, and the influence of the hierarchy has been with those who were over the people. There has been a kind of holy alliance between kings and priests, for the purpose of keeping the people in subjection, and this alliance has been none the less effective because it has left the parties to it apparently distinct. It is scarcely necessary for me to specify other instances of a similar character. The history of England, Old and New,* of Prussia† and the smaller German States, would illustrate the union of the two swords for the attainment of one and the same end. And in all these nations the practice of infant baptism made the partial or complete identification of church and state easy. For if the church can give to all the

---

* See Uhden's "New England Theocracy," Backus' "History of the Baptists," "Life and Times of Isaac Backus," "The Writings of Roger Williams," etc.

† The sufferings of Mr. Oncken in Hamburg, and of others in Prussia proper, illustrate the later and milder forms of religious persecution. Mr. Oncken's testimony as to the source of opposition to his work, namely (in a whisper) infant baptism! deserves notice.

people in their infancy a place in her sacred enclosure and a certain rank among her children, the state can easily endorse that act and make it a qualification for public service; nay, it can be persuaded to enforce the claims of the church upon the respect and support of all her children. But if men are admitted to the church on the sole ground of their personal faith; if it is deeply felt that religion is a service of God by the conscience and the heart, and that without this inward spiritual life, all outward forms are a pretence and a lie; in other words, if the door into the church is closed to all but those who enter of their own accord, with love to the Saviour in their hearts, it is plain that a union of church and state becomes practically impossible. For many worthy citizens will not bow to Christ; many who render to Cæsar the things that are Cæsar's, will not render to God the things that are God's. An honest faith in the Redeemer cannot be exacted by the civil power; but an honest faith in him is the one thing which qualifies a man for the church. Very soon, therefore, the state learns that its weapons are not meant for the kingdom of Christ, and that the only thing it can properly do is to care for the natural rights and temporal interests of the people. Let infant baptism give place everywhere to believers' baptism, and the union of church and state will soon come to an end.

But what evils flow from the union of church and state? Evils manifold and dreadful, from some of which we turn away with unutterable horror. Worldliness, ambition, strife, deception, persecution, massacre! these are the terms to be employed in characterizing the evils in question. But even these terms, quietly uttered in the sanctuary, fail to bring before our minds the terrible scenes which they represent in the history of the Christian religion. The secularization of the clergy, their love of power and display, their idleness and vanity, their disregard of sound doctrine and pure morals, have been largely due to their dependence on the state for support, to their acquaintance with political arts and intrigues, and to their commerce with ungodly magistrates. But the old adage is true: "like priest, like people." When their spiritual leaders become worldly, ambitious, corrupt, the people are almost sure to follow. So when the power and splendor of the Roman emperor were reflected upon the clergy, ambitious men began to seek office in the church, and the whole body was gradually leavened by their influence. Pagan temples, Pagan statues, and Pagan rites were dedicated to Jehovah, while the severe and holy simplicity of the early Christians passed away. And thereafter, down through the ages, an adulterous connection between church and state was the source of infinite mischief to the former, and, I fear, of little good to the latter. But I may not attempt to describe that mischief fully. It will be enough for me to recall a single feature of it. The Papal Church is careful to disclaim persecution. It is never her own act. The Pope, as a spiritual ruler, does not take the life of a heretic. How then, it may be asked, have the fires of persecution been kindled? The reply is at hand: by the state in close alliance with the church. By the state doing the sacred judgment of the church. By the Pope, as a civil ruler, executing the will of the same Pope as vicar of Christ. By godly magistrates drawing the sword in their civil capacity to suppress what they have condemned in their spiritual capacity. And so, tender and enlightened consciences have been mocked and flouted, gentle and saintly souls have been sent up to God from amidst the flames, and the best blood of Christ's earthly flock has flowed in torrents. But more cruel than the last act have often been the tortures that went before it. Confiscation, banishment, the dungeon, the rack, for a clear conscience and a pure life! in New England, in Old England, and throughout Europe! with now and then a Duke of Alva,* or a St. Bartholomew massacre! Such horrors kindled the soul of Milton when he prayed:

---

* Says Mr. Motley of the Council of Troubles, called also the Blood-Council, over which the Duke of Alva presided in the Netherlands: "So well did this new and terrible engine perform its work, that in less than three months from the time of its erection, eighteen hundred human beings (or twenty a day) had suffered death by its summary proceedings; some of the highest, the noblest, and the most virtuous in the land among the number; nor had it then manifested the slightest indication of faltering in its dread career." "Alva reserved for himself the final decision upon all causes which should come before the council, and stated his motives for so doing with grim simplicity. 'Two reasons,' he wrote to the king, 'have determined me thus to limit the power of the tribunal; the first that, not knowing its members, I might be easily

"Avenge, O Lord, thy slaughtered saints, whose bones
Lie scattered on the Alpine mountains cold;
Ev'n them who kept thy truth so pure of old,
When all our fathers worshipped stocks and stones,
Forget not: in thy book record their groans
Who were thy sheep, and in their ancient fold,
Slain by the bloody Piedmontese that rolled
Mother with infant down the rocks. Their moans
The vales redoubled to the hills, and they
To heaven. Their martyred blood and ashes sow
O'er all the Italian fields, where still doth sway
The triple tyrant; that from these may grow
A hundred fold, who having learned thy way,
Early may fly the Babylonian woe."

Persecution, however, is scarcely possible deceived by them; the second, that *the men of law* only condemn *for crimes which are proved;* whereas your majesty knows that affairs of state are governed by very different rules from *the laws which they have here.*'" But this was not enough. "Upon the 16th February, 1568, a sentence of the Holy Office condemned *all the inhabitants* of the Netherlands *to death* as heretics. From this universal doom *only a few persons, especially named,* were excepted. A proclamation of the king, dated ten days later, confirmed this decree, and ordered it to be carried into instant execution, without regard to age, sex, or condition. This is probably the most concise death-warrant that was ever framed. Three millions of people, men, women, and children, were sentenced to the scaffold in three lines." And this for heresy. I need not speak of the St. Bartholomew massacre the climax is horrible.

without the real, if not organic, union of church and state; but the union of church and state could not long be maintained, were believers' baptism to regain the place which has been usurped by infant baptism. And I cherish an honest pride in the colony planted by Roger Williams in Rhode Island, as the first civil community of modern times, which declined to meddle with religious belief or church life as such. The government of that colony was instituted by Baptists, who firmly held and plainly asserted, that religion is always, if genuine, a matter of personal conviction, that baptism should always express the subject's personal faith in Christ, and that the right of every one to worship God, peaceably, according to his conscience, should be held sacred by the state.

V. *Infant baptism divides the followers of Christ.*

Some who practise it plead earnestly for union, and denounce Baptists as the ringleaders of sedition in the Protestant world. In response to all this I would ask these loving friends, whether, in their opinion, their own voluntary separation from the Papal Church makes them the authors of schism in the body of Christ?

Whether the leaven of error in the Romish communion is not rather the divisive principle? Whether a company of believers in Jesus, loyal, sincere, truth-loving, can be justly called heretics or schismatics, simply because they insist on obeying the law of Christ, preserving intact the ordinances which he gave, or using them as he commanded? It is error, not truth, which is responsible for a divided church. If the Judaizers in Galatia had increased till they were a majority that could not be cut off, the faithful members would have been constrained by fealty to the Master to leave them and organize churches according to the gospel. And always, when a church, through error in doctrine or in practice, ceases to represent fairly "the gospel of the kingdom," when it so modifies its own constitution, or so turns away from the law of Christ as to make reform impracticable, then all who still hold the Head should withdraw themselves, and form a new body in harmony with the apostolic rule; and the responsibility of the division will rest with those who have abandoned or perverted the truth, not with those who leave the recreant church. Hence, if infant baptism is unauthorized by the New Testament, those who insist upon having it practised in their churches, must be accountable for the schism occasioned by it. I am unable to discover any authority for it in the word of God; nay, I am compelled to look upon it as the perversion of a Christian ordinance, subtracting from its meaning and adding to that meaning, moving ritualism into the foreground and personal faith into the background, permeating as leaven the whole constitution and work of the church, and, in a word, preparing it for papal usurpation, for union with the state, and for the infinite horrors of persecution. A firm adherence to believers' baptism only, would, by the blessing of God, have prevented all these, together with many of the ecclesiastical divisions which have distracted in a measure the kingdom of Christ on earth.

My task is now finished. It has been performed, I am sure, imperfectly, yet with an aim to speak the truth in love, to withhold no part of the large indictment through fear of giving offence, and to put down nought in malice. It has been performed, I may humbly say, as in the presence of One who is love itself, whose favor is of infinite value to me, and whose displeasure is worse than death. If I have added count to count, it has not been in heat or contempt, but with a feeling akin to that of the apostle when he described himself as "sorrowful, yet always rejoicing." For, though pained by what I think to be deviations from the law of Christ, and sometimes oppressed with sadness by differences among the servants of Christ, I believe in the power of truth to win its way into all Christian hearts at last; and though it is less agreeable to speak against error than to speak directly for truth, both must be done in the fitting time and place, both were done by our blessed and gracious Lord and by his inspired apostles; and we may well be content to follow in their footsteps. He who was himself faithful in reproving error, is able to make our feeble imitation of his fidelity a blessing to his people, as well as an honor to his name. And so, having an earnest good will to all, and a steadfast confidence in the Giver of truth, and in the truth itself, I commend what has been said to your prayerful regard.

HOWARD L. OSGOOD, D. D., LL. D.
1831-1911.
Professor of Oriental Languages, Rochester Theological Seminary.

PROTESTANT PEDOBAPTISM

AND THE

DOCTRINE OF A CHURCH.

BY REV. HOWARD OSGOOD, D.D.

PHILADELPHIA:
AMERICAN BAPTIST PUBLICATION SOCIETY,
1420 CHESTNUT STREET.

PROTESTANT PEDOBAPTISM AND THE DOCTRINE OF A CHURCH.

"But as many as received him, to them gave he power to become the sons of God, even to them that believe on his name: which were born, not of blood, nor of the will of the flesh, nor of the will of man, but of God."—*John* i. 12, 13.

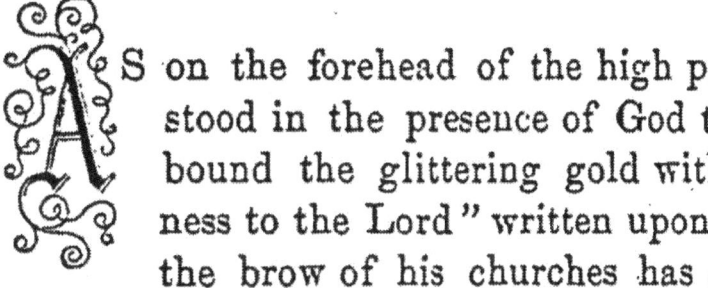AS on the forehead of the high priest who stood in the presence of God there was bound the glittering gold with "Holiness to the Lord" written upon it, so on the brow of his churches has Jesus inscribed these words of light, that they might herald to all the world, that his churches are the manifest miracles of his grace. These words proclaim the genealogy, in eternity and in time, of every soul known as his.

Mark the steps of approach—all who come—receive him by faith—they become sons of God—

are justified and adopted—and they do this, not by right of inheritance—not by the unaided exercise of any or all natural gifts—but because they are endowed with the very life of God—are born of him by the Spirit.

THE ONE WAY OF SALVATION.

There is but this one way of salvation for all men—for any man. Its oneness and its perfect adaptation for all speak the love and the wisdom of God. God sends his word either written, or spoken by human voice. This word, revealing God's way of salvation through Jesus Christ, is made powerful in the hearts of those that read or hear by the Holy Spirit. By that Spirit they loathe sin and believe in Jesus as their surety and atonement. With him they die and with him they rise. For his sake they are justified, accepted as righteous before God. He was made sin for them that they might be made the righteousness of God in him; and by the Spirit they live unto God, increasing in holiness and in knowledge of their God and Saviour. There is but this one way of salvation revealed. It is revealed for those who can hear and believe. We are never told how God saves those dying in infancy, or those who are bereft of reason. We believe that he does save *all* infants who die, and saves them through Jesus' blood, but in a way inscrutable to us. Certainly, so far as we have any means of judging, he does not save them by faith.

Within the sphere of our consciousness, and according to the Scriptures, the invariable order of the way of salvation is—*first*, the word, preached or read; *second*, faith; *third*, the life of faith. The order of God's gracious purpose and acts for the salvation of a soul is—*first*, he chooses; *second*, he calls by his Spirit through the word, communicating life and its exercise, faith; *third*, he justifies; *fourth*, he glorifies—receives into his eternal kingdom.

This is the Scriptural order, and all Protestant confessions of faith agree in this order. There is no evidence in Scripture that this order is ever reversed, or any step omitted or transposed. The confessions of all saints agree that this is the way by which they are led.

In giving salvation God never deals with men in the mass, always with individual souls. It is a testimony to the unspeakable worth of the soul, to the freedom and mighty responsibility of each man, that God condescends to deal with him as though there were no other man on earth.

With each one rests the decision of the question of questions—life or death.

FALSE VIEWS OF THE CHURCH.

For 1500 years there has hung around the word church and its synonyms in other languages an amount of mystery, to which the New Testament gives no warrant. With some denominations of Christians the church is often spoken of as though, apart from the individuals of which it is composed, "it were a moral person standing to Christians in the same relation in which a mother does to her children. To the church, Christians are said to owe their spiritual birth, the church educates her children, nourishes them with her ordinances, prays for them, and, if needs be, corrects them." That such an idea is a pure figment of the imagination; that no such thing exists as this corporate entity, this metaphysical abstraction, this abstract personality performing acts of thought and will distinct from those of the individual members who compose the body,—is patent to every reader of the New Testament.

With a church, as with each Christian life, there is an intimate, essential connection between the outward form and the internal spirit—between doctrine and life. The tree is known by its fruit. There can be no contradiction between God's doctrines and his precepts. The positive commands of God are—must be—in absolute harmony with his doctrines. There can be no contradiction between his doctrines of salvation and his precepts concerning his churches. What his churches are to be, how constituted, how maintained, is not a question of subordinate interest, but of paramount importance. One thing is certain, they must be, in their origin and continuance, in exact accordance with the doctrines of God's grace to man. They were to be the visible manifestations of those doctrines to the world—"the epistle of Christ written with the Spirit of the living God." If our constitution of a church is scriptural, it will be in harmony with the other doctrines of God's grace. If it is unscriptural, it will conflict with those doctrines, and before the world and on the minds of the members who uphold such a church will certainly tend to obscure, if not to efface those doctrines.

Both Luther and Calvin saw clearly that the central point of their controversy with Rome was just this doctrine of a church. Luther says: "What is the dispute between the Papists and us? It is the dispute about the true Christian church. The dispute is not whether we must believe the church—whether there is a church—but which is the true church." Calvin says: "We only contend for a true and legitimate constitution of the church, which requires, not only a communion in the sacraments which are the signs of a Christian profession, but, above all, an agreement in doctrine."

Luther and Zwingle and their followers separated from and condemned the Romish Church, not on account of the Romish constitution of a church, but on account of the false doctrines which Rome taught respecting salvation. In thus separating from Rome and preaching the truth, they deserve the highest commendation. But they retained essentially the Romish constitution of the churches.

The central point of the controversy between Baptists and Protestant Pedobaptists is not the doctrines of grace—for, thanks be to God, we generally agree there—but it is the constitution of a church. And this we hold to be a point of supreme importance for the free course of the word of God on earth. Baptists are thought to be great schismatics because, agreeing with evangelical Protestants on the great doctrines of the gospel, antecedent to the doctrine of a church, they refuse to acknowledge Pedobaptist churches as rightly formed, or to hold their administration of the ordinances as scriptural. Having granted so much, it is assumed we ought to grant everything else. We refuse to walk together where we think others offend against Christ's truth; but we joyfully walk with them where we are agreed. And this point of difference involves not merely that which is outward and subordinate, but draws in its train immediate consequences which affect the doctrines of God's grace to sinners.

The earliest Protestant divisions of the Pedobaptists were between the Lutherans and Zwinglians, afterwards Calvinists. They differed, and differ still, mainly in their views of the Lord's Supper.

The Presbyterians differed from the English Established Church mainly on the orders in the ministry and their powers.

The Independents differed from the Presbyterians on the powers of the individual churches.

The Methodists differ from other evangelical Protestants in their aristocratic form of church government.

But they all have at the base the same constitution of the churches. And the Baptist, existing before either of these denominations, stands opposed on deepest principle to that constitution. Our opposition is not like that between themselves, on points of acknowledged secondary interest, but on one point of primal fundamental importance.

The New Testament uses the word church only in two senses—one including all true believers, at all times and in eternity; the other including those who have professed to believe in Jesus and are united by the ordinances into separate local societies.

If the order and plan of salvation has been correctly stated, there are no materials on earth out of which to form a church—God's society—God's assembly—but those who are born of God. That unbelievers are found in the churches is not due to the defect in the model, but to the defect that inheres in human judgment.

THE CHURCHES, THE MIRACLES OF THE SPIRIT.

The churches, then, were to be the flower and fruit of salvation. God's choice, God's call by his Spirit and word, regeneration, faith, justification, adoption—such is the gracious process necessary to the formation of a church; for it is the process invariably pursued in the formation of all its parts. The churches were by their very existence to testify to all the way by which they were led. A church so formed is the constant manifestation of the Spirit. Let the Spirit cease to convert men and bring them to such a church, and it dies out with the first generation. How different would have been the story of church history if, instead of bringing into the churches by blood, by the will of the flesh, by the will of man, the churches had been kept to their original constitution, dependent only on the Spirit of God for increase.

The Baptist holding these views is compelled to object most strenuously against the constitution of all Pedobaptist churches, not simply in the interest of the form of baptism, but far more in the interest of the only way of salvation. Their churches are, to our view, formed in direct contravention of God's way of salvation; their constitution is at war with the doctrines of God's grace, and at war, too, with their own confessions of faith. We are exhorted to renounce our views of the form of baptism, so that there may be no division between us. But back of our view of the form of baptism there lie difficulties in the way of union far greater than any outward form. We do not mean to insinuate that we do not believe them Christians. God forbid that we should harbor such a thought of the thousands on thousands who in so many points have adorned and illustrated Christian life, and who are now zealous for God and his Christ. We believe them, as bodies, to be eminent in Christian virtues. We do not sit in judgment on their Christianity to condemn it. But this we say, that while we may so highly regard them, we are compelled to bear our testimony—unequivocal and earnest—against what we esteem to be grievous errors against the doctrines of God.

PEDOBAPTIST ERRORS.

1. *It is an error to admit unbelievers to church membership.*

While in all Pedobaptist confessions the very essence of the churches is made to consist in faith, they are guilty of the palpable contradiction of intentionally and constantly introducing those who do not believe—who cannot believe—as members of churches.

I know that each Pedobaptist denomination has its own mode of explaining this away—each differing from the other. Either one of two things they should do before inviting a Baptist to renounce his clear views and consistent practice concerning the church—either alter their confessions or cease their practice, which is at war with their confession. We agree with them that the very essence of the churches is faith, as it is the essence of the life of each member; and we rejoice that they confess this; and we beseech them, for the glory of our Master and Redeemer, to put away the inconsistency of their practice.

2. *It is an error to make church membership precede the hearing of the word.*

This leads us to notice another difficulty of much more moment. The Scriptures know nothing, we know nothing, and Protestant confessions know nothing, of churches which are not the body of Christ. To be in the church is, according to the New Testament, to be in Christ. Not that the church and Christ are synonymous; but because none were to be admitted but those who gave evidence of being in Christ. Now, the Scriptures represent the external instrument of our union with Christ and his church to be invariably his word. "We are born again by the word of God," Peter says, (1 Pet. i. 23); and Paul, "Faith cometh by hearing, and hearing by the word of God," (Rom. x. 17); "How shall they believe in him of whom they have not heard?" (Rom. x. 14); "Of his own will begat he us by the word of truth," (James i. 18). But if before hearing, before faith, before the apprehension of the word, either an outward ordinance or the collective church is placed as the means of union with Christ, there arises a positive contradiction between the Scriptures and the constitution of such a church. Nay, the union with Christ by that act is asserted to be, not internal and spiritual, but external and formal. The first thing needed is, not the word and faith, but the church. If the church ever rightly—according to God's purpose—precedes the word in the salvation of any soul, then why do we never hear the apostles exhorting men to join the church that they may come to Christ, but always hear them insisting on attention to the word, that men may be saved? By the constitution of Pedobaptist churches, a grievous injury is done to the word of God and to thousands of souls, in reversing God's order of salvation. The rightful place of the word is usurped by the church. The place of absolute truth for the enlightenment of the soul is taken by the broken lights of human representatives of that truth; and with thousands there is ever a film over their eyes as to the relation the word holds to the church and to their salvation.

Nor does the error stop here, as all church history shows us. When the word and its work are put away as prerequisites of church membership, and the church assumes the place of the word, and is the external means for uniting souls to Christ, that which is merely formal and outward becomes its greatest power, and that which is internal and spiritual is secondary. That which is outward in it assumes immense importance in the eyes of its upholders, and its polity and government are to be maintained at every expense for the good of souls.

It is one of the most marvellous, enigmatical facts of history, that all Protestant Pedobaptist churches, coming forth from the tyranny of Rome, and protesting against her tyranny over the consciences of men, should have become in a few years almost as bitter persecutors for their form of faith as Rome was for hers. Luther and Melancthon persecuted; Zwingle and Calvin persecuted; the Reformed Church of Holland persecuted; the Established Church of England, the Presbyterians of Scotland, the Presbyterians and Independents of England, the Congregationalists of New England—all fell into the same error as Rome had done, and defended it on the same grounds. Can this strange inconsistency be explained? There is only one solution apparent. Differing as they did from Rome, yet they actually formed their churches on the same basis as that of Rome. The church was put before the word; and, in their view, the salvation of souls demanded its existence; and with a quiet conscience its upholders could punish, with all bodily misery and deprivation of goods, those who denied its validity.

On the other hand, from the first hours of the Reformation till the present, no Baptist church can be shown which has ever favored or defended religious persecution. Nor can any Baptist author be found who has favored or defended the same. Their witness has been clear and unmistakable on the side of religious liberty, not tolerance—freedom, not sufferance—not for themselves alone, but for all men. This, surely, is not due to any intellectual or moral superiority on the part of Baptists, but must be due to a principle that inheres in their religious thinking; and I take it, that principle is to be found in just this holding the precedence of the word of God to the church. In their view every man must come face to face with the word of God. By that he must be convinced, and must decide the supreme question concerning his soul's life, before he possesses any qualification for membership in a church. Having referred him there, the decision is between him and his God—and no outward means of flattery or of punishment can effect the change, which is the work of God's Spirit alone.

When a Pedobaptist argues with a Romanist against the fundamental constitution of the Romish Church, he always takes the full Baptist position—but when he argues in favor of the Pedobaptist churches, he is compelled to take the Romish position and use Romish arguments.

3. *It is not in accordance with the Scriptural plan to make church membership precede regeneration.*

The church is according to the Scriptures a society of those born of God, regenerate persons. This birth, this regeneration, is the work of the Spirit alone; and its result, immediate, invariable, and indestructible, is life—not capacity for the reception of life—not powers which may develop into life, but life itself. So that they who are born again, born of God, live unto him a life which is totally different from their natural life; and by this life alone can the new birth, regeneration by the Holy Spirit, be recognized. But the wilful, persistent introduction of unregenerate persons into a church, and ascribing to them any interest whatsoever in it, is to do despite to the Creator Spirit who formed the world, and forms every soul that is born again. They are thereby asserted to have been born unto God by blood, by the will of the flesh, by the will of man; which to our eyes appears to be as flat a contradiction of God's plain word as it would be possible to make.

All who come to God, all who belong to him, all who have any part or lot with Jesus, are represented by the Scriptures as called by the Spirit—"called out of darkness into his marvellous light"—called according to God's purpose. This is the peculiar office of the Holy Spirit. All who are so called, do come to God. This word in its use in the Scriptures does not signify a mere external speaking the invitation of God, but it also means the sure operation of the Spirit on the heart, by which one is made gladly and longingly to hear the word of God. Those thus called are the sons of God. "For ye are not in the flesh but in the Spirit, if so be that the Spirit of God dwell in you. For as many as are led by the Spirit of God, they are the sons of God." But to teach or imply that those who have never known the gracious work of the Spirit, and of course give no evidence of it, are in any sense members of Christ, is to strike at the very root of salvation—the work of the Holy Spirit. The work of the Spirit precedes the reception of Jesus, which is accompanied with the gift of the privilege of becoming the sons of God.

And just as surely do the Scriptures teach us that where the Holy Spirit does not thus work to bring to life, and open the heart and the ear to long after and hear the word of God, there death reigns. There are, there can be, no neutrals between the state of death and life. Men are either dead in trespasses and sins, or they are alive unto God through Jesus Christ our Lord. That which is born of the flesh is flesh; or as another Scripture states it, is death, "for the mind of the flesh is death." And that which is born of the Spirit is spirit; or as Paul states it, is life, "for the mind of the Spirit is life." "Now if any man have not the Spirit of Christ he is none of his." But when the Spirit calls, then he "bears witness with our spirits that we are the children of God. And if children, then heirs, heirs of God and joint-heirs with Christ." If the Spirit has given one life, if the Spirit has called him out of darkness into marvellous light, then, but not till then, has he any qualification, or any right to admission to the household of God, unless we acknowledge that there may be dead members of him who is Life itself.

It may be objected to us that there are undeniably many members of Baptist churches who give no evidence of spiritual life. We grant it. But no Baptist church ever admitted them knowing them to be dead. They desired admission and gave credible evidence on their entrance that they were born of the Spirit—and on that evidence they were admitted. That afterwards they proved to be dead, only shows that men striving after God's model may often be led astray by Satan, transformed into an angel of light.

4. *It is an error to allow the church to take the place of faith.*

We have seen that the church cannot be put in the place of the word, that it cannot be put in the place of the Holy Spirit, for that would be to suppose the earthen vessel to be formed without clay, and without the potter's hand. Neither can the church be put in the place of *faith.* The word is the first external means of our union with Christ—it is the visible manifestation of Jesus. By the Spirit life is given to behold Jesus in his word, and to trust in him. The evidence of this work of the Spirit, and the only internal, spiritual means of union with Christ within our consciousness, is faith. By this—not as a meritorious cause, but as a prerequisite—by this alone are we justified, accepted as righteous for Jesus' sake before God. Without faith it is, and ever has been since the fall, impossible to please God. We "are children of God by faith in Christ Jesus," (Gal. iii. 16). And this faith, this spiritual apprehension of Jesus as our Saviour, is the sovereign gift of God. "By grace are ye saved through faith, and that not of yourselves—it is the gift of God."

In our thinking we may separate the work of the Spirit in regeneration, which is below our consciousness, from the result of that work, faith, which is our conscious act. But really they never are divided. The life the Spirit gives is the life that exists by faith. And of no soul in this world can it be said that it is saved, unless it believes in Jesus. Faith is the first opening of the eye as the dead comes forth from the tomb at the Spirit's call. It is the exercise of the resurrection-life. It is the conscious means and evidence that the soul lives. To produce faith in any soul is just as great a miracle, is just as marvellous an exhibition of omnipotence, as the resurrection of Jesus from the dead. And so the apostle prays that the Ephesians may know "what is the exceeding greatness of his power to us-ward who believe, according to the working of his mighty power which he wrought in Christ when he raised him from the dead."

Before the exercise of faith—before this conscious trust in Jesus as our sole surety and intercessor—whatsoever we do, however excellent it may appear, is sin, for it does not spring from the right motive. The Scriptures and the experience of every converted man teach this same truth. It is only faith in Christ, not our works, that renders us pleasing in the sight of God. Then we do, for the first time, put away our own righteousness, which is of the law, and trust only in that righteousness which is through the faith of Christ—the righteousness which is of God by faith.

This faith is inseparable from its fruit—works for God. The two are as closely compacted as regeneration and faith. But every Bible reader sees the vast difference between saying, that regeneration proceeds from faith, and that faith proceeds from works—or *vice versa*. In the one case salvation is man's work; in the other it is God's gift. In the one case we assert the merit of works; in the other the pure grace of God.

Most Protestant denominations hold these truths as strongly as we do, and have and do set them forth with power. Our controversy with them is not on these truths, but upon the utter inconsistency of the constitution of their churches with these most vital points. While holding these precious doctrines they do put their churches in the place of faith—for thousands of their members are taught that by the ligature of the church they are somewhat united to Christ, when they are sure, and the churches are sure, that they have no faith. Luther and Calvin, and their followers in Europe and England, contended with all their gigantic powers against Rome for the scriptural doctrine of justification by our faith only. Yet no sooner did they begin to constitute their churches than they practically denied all their words and justified Rome—for they admitted most of their members on the faith of others.

With perfect justice a German Roman Catholic author of this century, writing on the Reformation in Germany and the fierce persecution of the Baptists of that day by the Protestants, asks the Protestants, How such persecution in that century or in this can be defended by them? The Protestants, he says, left the Romish Church following their great dogma, justification by faith alone. They proclaimed the doctrine in words, but denied it in their churches. The Baptists formed their churches in perfect accordance with this central doctrine of Protestantism, and yet they were more bitterly persecuted by Protestants than by Romanists. So much so, that Baptists fled from Protestant lands to find a refuge in the tenderer mercies of Romanism.

When the church is put in the place of faith in the order of salvation—when one is said to be united to Christ, a member of Christ, before he exercises faith—they reverse the whole gospel scheme of salvation. By that act it is practically declared that salvation is of works, not of faith. It is not "of faith that it might be by grace." But the apostle declares that the promise of salvation is "by faith that it might be of grace;" "and if by grace, then it is no more of works, otherwise grace is no more grace. But if it be of works, then it is no more grace, otherwise work is no more work." We submit that that practice which makes salvation of works, and that confession which makes salvation of grace, are not exactly consistent; nay, they are contradictions of each other. And with all such imperious contradictions one or the other must obtain the mastery and banish its adversary.

Augustine held justification by faith, but he also held to a union with Christ by the church. His was the master mind of the ancient Catholic Church, and Rome has logically followed out his views of the church, and by necessity banished his scriptural doctrine.

To see the most pernicious effects of this gross inconsistency of practice with profession of the truth, we must go, not to the denominations of our own land, but to the Protestant churches of Geneva, France, Holland, Germany, England. Supported by the State, with all the citizens of the land members of the churches, with numerous ministers who savor of the charnel house, who have long forgotten and ceased to preach that salvation is "of faith that it might be by grace;" no confession of faith is required of the members, no discipline is exercised, so that you find great numbers of these members who deny the divinity of Jesus and the existence and our need of the Holy Spirit. Is it surprising that the idea of conversion to God with them is esteemed equivalent to lunacy; and a suggestion that they are not just such churches as the New Testament sets forth, is met with the scorn such ignorance deserves?

One of two things must be, as history teaches us it has been; either Protestant Pedobaptist churches must be truer to their confessions of faith and alter the constitution of their churches, or they must be truer to the constitution of their churches and put away their confessions of faith. We believe they will choose the first, and will exalt and proclaim and conform to the word of God.

5. *Entrance to the church was not designed to precede the evidence of God's choice.*

There is one more point where an insurmountable difficulty meets the Pedobaptist constitution of a church. They, for the most part, believe, as we also do, that all this scheme of grace, this use of the word of God, this regeneration by the Spirit, this gift of faith, is in consequence of God's gracious choice—his predetermination to bestow salvation upon certain souls. Why he should choose one and pass by another, we can assign no reason, while at the same time we fully believe that there is no unrighteousness with him. The Scriptures assert the fact that he does so elect, and the result in actual experience is in perfect accordance with the statements of

Scripture. This choice, this election, does not interfere in the slightest degree with man's responsibility, or with the perfect freedom and assurance of the gospel call to all. Every man knows he is responsible to God. The sense of direct responsibility to the Supreme Ruler of all is planted so deep in the mind of every human being, that the most degraded Hindoo, or Chinese, or Fetish worshipper of Africa, or the brutalized Australian or Feejee Islander, as well as all the inhabitants of lands called Christian, proclaim it by deed if not by word. Man's, every man's, responsibility to God for all his words and works and thoughts, is asseverated by Scripture just as strongly as God's choice of his people.

It is not for me to enter into a proof of this Scripture doctrine here. It is sufficient for us now that Calvinist and Lutheran, Presbyterian and Independent, the English Church and Dutch Reformed, have all proclaimed their belief in it by their authoritative confessions. The great majority of Baptists have held the same, to wit: that all the means of salvation flow out from God's sovereign, unconditioned, election of his people. Let me quote the excellent statement of Dr. Hodge, in his second volume on Theology, p. 333: "The ground of this election is not the foresight of anything in the one class (the saved) to distinguish them favorably from the members of the other class (the lost), but the good pleasure of God. . . . That all those whom God has thus chosen to life and for whom Christ specially gave himself in the covenant of redemption, shall certainly (unless they die in infancy) be brought to the knowledge of the truth, to the exercise of faith, and to perseverance in holy living unto the end."

I quote from Dr. Hodge (p. 314, vol. ii.) another statement quite as true as the preceding, which is important just here. "The order of the divine decrees, or in other words the relation in which the several parts of the divine plan stand to each other, is very far from being a matter of idle speculation. It must determine our theology, and our theology determines our religion." We believe that. If, as the Romanist teaches, faith results from good works—if the gift of salvation is bestowed upon us for any good work or any worth in us, then man is not helpless or ruined or lost. If I fall down a precipice and am bruised and broken in some parts, yet able to climb up again and reach a point of safety, I cannot be said to be utterly ruined and lost. If salvation is a rope let down from heaven which one may catch by a bound into the air—just the strength required both of mind and body to make that bound, measures the good yet remaining in us, and measures too just the amount we are required to supplement to the work of God for our salvation. Christ in that case did not come to save the dead and the lost, but to help man save himself. And the Spirit does not make alive from the dead, but only arouses the drowsy. But if that which is born of the flesh is dead, destitute of all spiritual life to God; if the mind of the flesh, its whole course of thought, runs in the way of and issues in the ocean of death, then every one born again to God by the Spirit, must be so made alive, because God—while the soul was dead—predetermined to make it alive, and also predetermined all the means to that end. This purpose of God's mind, as it stands written broadly on every page of God's word, and in the experience of all who come to him, must, in all right thinking, stand as the antecedent cause of life and faith. In Scripture, to be elect, and to be called of God, are convertible terms. The elect are the called; the called are the elect. On two points the Scriptures warn us. We are not to pry into this eternal counsel of God as though by searching we could find it out; and we are not to deny the fact, but are to ascribe his work of grace to "his good pleasure which he purposed in himself."

How is this gracious choice made known? By the work of his Spirit in the heart and life of the individual, and we judge of this work by the evidence furnished by the life and profession of the individual. It would seem, then, near akin to monstrous presumption—and nothing but hoary false tradition could ever blind good men to that fact—to lay our hands upon any one and say, this is one of the elect of God, before God has given us any evidence of the fact by the work of his Spirit. Of no one born of flesh can this choice be affirmed till God's work appears in him. He or they who make men believe that they are united to Christ, are members of his body, in any sense, before the work of the Spirit is manifested in faith in them, take their presumptuous stand beside the sovereign, secret will of Jehovah, and profess to declare it, before he has made it known, and by their act profess to bind that free and sovereign will to the sinful work of a lost, dead soul.

To put the church before faith, to put it before the work of the Spirit, to put it before the word, is to attempt to put it in the place of God's sovereign, secret will, and there it breaks upon the bosses of Jehovah's buckler.

The constitution of that church cannot be scriptural which thus wages incessant war, not only with distinct and separate truths of God's word, but (in Dr. Hodge's words) "with the relation in which the several parts of the divine plan stand to each other." This relation, Dr. Hodge says, "determines our theology, and our theology determines our religion."

A CHURCH THE CULMINATING POINT OF GOD'S VISIBLE WORK OF GRACE ON EARTH.

The Baptist holds to the simple Bible truths, that man is born spiritually dead—that life can come, does only come, through the effectual working of the Holy Spirit, and this life is given by God in accordance with his purpose. Joyfully, earnestly, does he carry the gospel call to all, and urge each one to believe in Jesus, assuring each one that if he believes he shall be saved. But before he dares to assure any man that he is a member of Christ or has any part or lot with him, he must see the evidence of the precious work of the Spirit in that man. The assembly of God's people, the church, is the gathering together of those who have thus given credible evidence of being born again; and so it is the culminating point of God's visible work of grace on earth. The scriptural doctrine of a church does not conflict with, but follows and depends upon and honors, each doctrine and the relation of the doctrines of God's grace to man. A church can be rightly composed only of those who have "received Jesus, and to whom he has given the privilege of becoming the sons of God, who are born not of blood, nor of the will of the flesh, nor of the will of man, but of God."

These are the radical differences between the Baptist and Pedobaptist constitutions of a church. Put the ordinances of a church entirely out of view for the moment, and beyond them how wide is the difference between us. What puny superficiality then to assert that the form of one ordinance is all that makes a Baptist church to differ from others, or that Baptists exist merely to uphold that form. If there are any Baptists so blind as to acquiesce in a statement so far short of the truth, I pity them. We are set for the defence, not of one part of the truth only, but of the churches of the living God according to the New Testament model. And not merely for the form of a church, but for that form as it is connected with all the truths of salvation, as well as for all those truths as they are related to a church.

"The difficulties of Protestant Pedobaptism touching the doctrine of a church" are, that, holding what are usually termed the doctrines of grace, they constitute their churches in indefensible contradiction to these truths.

Our refusal to walk with them in their churches is based not merely upon their change of the form of baptism—for neither historically nor logically is that true. Suppose all Pedobaptist denominations to-day returned to the scriptural form of baptism, but still retained their peculiar constitution as churches, we should be compelled to protest against them and deny that they were formed according to the word of God. Our refusal to walk with them in their churches is not based upon any belief among us that they are not excellent Chistians, taught of the Spirit of God in many ways, zealous in good works, who hold communion with our Lord Jesus Christ, and have a blessed hope of life eternal with him. Let this be stated in its broadest form—let it be proclaimed from the house-tops—let it be known in every Pedobaptist household in the land, that in other things we can bid them God speed, but not in their constitution of churches. Here we see an error against God's truth, and as we love that truth, we protest in word and life.

God forbid that by this protest we should seem to lay our hands on our hearts and say to Pedobaptists stand off, we are holier than you! Paul had no such feeling when he withstood Peter to the face because he was to be blamed. It was in the interest of that truth which was dearer and more precious and vital than all earthly ties, and I do now believe many pious Baptists live who have any pleasure in this protest for itself; but as they have been saved by Jesus and taught his truth, they must uphold that, whatever opposes. Nor can those now antagonistic, be one in churches till all churches are by their constitution brought into entire harmony with that truth. God grant that day may soon come.

Brethren, these facts are burdened with lessons for us. If we have more truth on our side, by that we are placed under a mightier responsibility—a responsibility not answered by a mere blatant protest, but demanding of us lives wholly consecrated to God. The worldly Baptist has no excuse, and so far as we can judge will be worthy of a deeper condemnation than those who have not seen God's truth so clearly. Our churches must proclaim their protest against error much more by the lives of the members than by mere assertion, or the assertion of the error of others will be their own condemnation. Our churches must be pure in doctrine—living in faith—strict in discipline, if they are to be true witnesses for our God and his Christ.

HENRY HOLCOMBE TUCKER, D. D., LL.D.
1819-1889.

President of Mercer University and
Chancellor of the University of Georgia.

THE

POSITION OF BAPTISM

IN THE

CHRISTIAN SYSTEM.

BY HENRY H. TUCKER

PHILADELPHIA:
AMERICAN BAPTIST PUBLICATION SOCIETY,
1420 CHESTNUT STREET.

THE POSITION OF BAPTISM

IN THE

CHRISTIAN SYSTEM.

"Thus it becometh us to fulfil all righteousness."—MATTHEW iii. 15.

"Go ye therefore and teach all nations, baptizing them in the name of the Father and of the Son and of the Holy Ghost."—MATTHEW xxviii. 19.

"He that believeth and is baptized shall be saved, and he that believeth not shall be damned."—MARK xvi. 16.

MANKIND are prone to two evil intellectual habits: one is to look at only one side of a question, and the other is to carry the partial view thus obtained to an extreme. Nowhere are these unfortunate tendencies more conspicuous than in the domain of religion, and on no subject, perhaps, more than on the subject of baptism. Owing to extreme and one-sided views, its importance is overrated by some, and underrated by others.

The former class attribute to it a power which is supernatural, miraculous, omnipotent. In their view, it has the power of creating the soul anew. If any man be in Christ, he is a new creature; and baptism brings him into Christ. Baptism is essential to regeneration, or rather it *is* regeneration. Without regeneration there is no salvation, and without baptism there is no regeneration. All who are regenerate are saved, and all who are baptized are regenerate. Baptism is therefore all in all. More is not needed; less is perdition. In the last day, those to whom the Judge will say, "Come, ye blessed," are the baptized; and those to whom he will say, "Depart, ye cursed," are the unbaptized.

Some of the greatest extremists might accept these results; others, less logical, will not accept the results, while yet they hold to the principles that lead to them. Having merely stated this view, without argument either for or against it, it is enough to say that, in the opinion of those who are called Baptists, it greatly overrates the value of baptism, and is wholly unsupported by Scripture.

Another class regard baptism as a mere form. The most consistent of them regard it as a useless ceremony, and discard it altogether. Others retain the rite, but lay little stress on it. In their opinion, the place it occupies as a human duty is an insignificant one; they speak of it as a non-essential, and therefore as a thing not worthy of any very great consideration. Many persons are lost with it, and many are saved without it, and hence any great time or attention bestowed on this is so much taken away from the weightier matters of the law. Without arguing the question, suffice it to say that, in our opinion, this view underrates the value and importance of baptism, and is not countenanced by the word of God. Strange to say, however, persons who entertain this view are sometimes in haste to administer the ordinance of baptism to a dying person; and this shows that, after all, they are unsettled in their minds, and also that the transition is easy from one extreme to its opposite.

But what *is* baptism? Certainly it is a form, but it is not a *mere* form. The word *mere* strips the form of all its adjuncts, and leaves nothing *but* the form. Baptism is clearly more than this; for,

1. It is an act of obedience. Now, obedience to God is as high a function as any moral being can perform. It is the carrying out of the purposes of infinite wisdom and goodness. The least act of obedience is a great act. Not one jot nor tittle of the law of God is unworthy of the source whence it came; and he who obeys in the least particular is thus far in harmony with the Almighty; and, in doing the will of the Supreme, he is doing that which ennobles himself and glorifies his Maker. In what way can a man or an angel more grandly exalt himself? In what way can he better serve his God? To say that such an act is a

mere form because it *involves* a form, is to lose sight of the God who has commanded it.

2. It is but a slight variation from the preceding thought to say that, so far as baptism is a form, it is a *prescribed* form, and therefore the peer of anything else that is prescribed. "Whoso shall keep the whole law, and yet offend in one point, he is guilty of all. For he that said, Do not commit adultery, said also, Do not kill," and he also it is who has prescribed the form we have spoken of. There is the same authority for this that there is for any other duty. It is part of the law of God; and to disparage any part of that law is to disparage the whole of it. God's law is a unit; God's law is virtually himself; it *is* himself expressed. To speak lightly of *it* is to speak lightly of *him;* and to say that anything which he has commanded is simply a form, a *mere* form, a naked form, and *nothing but* a form, would seem to be a shocking irreverence. If it is not taking the *name* of God

in vain, it is at least speaking vainly of the *law* of God; and if there be a distinction in these kinds of profanity, it is not needful now to trace it.

3. Baptism is an act of worship. All work is worship; especially all righteousness is worship; and especially is *this* act of righteousness an act of worship, because there is nothing in the nature of things which requires it; in this act we obey no instinct, no dictate of mere reason, nor of unenlightened conscience. It is done in homage to no abstract principle of right, if there be any such principle; it is done as unto God. It is done *purely* for him, and therefore would seem to be worship in a higher sense than almost anything else that we do. If it is glory to the angels to cast their crowns at his feet, so also it is glory to us to cast ourselves at his feet, as we do when, subjecting our wills to his, we obey his word. Worship formulated is none the less worship; and if God himself is the formulator, that fact would

seem to invest the worship with higher dignity and greater acceptableness.

4. Baptism is also an act of imitation. The Son of God set us the example, and in so doing he uttered the word "Thus." True, this word was addressed directly to John, and had reference to the act immediately to be performed. But what was duty for the actors in that scene is duty for all; what was duty then is duty now. The disciples afterwards baptized under the immediate order of our Lord, and hence we know that what he then inaugurated he intended to be continued; and if the act is continued, why may we not couple with it the words which first accompanied it? May we not extend the meaning of the word *thus*, and consider it as addressed not only to John, but to all of us? Otherwise, why was the record made? If any lovers of our Lord had stood on the banks of the Jordan and witnessed the scene, would they not have understood him, in the use of the word *thus*

accompanied by the act, to describe duty for them? *We* stand on the banks. We witness the scene. We witness other baptisms administered by his order, and doubtless in his presence, and hence may consider ourselves addressed in the word *thus*. It is as if Christ had said, "I am your model; here is your pattern; what I am doing, it becomes you to do." If there be any doubt in language, there is none in action. The act, the fact to be witnessed, is the thing to be done. It is always safe to follow the example of Christ, and perilous it is to refuse to do so, when he has declared that he *intended* it to be followed. Not to obey is to disobey; and if obedience to God be our highest glory, disobedience is our greatest disgrace and our greatest destruction. To disobey when we are *told* what to do is a certain grade of crime, but to disobey when we are not only told, but *shown* what to do, would seem to be a higher grade of crime. When he who was the brightness of the Father's glory and the express image of his person, submitted to the ordinance of baptism, and, virtually summoning the whole world to hear, said "THUS," he dignified the form into something *more* than a form. He made it a part of His history, and thus glorified it for eternity; and at the same time he made it part of our duty, and thus exalted us to the privilege of being so far, at least, in union with him. It is no small thing to say that his history is our history. It is a privilege to know that in any one single thing we have done exactly what he did. That far, at least, we know our record is honorable and glorious. Christ said to Simon and Andrew, "Follow me!" Shall we confine the call to these? His whole life is an embodiment of the same words as addressed to us all. Follow thee! Yes, precious Saviour! we follow thee with joy! Blessed are they who follow! Blessed are they who walk in his footsteps! If we would be conformed to his image, let us conform to his actions. If God said once to Moses, "See thou make all things according to the pattern shewed to thee in the mount," and if Moses showed his greatest wisdom in exact obedience, and if he would have shown greatest folly in speaking of this as a mere form, so when Christ has said to us, as he does by the word *thus*, "See thou do all things according to the pattern I showed thee in baptism," we shall be wise indeed if we copy the pattern, and foolish indeed if we speak lightly of it. No, it is not a mere form; it is an adaptation of ourselves, thus far, at least, to him.

5. Baptism is an act of consecration. It is the outward expression of an inward act. It is the visible embodiment of a sentiment—the sentiment of consecration. The body is made subservient to the behests of the soul, and gives itself to baptism as the soul gives itself to God. Admit that this inward consecration might exist without the outward act, it is still true that no sentiment takes as thorough pos-

session of us unexpressed as when expressed; and be sure that the form of expression which God has selected will most intensify the sentiment, and better than any other subserve its purpose

6. But baptism is more than an act of private consecration; it is an act of public profession. It is an announcement to the world that we are Christ's. It is the act by which we commit ourselves openly to him and to his cause. It is the public putting on of Christ; and surely to put on Christ is not a mere form. Putting on Christ is what an angel cannot do. It is what cannot be done in heaven; in no part of the universe except on *earth* can this glorious deed be done.

7. Baptism is an act of symbolic meaning, and while it is a profession of faith, it also teaches by emblem the principles of the faith that is professed. Divine truth is taught in *actions* prescribed by the divine will, no less than in *words* so prescribed. Baptism is an

expression, brief but comprehensive, of the leading doctrines of the New Testament. It is itself a Testament; it is itself the word of God. Pregnant with infinite meaning, it is the most condensed and most intensive utterance, in symbol, of revealed truth that God has vouchsafed to us; or, at least if it has a peer, it is found only in that other ordinance in which we show forth the Lord's death until he comes. To speak lightly of this, to regard it as a form and nothing but a form, is to be blind to almost heavenly glory.

When the King of kings and Lord of lords issues sovereign mandates to his holy angels, can we suppose that they regard any one of them as a mere form? Would those glorified ones so trifle with that which has for its authority, *Thus saith the Lord?* How much better is the case when man, whose breath is in his nostrils, thus impeaches the wisdom of the All-wise, Supreme, and Eternal Lawgiver of the universe? Is it conceivable that the great God could possibly lend the sanction of his authority to that which is nothing but emptiness? or that he would command us to do that which might well be left undone? Does disobedience of any part of his law make no change in our relations to him? A mere form is an insignificant thing and unworthy of respect. Has God commanded anything that is insignificant or unworthy of respect? Is any part of his law contemptible? The soul takes fright at the very thought. God's commandment is exceeding broad; each part of it is jealous of the honor of every other, and each is invested with the majesty of all.

A blessed thing it is to obey, but when we obey in a manner prescribed, and when we worship, and imitate our Lord Jesus Christ, doing just what he did, consecrating ourselves to God, putting on Christ before men and angels, and by the self-same act symbolize all the essential principles of the gospel, surely the act must be one which outranks in dignity any other outward act of which human beings are capable, and one on which an intelligent universe must gaze with admiration and delight. Impressed with these views of the dignity of baptism, the candid inquirer, shocked at the impiety of calling it a mere form, thus casting dishonor on the Almighty, may naturally incline to the other extreme. It need excite no surprise if one should say, "Surely the performance of such a deed will ensure the salvation of the soul; for it is not to be supposed that any of those can be lost who are admitted to such a privilege; and surely the neglect of such a solemn duty must lead to destruction; surely there can be no forgiveness for such flagrant sin."

The lover of evangelical truth needs not to be reminded that nothing that we can *do* is the groundwork of our salvation. "A man is not justified by the works of the law, but by the faith of Jesus Christ; . . . by the works of the law shall no flesh be justified." Gal. ii. 16. All deeds of the law, that is, all acts of obedience, are here classed together, and of course baptism is included; and if the whole of them together are declared to be worthless as a ground of justification, of course any one of them must be so.

But even if the baptism prescribed *were* meritorious, and possessed of saving efficacy, it does not follow that everything that is called by the name of baptism would be of equal value. Suppose the outward act to be done; but if it is *not* done as an act of obedience; and *not* because it is a form prescribed; and *not* as an act of worship; and *not* in imitation of our Lord's example; and *not* as an act of private and personal consecration; and *not* as an act of public profession; and *not* as an act of symbolic meaning; then indeed it is not only a form but a *mere* form; its spiritual character is gone; it is simply mechanical, and has no more value nor dignity than a washing of the body which might happen to one by accident. If the *word* fails to profit when not mixed with faith in them that hear it, so neither does baptism profit when not mixed with faith in them that receive it. Indeed, "*whatsoever* is not of faith is sin." Rom. xiv. 23. And surely what is done in the name of the Holy Trinity, if without faith, must be sin in most aggravated form. The baptism which is required of us involves all the religious elements heretofore described; hence a baptism so-called which has *none* of those elements is clearly not the same thing; and even if there were saving power in genuine baptism, which there is not, there could be none in this. Doubtless many have been baptized with a spurious baptism, and have discovered at last that it was indeed a mere form. But it can never be too often repeated, that baptism however genuine and proper, and however exalted in rank as a duty is after all only a duty; and we must not make the fearful mistake of substituting corporeal washing in water for spiritual washing in the blood of the atonement.

The intelligent inquirer may still say, "I know that baptism is not our saviour; Christ is our Saviour; I know that the duty of baptism whether discharged with faith or without faith, is like all other duties, and is neither the reason of our being saved, nor the means of our being saved, nor a certain evidence that we are or will be saved; but is not the *neglect* of it a certain evidence that we are lost, and also a good reason why we should be lost?"

In reply to this let it be said, that where sin abounds, grace does much more abound; and that there is no sin so dreadful that the blood of Christ has not power to wash it out. True, there is such a thing spoken of as an unpardonable sin, but it is not implied that this is because there is any failure in the efficacy of the atonement; and above all, there is not the least hint that this sin consists in the neglect of baptism. It is possible indeed that baptism, *like any other duty*, might occupy such a position in the life of an individual man, as to be *in his case* a turning-point; a test question, on the decision of which, it is to be settled whether or not he will yield unqualified obedience to God; and *in his case* neglect of this particular duty might be *an* unpardonable sin; but to say in general terms that the neglect of baptism is an unpardonable sin, is to say that which has no shadow of warrant in the New Testament. Neglect of baptism is like neglect of any other duty —sinful. But sin does not stand between God's elect and heaven: Christ has removed it; his blood has washed it into nothingness.

Again comes in the honest seeker for truth and says, "You tell me that the duty of baptism is one of vast importance, and yet that its observance will not save, nor its neglect destroy. How can these things be reconciled?

What is the exact relation of the duty to the salvation of the soul?"

The relation is the same as that of any other duty, neither less nor more. Its importance as a duty does not give it the least importance as a saviour. It holds high rank in one department, and no rank at all in the other. Duties may vary in their relative importance, but they do *not* vary in their universal want of power to save, or to do anything *toward* saving. In that respect duties are all alike.

It may throw some light on the whole subject to answer the often-asked question, "Is baptism essential?" The answer to this question will be nothing more than repetition, in different form, of what has been already said; but difference of form may be exactly what is needed.

The question as it stands is unintelligible. The word *essential* implies relationship; and relationship implies two objects of thought, for if there were only one object, relationship would be impossible; and in the question asked only one object is presented—namely, baptism; it is therefore incomplete and cannot be answered. He to whom it is addressed may well ask, Essential to *what?* If the inquiry be as to whether baptism is essential to salvation, the answer has already been given, It is *not* essential. If the inquiry be, Is baptism essential to duty? the answer has also been given, It *is* essential.

Another inquiry suggests itself, and that is, How can a thing be essential to duty and yet not essential to salvation? This question implies forgetfulness of the whole scheme of redemption. Absolute obedience in every jot and tittle is essential to duty; but if absolute obedience be essential to salvation, then none will be saved, for there is none righteous, no not one. Our only hope is that our shortcomings in regard either to baptism, or to anything else, are atoned for by the precious blood of him who died for us, and gave himself for us, and bare our sins in his own body on the tree.

It is aside from present purposes, but it may not be amiss to say to those who speak of non-essentials, that if the word *non-essential* is not connected in their minds with some other word, their language is meaningless, and they deceive themselves by supposing that they are saying something when they are saying nothing. Non-essential to what? *That* is the question. Without an expressed or implied answer to this, the word *non-essential* conveys no idea whatever. When they speak of this or that being non-essential, do they mean non-essential to salvation? If so, let them remember that it may still be essential to *duty*. And to speak lightly of duty is to speak lightly of law, and to speak lightly of law is to speak lightly of God. Let us therefore be careful in speaking of non-essentials, lest we fall into the folly of talking about nothing, or into the sin of casting contempt on the holy law of God.

The exact relation of baptism to the salvation of our souls has now been set forth; we have seen that in *this* relation it differs from no other duty; and now, avoiding on the one hand the error of those in whose extreme view it is endowed with the miraculous power of regeneration; and on the other hand the error of those who look on it as a mere form; and avoiding too the strangely illogical error of those who speak of it as a trifle and yet hasten to administer it to the dying; and for ourselves regarding it simply as an important duty, but not as a saviour, nor possessed of any merit whatever, —let us examine the Scriptures, to ascertain the *degree* of importance as a duty, which is there attached to it.

1. Let us begin by saying that we are always greatly influenced by first impressions. There is a reason why this should be so.

The mind is in good condition then to form clear conceptions. To that which is first there can be nothing previous. Hence there are no disturbing influences, and nothing interferes with or modifies the full force of any thought that may be presented. When a public speaker rises to address an assembly, his very attitude and look, before he has said a word, will influence the minds of his hearers favorably or unfavorably. His first sentence is sure to be listened to, and on its effect, to no small extent, depends his success. The preacher begins by announcing his text. This always commands attention. The sermon is supposed to come from the text; hence the sermon must be *in* the text. Sermon and text are in a sense the equivalents of each other; as it were the opposite sides of an equation; the text is the sermon in brief; the sermon is the text expanded.

Now what is the text of the ministry of Jesus Christ taken as a whole? What is his attitude when he is first presented to the world in his public character? What is the first impression that he makes?

For ever be it remembered that the very first recorded utterance of Jesus Christ, which by extension of meaning may be applied to us all, and which certainly applied to himself, was his testimony for baptism. Let the human race turn their eyes upon him as he introduces himself at once to his work and to the world, and they behold him in the act of baptism. This is at once his first utterance and his first attitude. "Thus it becometh us to fulfil all righteousness," are the first recorded public words that fell from the lips of the Son of God. Suiting the action to the word, he yields himself to the rite, and calling upon mankind to remotest generations, as it were with a shout that will resound to the end of time, he said "THUS"!

Here, then, is the text of the whole ministry of Jesus Christ, both spoken and acted. Here is an epitome, in word and emblem together, of all that his future ministry is to develop. He knew the power of first impressions, and selected, as the first that he would make, that which is made by baptism. It may amaze us, but still it is true, that baptism has been selected by Infinite Wisdom as the initial of the grand and glorious work on earth of the Redeemer of mankind. Does all this seem to be too wonderful to be true? Look to the record and see if a public word was ever spoken by him prior to the word "*Thus;*" or if a public act was ever performed by him previous to baptism. Here, then, is both the title-page and the frontispiece of his ministry. There are the recorded words; there is the picture of the act. If Christ has honored baptism thus, by putting it in the foreground of his work, let those beware who speak of it as a thing of little moment.

2. First impressions are strong; perhaps last impressions are stronger. We may forget

our first introduction to a friend; we are not likely to forget our last and parting interview. Especially is this the case when we know, at the time of the interview, that it is to be the last. Dying words are apt to be undying words. We cherish them with peculiar interest and with utmost tenderness; and, even if they were *not* cherished, even if we try to obliterate them, they fasten themselves upon our memory and seem to sink through our whole nature. Jesus Christ knew what was in man, and he knew the power of last impressions, and among the last words he ever uttered were these: "Go teach all nations, baptizing them in the name of the Father and of the Son and of the Holy Ghost." This was after he had risen from the dead; it was after forty days of mysterious existence before he had ascended to his Father, between the lowly sepulchre and the heavenly throne, and in his last moment on earth, just before he was received into a cloud up into heaven out of sight.

Surely the occasion was a grand one, and the words then spoken ought to have been worthy of it, and they *were*. They were words that spoke of baptism. If baptism was the text and exordium of his ministry, so now it has become its peroration. He closed as he began. The initial adumbrated the conclusion. The orator prepares with care his closing words; the lawyer wishing success strives to get the last word; the dying friend, knowing his words to be the last, and with eternity right before him, speaks words of tenderness and truth; and Jesus Christ, closing his ministry, and closing his personal intercourse with his people, and knowing that they would never hear his words on earth again, spoke of baptism. Let the lip quiver when it utters the word *mere*.

Is it not wonderful that the mention of baptism is both at the beginning and at the end of the ministry of Jesus Christ? Ought not these two God-spoken announcements to arrest the attention of mankind? Are they not like two sentinels, one at either end; like two great watch-towers over against each other; like two huge pillars parallel and opposite, based on earth, and reaching to heaven? Let those reject these figures who please, but the world is challenged to dispute the *facts*. Nor is it any relief to say that the facts were accidents. Accidents do not happen with God. Nor is there any relief in saying that the facts are unimportant. If the beginning and the ending of the public career of incarnate Godhead are not important, it would be in vain to search the annals of time or of eternity for that which *is* important.

3. But another view awaits us. When one person is giving directions to another in regard to a multitude of things, he mentions a few of the most prominent and important, particularly and by name; the rest he groups together, in phrases which describe them all *as a whole*, but no one of them as a unit. Especially is

this the case if the directions are the last that are to be given. In such a case, to mention and make conspicuous trifling matters of detail, to the forgetfulness or neglect of the main and leading points, would be unnatural, and, to a well-constituted mind, impossible.

Just before our Lord parted with his disciples for the last time, he held a conversation with them, in which he gave them his final directions for the great work that lay before them of evangelizing the world. All the words that he spoke, it is to be presumed, were not recorded; but we may judge of what was said by what is written. The record shows that, in speaking of various and multiform duties, he used generic terms, saying comprehensively, and without particular description of any one thing, "Teaching them to observe all things whatsoever I have commanded you." But, from out the long catalogue of the "all things" which they are commanded to teach, one thing is mentioned by name, and *only* one, and that one is baptism: "Go ye and teach all nations, baptizing them." Why this particularity? Why was specific mention made of this? Why was this segregated and made to stand out in bold relief, while the "all things," grouped together, formed the background? Suppose the thoughts to be presented to the mind by the act of painting rather than by words. Which would be the conspicuous figure on the canvas? Which would be the key to the picture? What means this, that baptism stands alone, and flooded with light, while the "all things" cluster together in the shade? It may not be easy to answer this last question, but, whatever the answer may be, he must be audacious indeed who supposes baptism to be anything less than a *great* commandment.

4. Let it not be supposed that imagination has outstripped the reality. Our ideals never exceed, but always fall short of, God's reals. Another fact confronts us, more astounding

than any that have yet been named. There are many, many things which we are required to observe and do; but there is only one duty devolving on any member of the human race, which he is required to do "in the name of the Father and of the Son and of the Holy Ghost," and that one duty is baptism. Why should the act be coupled with this dread and awful formula? What else can it be than to give it the emphasis of the Infinite? If baptism is an expression, are not the tremendous powers of Eternity summoned up to infuse the energy of Godhead into it? Why is no other duty required to be done in a manner so deliberate, so solemn, and so awe-striking? By withholding the dread sanction from other duties and giving it to this, are they not relatively depressed, and is not this made to loom up as, in some respect at least, a duty without a peer? True, when the sick are anointed with oil, and the issues of life and death are at stake, it is to be done "in the name of the Lord," but not "in the name of the Father, and of the Son, and of the Holy Ghost." There is no calling up of the three separate Persons of the Trinity; God is appealed to as God; but the three glorious Witnesses, each by name, and one by one, in mysterious unity, are not displayed as in baptism. Actions are dignified by deliberation; actions are dignified by being done in the immediate presence of God, and in the name of God. That the idea of God may fully occupy the mind, and that the thought may be detained, that his glory may spread over all, and his majesty make all sublime, he unfolds himself as Father, Son, and Holy Ghost in the ordinance of baptism. Why is it that one duty, and only one, is accompanied by these august honors and these terrible sanctions? Whatever the reason may be, the fact is undisputed and immovable. In the light of this fact, let scoffers turn white as snow!

Modern scholarship seems to have most

clearly decided that the word translated *in*, in the formula of baptism, should have been translated *into*. What the words may mean, when thus translated, we cannot precisely conceive. But there is something awful about them. Baptized *into* the name of the Father, and of the Son, and of the Holy Ghost! There seems to be a hidden significance in the word *into*, before which the meaning of the word *in* melts away to nothing. Is it too much to say that the name of God *is* God? And are we baptized into him? Are we plunged into that ocean of Eternal Being? Whether it be so or not, we are drowned in this ocean of thought. Overwhelming as these conceptions may be, and inadequate as must be our view of the truth of God, yet the *fact* stands out on record, on the living oracles of the living God, that we are baptized into the name of the Father, and of the Son, and of the Holy Ghost.

Possibly, angels may comprehend what to us

is an insolvable mystery; and, if they do, must they not look on with amazement as upon one of the most wonderful phenomena of Eternity when they behold a sinful man baptized into the name of God? Without pretending to explain what surpasses human powers of thought, it is enough to say that baptism would not be the only duty commanded to be done "in the name of the Father, and of the Son, and of the Holy Ghost," if it were not a duty whose importance and whose rank should command the awe-struck reverence of all created intelligences.

5. But we have not reached the greatest wonder yet. Our nature is not poured out into words as it can be into acts; and neither our words nor acts are like those of the Almighty. In the formula of baptism we use his sacred name. True, it is by his command that we do it; still, it is *we* who do it. On one stupendous occasion the formula was

not spoken, but acted, and it was God who enacted it. Once only, in the history of the world, has God in his triune character manifested himself to his creatures, and that was on the occasion of baptism. Father, Son, and Holy Ghost were each separately manifested at the river Jordan. The glorious Son was baptized; the glorious Father spoke from heaven; and the glorious Holy Spirit descended like a dove! The words of the formula were embodied into the acts of the Trinity! For ever sacred, for ever awful, for ever fearful words! Oh, sublimest drama of Earth! Never before, never since, has the world witnessed such a spectacle. Once the world was visited by more than twelve legions of angels, but these were only the messengers of the Throne, and not its Occupant. Gethsemane was a place of lonely agony. Calvary resounds with the cry, "My God! my God! why hast thou forsaken me?" But in baptism the triune God has set his Earthly Throne, for there only has he been manifested to the world. Perhaps the facts of that occasion are the basis of our present formula; these words are the echoes of those facts; and they may have been prescribed to keep us ever in remembrance of that moment of transcendent majesty, the most conspicuous and exalted moment of all Time. But why was baptism singled out as the occasion for such amazing display? We may not be able to say, but the fact stands up as a witness with a voice louder than ten thousand thunders as God's testimony in honor of baptism.

6. It will relieve the strain upon our minds to take a view less overpowering. We judge of a man by the company he keeps. The same principle that prevails among animals of lower order seems to hold good among men,— like consorts with like. Hence to know a man's associates is in a certain sense to know him. Knowing the class to which he belongs, we know at least his rank and

his general characteristics, even if we remain ignorant of his individual peculiarities. So also we judge of the opinion which a man has of anything by the classification which he awards it; or by the connection in which he speaks of it, and especially if he *always* speaks of it in that connection. Thus if one speaks of angels and archangels, cherubs and seraphs, we take it for granted that in his opinion these different orders of beings are in some way related to each other, and that in some respects they are, if not equals, yet worthy of being named together. There may be differences among them; still, he looks at the resemblances rather than at the differences, and places them all in the same category. So, too, when in the Apocalypse mention is made of dogs, and sorcerers, and whoremongers, and murderers, and idolaters, and liars, we suppose that however these may differ from each other, they are all measurably on the same footing, because the classification groups them all together as members of the same family. What minor differences there may be among them are ignored because of their general similarity; and we are confirmed in this view because elsewhere the same classes with others of like character are named together, and the same destiny is assigned them. In fact, every man's mind is so constituted that he cannot help being influenced in his opinion of a thing by the classification in which it is found. The principle is founded in nature, and as the Bible was inspired by the God of nature, it cannot be wrong to apply the principle to the interpretation of the book. What classification is awarded by the word of God to baptism? Let the record speak for itself: "He that believeth and is baptized shall be saved, and he that believeth not shall be damned."

Five things are here spoken of; believing, — not believing, — salvation, — damnation, —

and baptism. The first subject named—believing—is one of infinite importance, for "Without faith it is impossible to please God." The second—not believing—is the peer of the first, for the unbeliever makes God a liar, and unbelief is the seed-sin of all sins. The third—salvation—is a thing of transcendent importance, for it involves all the eternal joys that are at the right hand of God. The fourth—damnation—is fit to be mentioned in frightful antithesis to what precedes, for it involves infinite ruin in everlasting fire prepared for the devil and his angels. These four themes, towering in gigantic importance, are fitly named together, and the fifth—baptism—is fit to be named in this colossal companionship or it would not have been so named. It is not a case of accident, where a small thing has by inadvertence been slipped in among the great. It is by divine intention that these five things are classified together. It is the grouping of

Infinite Wisdom. Nor is it conceivable that either God or men would put a trifle in connection with the most stupendous themes of eternity.

Judge of baptism by the company it keeps in the word of God, and decide whether it is a thing of small moment. There must be something in the nature of the facts which makes their association proper. God would not associate things together in a kind of union which ought not so to be associated. Hence from the very fact that they are named together, we know not only that there is a propriety in the combination, but we also know that there must be something in the nature and essence of things which is the foundation of this propriety. What this something may be, which brings close together things which in our conceptions are far apart, we do not know, and have no means of ascertaining. But our conceptions are not to be our guide. God's conceptions are eternal truth. And if in his conceptions belief and unbelief, and salvation and damnation, and baptism, are so connected as to be named conjointly, then what God hath joined together, let not man put asunder.

It adds force to the argument to remember what has been already said, though on a different topic, that baptism is also named in connection with "the name of the Father, and of the Son, and of the Holy Ghost." The association is one of supremest dignity, nor is it less than sacrilege to suppose for a moment that such association would find place in the word of God, if it had not foundation in the everlasting law of right. He who scoffs at baptism, scoffs at that which keeps glorious company. If an insult is offered to one's associates, is it not offered to him?

7. The words small and great are relative in their meaning; and things small and great are so only by comparison. The bap-

tism of a believer is in some respects a small thing; it is a small thing when compared with the baptism of Jesus Christ. "Thus it becometh *us* to fulfil all righteousness." If there be any doubt as to whether the word *us* includes ourselves, there can be no doubt that it included him who uttered it. If he had said, "thus it becometh *me* to fulfil all righteousness," the words would have expressed real truth. From this we learn that if our Lord had not done what he did, his righteousness would not have been fulfilled; and if not fulfilled, it would have been incomplete; and if his righteousness had been incomplete, he would have been incomplete, and the world would have had no Saviour! Hence *his* baptism *was* essential,—essential to the salvation of the world! What a moment was that in the history of the universe, when on its action hung the destinies of eternity! No wonder it was honored by sublimest manifestations, and elicited expressions of divine pleasure, and displays of glory from the Throne itself. True, indeed, *every* moment of Christ's life was pregnant with eternal destiny, but this particular moment has been singled out for pre-eminent distinction, above every other moment in the earthly career of the Son of God. Perhaps it was because in that act of consecration, he took upon him the vow to do and to suffer his Father's will to the uttermost, and all his future work was constructively and concentratively present in that one germinal deed. In our own baptism, although our salvation does not depend on it, let us remember that it is the imitation and the counterpart of that on which the salvation of the world *did* depend. Let this fact invest it with profoundest solemnity and dignify it into awful majesty. And if not in the letter, yet in spirit, Christ includes ourselves with him in the word *us*, elevating us thus to the heavenly peerage of the sons of God, let us so observe the duty as to be worthy of the glorious companionship, and let our baptismal vows be like his whose promise was equivalent to performance.

8. Another fact worthy of our most devout attention, is the fact that baptism is the only duty of all the duties enjoined upon us, which we are required to perform but once. This fact gives it a distinction which it enjoys all alone. The observance of the Lord's Supper may be, and ought to be, often repeated. Many other duties continuous in their nature seem to be part and parcel of our daily lives, and in their discharge we may from time to time improve. But on baptism there can be no improvement. It is the act of a moment, and when done it is done for eternity. If we are to be judged for the deeds done in the body, and if this one deed invested with the most awful and most glorious, and most dreadful sanctions of the Almighty, is to be done but once, and once

for al., with what solemn preparation, and with what unutterable reverence should it be done! Is it not the greatest visible crisis in life? Is it not a turning-point to which we should look both forward and backward with trembling interest? May it not be the era from which some of the grandest interests of eternity are dated?

9. There is a difference between truths and facts. It is not easy to give a definition of truth, but the word fact may be more easily handled, and it is with this chiefly that we have to do. It is from the Latin word *facio, factum*, and means that which is *done*. Truth is not the result of action, but fact is. Truth may be spoken, truth may be believed, but it cannot be *done*. No agent is necessary to its existence. Not so with fact; for, before anything can be *done*, there must be a *doer*. Truth is eternal; facts date only from the time when they became facts; that is, from the time when they were *done*. Truth is much more vast

than fact, and oftentimes not so easily comprehended. Truth is matter of principle, which may not be clearly understood. Fact is like that which is the object of sense. Truth may often seem to evade the grasp of the wisest. Fact is within the reach of all, even the feeblest. These differences, and others that might be named, are such that the presentation of truth often fails to make as clear and as strong an impression on the mind as the presentation of fact.

Now, in what has been said of baptism, there may have been a mixture of truth and fact; but every point that has been presented as a topic is distinctly matter of fact. If, in connection with these facts, truths have been uttered, so also there may have been intermixture of error; and some of the inferences drawn from the facts may not have been drawn correctly. But in the facts themselves there can be no error; nor, I presume, will the statement of them be disputed. Let us recapitulate them. 1. It is a *fact*, that baptism was the initial of the ministry of Jesus Christ. 2. It is a *fact*, that he closed his ministry as he began it,—with baptism. 3. It is a *fact*, that the record of his last conversation on earth shows specific mention of this duty and of no other. 4. It is a *fact*, that this is the only duty which we are required to perform in the name of the Trinity. 5. It is a *fact*, that once only was Godhead displayed to earth in triune character, and that this was done on the occasion of baptism. 6. It is a *fact*, that baptism is classed in the Scriptures with things of most tremendous import and of infinite dignity. 7. It is a *fact*, that the baptism of Christ was essential to the fulfilment of all righteousness. 8. It is a *fact*, that baptism is the only duty of which one single moment in the life of an immortal being has a monopoly.

Whatever may be thought of the inferences that have been drawn, the *facts* are immovable. Statement of truth might be disputed, for there might be difference of opinion as to what *is* truth; but there can be no difference of opinion as to the *facts*. The facts are their own witnesses; they speak for themselves.

In forming theories on baptism, if one disregards these facts, he is not even building a house on the sand; he is trying to build in the air. On the other hand, a theory which is built on the facts,—on these solid rocks,—is worthy of this respect at least, that it is built on a good foundation.

Why not apply the principles of the Baconian Philosophy to the interpretation of Scripture, and take the facts as starting-points? With these facts spread out before the eyes of mankind, it is surprising that any should think of baptism as a thing of small importance, and so signally undervalue that which God has so signally honored. It is equally astonishing that any should incline to overrate that which it would almost seem cannot be overrated. Not satisfied with the exalted rank which the facts of Scripture accord to baptism, they must even go farther, and (incredible to relate) claim for it something *more;* they claim for it the power of regenerating the soul, which belongs only to the Holy Spirit; or, if not so wildly extreme as this, they claim that it is the *means* by which the Holy Ghost renews the soul, thus substituting the mere water used in baptism for the truth of the word, and for the blood of the covenant.

Let us avoid both extremes; and let us remember that the fact that baptism holds high rank as duty, gives it no rank whatever, and no *place*, as the groundwork or means of our salvation. Christ is our righteousness. His blood cleanses from all sin. Neglect of baptism must be sin; and failure to hold it in proper esteem must be sin; but the precious blood of the Lamb of God has power to wash away *all* sin. No sin is so great as to defy the power of the blood of the everlasting covenant. Christ is all; Christ is enough.

If any man be in Christ, whether baptized or not, he is a new creature. If any man be not in Christ, whether baptized or not, his doom is perdition.

Let us thank God that, while our salvation is made secure by the merits and mediation of his Son, we are permitted to obey his commandments, in keeping of which there is great reward.

INDEX
(for Pages 1-350)

	PAGE
Baptism a positive or legal institution	40
Baptism—Early historical statement about it	196
Baptism a prerequisite to the Lord's Supper	201
Baptism required of both Jew and Gentile converts	34
Baptism—What it expresses symbolically	176
Baptists and Religious Freedom	125, 245
Baptists must teach their principles	259
Baptist Progress in the nineteenth century	333
Believers the only subjects of baptism	39
Communion at the Lord's table confined to Church Members	101
Compromise: there can be none	287
English Baptists and Open Communion	112
Greek word translated baptize—its meaning	169
Household baptisms on record give no support to infant baptism	45
Immersion only is Baptism	62
Leading men of A. D. 1800	346
Membership in a Baptist Church—requisites for	119
New Testament, common version, best book to guide honest inquirers about baptism	92
Persecutions of Baptist	345
Regenerate church membership at the foundation of all Baptist peculiarities	18, 147
Reasons for becoming a Baptist—Dr. Peters	307
Sunday Observance and Religious Liberty	333
Testimony of Candid Scholarship	317
Value of Baptist Principles to the world	277
Washings among the Jews	187

THE BAPTIST STANDARD BEARER, INC.
A non-profit, tax-exempt corporation
committed to the Publication & Preservation
of The Baptist Heritage.

SAMPLE TITLES FOR PUBLICATIONS AVAILABLE IN OUR VARIOUS SERIES:

THE BAPTIST *COMMENTARY* SERIES
Sample of authors/works in or near republication:
John Gill - *Exposition of the Old & New Testaments (9 Vol. Set)*
John Gill - *Exposition of Solomon's Song*

THE BAPTIST *FAITH* SERIES:
Sample of authors/works in or near republication:
Abraham Booth - *The Reign of Grace*
John Fawcett - *Christ Precious to Those That Believe*
John Gill - *A Complete Body of Doctrinal & Practical Divinity (2 Vols.)*

THE BAPTIST *HISTORY* SERIES:
Sample of authors/works in or near republication:
Thomas Armitage - *A History of the Baptists (2 Vols.)*
Isaac Backus - *History of the New England Baptists (2 Vols.)*
William Cathcart - *The Baptist Encyclopaedia (3 Vols.)*
J. M. Cramp - *Baptist History*

THE BAPTIST *DISTINCTIVES* SERIES:
Sample of authors/works in or near republication:
Abraham Booth - *Paedobaptism Examined (3 Vols.)*
Alexander Carson - *Ecclesiastical Polity of the New Testament Churches*
E. C. Dargan - *Ecclesiology: A Study of the Churches*
J. M. Frost - *Pedobaptism: Is It From Heaven?*
R. B. C. Howell - *The Evils of Infant Baptism*

THE *DISSENT & NONCONFORMITY* SERIES:
Sample of authors/works in or near republication:
Champlin Burrage - *The Early English Dissenters (2 Vols.)*
Albert H. Newman - *History of Anti-Pedobaptism*
Walter Wilson - *The History & Antiquities of the Dissenting Churches (4 Vols.)*

For a complete list of current authors/titles, visit our internet site at
www.standardbearer.com or write us at:

The Baptist Standard Bearer, Inc.
No. 1 Iron Oaks Drive • Paris, Arkansas 72855

Telephone: (479) 963-3831   Fax: (479) 963-8083
E-mail: baptist@arkansas.net
Internet: http://www.standardbearer.org

Thou hast given a *standard* to them that fear thee; that it may be displayed because of the truth. -- Psalm 60:4

www.ingramcontent.com/pod-product-compliance
Lightning Source LLC
Chambersburg PA
CBHW020300010526
44108CB00037B/160